TOBY ALES

Created and Directed by Hans Höfer

INSIGHT GUIDES
LonDon

Edited and Produced by Andrew Eames

Executive Editor: Brian Bell

HOUGHTON MIFFLIN COMPANY

APA PUBLICATIONS

LONDON

New Edition
© 1995 APA PUBLICATIONS (HK) LTD
First edition published in 1988
All Rights Reserved
Printed in Singapore by Höfer Press Pte Ltd

Distributed in the United States by:
Houghton Mifflin Company
222 Berkeley Street
Boston, Massachusetts 02116-3764
ISBN: 0-395-66209-5

Distributed in Canada by:
Thomas Allen & Son
390 Steelcase Road East
Markham, Ontario L3R 1G2
ISBN: 0-395-66209-5

Distributed in the UK & Ireland by:
GeoCenter International UK Ltd
The Viables Center, Harrow Way
Basingstoke, Hampshire RG22 4BJ
ISBN: 9-62421-059-4

Worldwide distribution enquiries:
Höfer Communications Pte Ltd
38 Joo Koon Road
Singapore 2262
ISBN: 9-62421-059-4

ABOUT THIS BOOK

This latest edition of *Insight Guide: London* has been produced by the team behind the original book. In the interim, both the city and their lives have changed considerably. When they first met, **Brian Bell** was deputy editor of the colour magazine accompanying the *Observer* newspaper and **Andrew Eames** was a freelance writer and photographer; now Bell is Apa Publications' executive publisher in London and Eames is contributing editor. Their first meeting took place in El Vino's wine bar, then a favourite haunt of Fleet Street journalists; now all the national newspapers have relocated and Fleet Street is just another avenue of shops and offices.

Whether or not London is "chaos incorporated", as George Mikes once described it, the initial problems in producing this book had seemed daunting. How, after all, does one squeeze the whole of London into 260 pages? A new book on some aspect of London is published every five days, so the challenge facing Apa was to produce one that distinguished itself from the crowd. However, anyone who works on an Apa guidebook has an advantage from the start. The books' format, with dual emphasis on informative, entertaining, up-to-date and well written text twinned with the vision of today's most exciting photographers, has long been innovative in the world of travel guides.

Apa Publications is the brainchild of founder **Hans Höfer**, who came to Asia in the late 1960s from West Germany, after graduating in printing, book production, design and photography. There are now well over 180 *Insight Guides*, the popular series of *Insight Pocket Guides*, and the London office has become the main editorial centre.

Eames, taking on the task of project editor for the London book, was no stranger to the Apa philosophy, having contributed to Apa's *Insight Guide: Great Britain*. He first became aware of Apa's existence in that company's early years when he, like Apa, was based in Singapore. Out of his spell in Asia Eames produced an autobiographical book, *Crossing the Shadow-Line,* and in recent years has followed that with *Four Scottish Journeys.*

Once the overall structure of *Insight Guide: London* was established, Eames sought out writers with the right combination of affection and detachment from their subject that distinguishes the Apa guides.

A former colleague on *The Times*, **Tim Grimwade**, an Australian who had lived in London for 10 years, poured many of his observations into the section on the West End, which kicks off the Places section of the book. "It is the underlying humour of the people which makes London special for me," says Grimwade. "The cynicism of street traders, the over-officiousness of bureaucracies, the pursuit of traditions being outdated."

Also at *The Times* was **Srinivasa Rao**, who distinguished himself first on the *Times of India*. Rao came to London in 1965 and became one of the elder statesmen on the home desk of *The Times* and universally known as "Sonny". He proved the ideal person to write the section on race, "A Melting Pot".

Also recruited from the desks of the *Times* was **Allison Lobbett**, who researched and wrote the chapter on London's financial quarter, The City, before moving to the *Financial Times*. Lobbett was born in Wales and distinguished herself at Cambridge University. She says The City is still a bastion of men in suits, but it is also a place of far more

Bell

Eames

Grimwade

Rao

wit, beauty and interest than the business label would suggest.

When pushed, **Lynne Truss** will admit to bringing dinner-party conversations around to the two subjects of London taxis and taxi drivers, about whom she has a feast of anecdotes, some of which are retold in the chapter on the Cabbie. Truss, former literary editor of the *Listener* and now a novelist, arts reviewer and columnist for *The Times* is a born and bred Londoner.

An aversion to "anywhere where the daytime temperature gets above 72° Fahrenheit" did not prevent Scotsman **Brian Morton** from moving south to London, which he still considers to be "abroad". In between his job as literary editor of the *Times Higher Education Supplement* and writing three books, Morton penned the chapters Modern Metropolis, London's Parks, and Wigs and Pens.

Apa's stalwart historian **Roland Collins** produced the three historical chapters in this book. When not pursuing his lifelong interest in the social history of the British Isles, he is an accomplished artist with London exhibitions. Collins, who was born, educated and spent his working life in London, describes the city as a "renewable feast. Its old delights never fail, but the city has to change to live and young London is coming along fine."

For the tricky chapter "Official London", the London most dense with the heavier of the tourist attractions – Parliament, Downing Street, Westminster Abbey – Eames turned to **Victor Bryant**, a lecturer on ceramic history. Bryant is a trained tourist guide lecturer on London, particularly its more historical elements. Bryant also wrote the panel story on London's Museums.

Undoubtedly the most prolific of the writers assembled in this book is **Roger St Pierre**, who penned the chapters on Village London and Day Trips. St Pierre is responsible for 17 published books from the *Book of the Bicycle* to the *Illustrated Encyclopedia of Black Music.* He was educated in London and has lived in the city ever since, which he nows knows "better than any taxi driver".

The fact-packed Travel Tips section was ably assembled by **Andrea Gillies**, the first female editor of the *Good Beer Guide*. For this edition, it has been updated and expanded by **Beverley Harper**, a regular contributor to *Time Out* and the *Sunday Times Magazine*.

Editorial research and the one-page panels on Parliament, royalty and pubs were the responsibility of **Simon Dennison**, an Oxford graduate who has freelanced widely.

Many of the photographs in this book are the vision of **Richard T. Nowitz**, an American now living in Washington DC who contributed to several Apa guides. Other photographs were contributed by **David Gray**, a freelance market researcher with a passion for photographing London, and **Neill Menneer**, a professional with a history of photography that includes an exhibition *Images of London.* Many of the paintings in the early part of the book are reproduced by courtesy of the Museum of London.

Eames wishes to thank **Judy Lehane** for her sterling work on picture research, **Elspeth Sinclair** for her editing skills, **Tim Baker** for assistance with the book's maps, and **Martin Symington** for supplementary editorial.

And so to London. What Dr Johnson actually said was this: "Why, Sir, you find no man, at all intellectual, who is willing to leave London. No, Sir, when a man is tired of London, he is tired of life; for there is in London all that life can afford." No guidebook could wish for a better dedication.

Lobbett

Collins

Gillies

Nowitz

CONTENTS

History and People

15 The Streets of London
—by Andrew Eames

21 Beginnings
—by Roland Collins

25 The Golden Age
—by Roland Collins

29 Splendour and Sweatshops
—by Roland Collins

35 Modern Metropolis
—by Brian Morton

38 *The Bobby*
—by Andrew Eames

45 A Melting Pot
by Srinivasa Rao

51 The Cockney
—by Andrew Eames

53 The Cabbie
—by Lynne Truss

57 Theatreland
—by Lynne Truss

The Main Attractions

69   The West End
—by Tim Grimwade

78   *Pubs*
—by Andrew Eames

93   Official London
—by Victor Bryant

93   *Parliament*
—by Simon Dennison

98   *Royalty*
—by Simon Dennison

109   London's Parks
—by Brian Morton

119   Posh London
—by Andrew Eames

124   *Night Sites*
—by Andrea Gillies

A Pick Of Places

132 *Museums*
—by Victor Bryant

137 **City Villages**
—by Roger St. Pierre

142 *Blue Plaques*
—by Andrew Eames

148 *Markets*
—by Andrew Eames

153 **Wigs and Pens**
—by Brian Morton

181 **Docklands and the River**
—by Andrew Eames

191 **Day Trips**
—by Roger St. Pierre

Maps

64 London
66 London and Environs
70 The West End
94 Official London
120 Posh London
138 London's Villages
154 Wigs and Pens
168 The City
184 The River and Docklands
192 Country and Sea
208 The Underground

TRAVEL TIPS

202 *Getting Acquainted*

202 *Planning the Trip*

204 *Practical Tips*

206 *Getting Around*

209 *Where to Stay*

215 *Eating Out*

222 *Attractions*

244 *Further Reading*

**For detailed information
see page 201**

THE STREETS OF LONDON

Let me take you by the hand and lead you
through the streets of London.
I will show you something that
will make you change your mind.
　　　　　　– Ralph McTell, *Streets of London*

Threadneedle, Throgmorton, Bread and Milk Streets; Yukon Road, Zampa Road, Zander Court and Cosmo Place; Manchuria Road, Morocco Street, Max Roach Park and Bohemia Place; all are street names of London which portray some part of London's history, some snippet of world events, of empire building, of television fashions, or simply of the street planner's own politics. They are names that can reveal more than the buildings themselves: whole areas are named after colonial leaders, regions of Australia and highpoints in the Boer War. There are 12 Churchills and four Dallases.

There is no single underlying logic behind street naming. The very multi-influenced nature reflects the city itself and something of its fascination. Taxi drivers probably learn more English history from these names than they did at school. The British love their capital's streets and have even modelled boardgames around them.

Always changing: London is not uniform. It is patchy, even blotchy. This is not a city of grand vistas, but everyone finds their own favourite holes and corners. While it has a long and venerable past, that past is often not visible. Over the centuries the ripples of history have repeatedly destroyed parts of the city and the rebuilding has resulted in streets that reflect something of everything.

Queen Boadicea burnt the place in AD 60, but this was just the first of a succession of serious setbacks. The plagues of 1665 claimed 100,000 Londoners and a year later

the Great Fire destroyed much of the city.

In the Blitz of the World War II, 29,000 Londoners were killed, and 80 percent of the city's buildings were damaged, with a third completely destroyed. The hurricane of October 1987 destroyed an estimated 15 million trees in the southeast, and another fierce storm in 1990 wreaked further havoc.

In this process of change something good comes out of each disaster. So dark and narrow were the streets in the old City of

London that shopkeepers had to erect mirrors outside their windows to reflect light into the shops. The Blitz allowed widening and lightening, slums disappeared and the level of street crime declined.

Vital statistics: London is not one of the world's most dangerous capitals. In 1991-2 there were 185 murders in Greater London, compared with 1,905 in New York City. However, there are large numbers of street robberies (more than 22,000 a year). It is said that in Petticoat Lane the pickpockets are so fast that you can buy your own handkerchief by the time you reach the end of the market

Preceding pages: open-air eating in Covent Garden; Tower Bridge ironwork; men of metal; Whitehall from St James's Park; the financial district from the river. Left: greetings from a traditional pub. Right: a Pearly Queen wears her robes with pride.

stalls. And yet this is the city where the milkmen can leave pints of milk on doorsteps in perfect safety.

London is tremendously dominant within the United Kingdom, and always has been. In 1605, 6 percent of the of the country's population lived in the city. Today the population of the 625 square mile metropolis stands at 6.8 million (with a slight majority of women). The figure is 12 percent of the country's total population.

London is still the largest city in Europe. It hosts 18 million tourists a year and 25,000 street-people sleep within its confines. A million commuters use public transportation

is a collection of communities or villages which the expanding metropolis has swallowed up with the countryside. At the centre of this patchwork city is a common area of shared London, a London of work and play. This book deals primarily with shared London, which is the essence of London, although to it the writers add their own little corners of interest.

As with any city the impression of London projected by guidebooks is not always a realistic interpretation. Any visitor with a traditional guidebook in hand, wandering the streets, will be eternally frustrated by the fact that the site where a famous old author

daily into Greater London, with another 250,000 travelling independently. Overall the Underground network (the oldest in the world) carries 750 million passengers a year and the buses three million a day. Sadly, the Underground in particular has not stood up well to the strain.

London's weather is by no means as bad as Londoners make it out to be. The city averages three hours and twenty minutes of sunshine a day on a yearly basis. While New York's rainfall is double, London's comes down more slowly and lingers longer.

Shared London: To most Londoners the city

lived is now a glass and steel block. The reader may also feel the rich history which the book so emphasises is barely apparent on street level.

Even for Londoners, weekly publications such as *Time Out* create a false impression by implying that Londoners participate in a morass of entertainment into the wee hours, using a language only other like-minded youngsters would understand. In truth, many Londoners never go to fringe theatre productions, and rarely go to the West End.

Henry James described the capital as a "giant animated encyclopaedia with people for pages". With all the variety and history in this city, it is difficult to know where to start as a tourist, but James's emphasis is a good one. The people and the culture matter as much as the buildings. Left in the hands of tourist organisations, there is a danger that any city becomes a string of tourist buildings. Following are a few suggestions of venues to fill in the colour between the sights and make the city real.

London revealed: Try the balcony of the Royal Festival Hall (the South Bank) after dark for a glorious view of the Thames lights; a round trip on the Docklands Light Railway to view the revitalisation of what

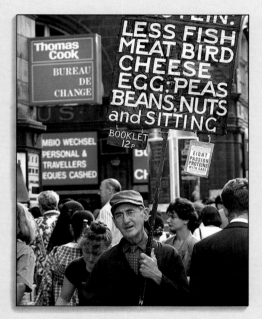

was the warehouse of the world, and what is now becoming a tourist attraction; and tea dances at the Waldorf Hotel.

For a spectacular view of London, go to the top of Westminster Cathedral (not the Abbey) spire or view the City's worker ants from the gallery in the Lloyds building (a magnificent modern structure detested by those who work in it). Have lunch at Fortnum and Mason's on Piccadilly, or take in an open-air performance of Shakespeare in Re-

gent's Park theatre, which you might precede with a cruise along the Regent's Canal.

Have a drink at the Grenadier public house on Wilton Row, off Knightsbridge; amble around Harrods; enjoy Sunday lunch at the Roof Garden in Derry Street, off Kensington High Street; visit Camden market, which reflects trendy modern London, on a Saturday or Sunday and Brick Lane market, which reflects downtrodden and dodgy London, on a Sunday. Try a fringe theatre production or a late-night cabaret; stroll through Leicester Square and Covent Garden on a Saturday night for the international flavour of the city.

No-one should attempt to see London without walking, but only shared London is accessible this way. For a vision of real London sit upstairs on a double-decker bus and travel through the layers of the metropolis to the perimeter.

When public transport first began to operate at the beginning of the century, only the rich could afford to commute, leaving the poor to settle in central London. In recent years that trend has reversed, and house prices have pushed the lower-paid out into the suburbs.

This "gentrification" of inner London terraces has halted. The last decade saw some grand developments along the banks of the river, which is at last becoming more of a feature of daily life.

Meanwhile, the broad-brushstrokes of London's image remain the same. This is the city where secret agents in overcoats exchange envelopes through wastepaper bins in the parks; here royalty rides in coaches and gets splashed over the front pages of the newspapers; here politicians pay off prostitutes at railway stations and a swastika is projected onto the top of South Africa House in Trafalgar Square for months without being officially noticed. This is the City that is still the financial centre of Europe (though Frankfurt has been creeping ever closer).

In these pages you will learn about all of this and more: when the first public lavatory opened in London; where to buy jellied eels; why taxi drivers don't like their passengers to interrupt; and how to find the hidden police station in Trafalgar Square. Here, in short, is London revealed.

Did London begin in Creffield Road? During the Stone Age, this undistinguished street in the West London suburb of Acton was home and workshop to prehistoric flint workers. They left behind 600 worked flints and the discovery is one of the few on which our limited knowledge of pre-Roman London is based.

Together with the scant evidence of a hand-axe from Piccadilly Circus, the locations are spots on an archaeologist's map through which an ancient river flowed and created gravel banks in the clayey basin on its way to the North Sea.

Not until AD 43 does the story of London proper begin, when the invading Roman army chose those gravel banks between what is now Southwark and the City as the site of their bridge. Roman London, which may be the Celtic "Llyn-din", the fort by the lake, quickly took shape, but suffered a setback 17 years later when British guerrillas under Queen Boadicea attacked and burned areas we now identify as Lombard Street, Gracechurch Street and Walbrook.

A rebuilt Londinium, as the Romans called it, had by AD 100 supplanted Colchester as the capital and military and trading centre of Britain. It had a timber-built bridge, quays, warehouses and domestic buildings. Wattle and daub were faced with plaster; Kentish ragstone was brought by boat for public buildings and the necessary defensive wall constructed to resist raids by marauding Saxons from the Continent. Roads radiated to Colchester, York, Chester, Exeter, Bath and Canterbury.

Decline and fall: By AD 288 the settlement's importance had been recognised by Rome. It was given the proud name "Augusta", but that pride went before a fall. In 410, threatened by the Germanic races from the North, Rome had no alternative but to recall its garrison from England, with the result that culture withered and the very fabric of Londinium crumbled.

Under the Saxons it eventually recovered its place of importance. And in the early 8th century Bede called it the "Market of the World". South of the original wooden London Bridge the Borough came to independent existence.

By 900, Alfred, King of Wessex, had resisted Danish invasions, but subsequent att-

acks ended with Sweyn as King of England. After his death Canute was crowned in the palace of the Saxon kings which the City's Aldermanbury is thought to perpetuate.

Meanwhile, 2 miles (3 km) up river on Thorney Island, the Monastery of St Peter, later the great West Minster, was established. Following his accession in 1042, Edward the Confessor moved his court to Westminster, thereby creating the division of royal and mercantile power which had a profound effect on the character and growth of London. Edward, in lieu of his pilgrimage to Rome, set about rebuilding the Abbey, and

Preceding pages: *Trafalgar Square by Moonlight,* by 19th-century artist Henry Pether. **Left:** detail from an artist's impression of Roman London. **Right:** early Roman mosaic found under the City.

it was there that succeeding kings were crowned, married and, until George III, were buried.

City landmarks: In 1066 William the Conqueror brought the laws of Normandy to England, but promised the City of London privileges that are still honoured today. Self-direction in local affairs was satisfied by the election of a first mayor in 1192, with aldermen and a court. A new St Paul's Cathedral was started and the great keep of the White Tower completed in 1097. Westminster Hall, probably the largest building of its kind in Europe, followed. By 1176 work had begun on a stone London Bridge, houses had

appeared on it and the suburb on the south bank was growing. Though the Roman wall, now with six gates, still formed the city boundary, that part on the river bank had been replaced with wharves.

Trading ships sailed up the Fleet and Walbrook rivers to quays now long buried but remembered in local street names. Narrow lanes between old manors and religious houses within the city wall set the pattern for the later congested, haphazard arrangement of streets and alleys that has persisted to our time. The only surviving landmark is Crosby Hall, a typical merchant's mansion built

originally in Bishopsgate and then re-built on Chelsea Embankment.

Along the riverside road to Westminster, fine houses with gardens running down to the water brought early ribbon development. Bridewell Palace at Ludgate was built alongside a bishop's palace at Salisbury House near St Bride's. In the Strand, the Palace of the Savoy stood next to Durham House.

London was now home to more than 25,000 people, worshipping in over 100 parish churches within the walls and almost within the shadow of a medieval St Paul's.

Union and plague: By the 14th century the city's merchants had joined together in craft associations for protection and trade promotion and built their "gild" halls. The 15th-century Guildhall followed, and fire, bombing and restorers have failed to diminish it as one of the City's key buildings.

Lawyers now got together in Inns west of the City and bishops further afield in palaces at Lambeth, Holborn, Fulham and Southwark. London still had farms, smallholdings and marshy wastelands an archer's shot away from its walls.

Chaucer's city had grown to 50,000 inhabitants despite the "Black Death" of 1348, when, in one day alone, 200 dead were taken outside the city and buried in mass graves.

London stopped growing in the 14th century. The City (now with a capital C) quite simply had no ambitions to get any bigger. Had it wanted to, it would have had to change its character, perhaps endanger its hard-won privileges and sacrifice its unique position as a major European market and port. Whatever was happening outside the walls, the City was in blinkered detachment that was not to be disturbed until Queen Victoria's reign.

Attempts were made to restrict the growth of London and Westminster. No more houses were to be built. Enforcement, however, was ineffectual and parishes continued growing until common purposes dictated a common form of government and the County of London was born.

Left: London Bridge as depicted in Visscher's *Long View of London*, 1616. **Right**: Charles d'Orléans in the Tower of London.

Much married and celebrated divorcee Henry VIII almost qualifies as the "father" of modern London, though the changes he brought about were the accidental outcome of a bid for personal freedom from the power of the Church.

In 1536 Henry persuaded Parliament to authorise the dissolution of the monasteries. Their property and revenues were granted to the Crown, and Henry either made them a gift to close supporters or sold them. Cardinal Wolsey's house was added to an expanding palace in Whitehall. Hyde Park and St James's were enclosed as deer parks.

When foreign visitors commented on the depressing ruins of the churches and monasteries, the areas became "ripe for development". The City fathers took on the church's humanitarian work, buying St Thomas's to care for the sick and elderly, Greyfriars for orphans, Bridewell for criminals and beggars, and Bethlehem ("Bedlam"), to house lunatics.

Convent (Covent) Garden and Clerkenwell, Stepney and Shoreditch, Kennington and Lambeth all succumbed to population increases, taking the total of London's inhabitants from 50,000 in 1500 to 200,000 by the end of the century. Today, little survives of Tudor London's typically wood-framed houses with oversailing upper storeys. A fair idea of the character of the old-time street scene can be seen in the Old Curiosity Shop at 13 Portsmouth Street, near Lincoln's Inn.

Henry VIII's daughter Elizabeth, who came to the throne in 1558, was truly London's queen and the "golden" age began, not only in a commercial sense, but also in education and the arts.

Reminders of the city at this time remain in today's street names. Bread, Milk and Wood Streets recall Cheapside market, while Cheapside Cross and St Paul's Cross remain as testaments to Edward I's devotion to Eleanor. In all, he set up 12 crosses to record

EST. CIRCA 1735

the resting places of her body in the slow march to Westminster Abbey.

At St Paul's, much of the preaching was still done outside the Cathedral. By this time the trading which had been carried out inside the nave, known at the time as "Paul's Walk", went to Sir Thomas Gresham's new Royal Exchange.

One man, a Londoner by adoption, came to dominate the Elizabethan scene—William Shakespeare. At the time, however, he was not officially very popular. The Lord Mayor banned theatrical performances from London. Shakespeare and his fellow playwright Ben Jonson moved to new sites on the south bank of the Thames: the Globe, Swan and Hope, which they shared with bear pits, brothels and prisons.

Revolution and style: Queen Elizabeth's deathbed choice of her Protestant son James to succeed her nearly brought about his death and the dissolution of Parliament. In a thwarted attempt to blow up Parliament, Robert Catesby attempted to further the Roman Catholic cause. November the 5th, Guy

Left, Elizabeth I, queen of the Golden Age. **Right**, Shakespeare remembered in London today.

Fawkes Day, is still commemorated today with fireworks.

Against a background of conflict between King James and Parliament, the look of London responded to a new influence: the Italian architecture of Palladio as seen through the profoundly individual work of Inigo Jones. The purity of Jones's style is best seen in the Queen's House at Greenwich, begun in 1613. Six years later came the Banqueting House in Whitehall, the first time Portland stone was used in London. Throwing Gothic to the winds, he went on to design the little known Queen's Chapel at St James's Palace.

His most significant contribution to the new city was his work on the old Convent Garden for the Duke of Bedford. The great Piazza he created there was the prototype for the most loved and typical feature of the city, the London square. On the east side, behind a massive portico is "the handsomest barn in England". His St Paul's church. Jones also had a significant influence on the architects who followed, such as Sir Christopher Wren.

Water, pestilence and fire: At the beginning of the 17th century, London's rapidly expanding population began to make demands on water supplies that the city could not satisfy. Private, though necessarily self-interested, benefactors set up conduits in various streets and restrictions were put on brewers and fishmongers to prevent waste.

By 1600 a source of pure water was vital, and for one man, Hugh Myddleton, an obsession. A Welshman, goldsmith and banker, he conceived the idea of bringing a "New River" to London from springs near Hertford. At his own expense he started work on the man-made river in 1609 and brought it as far as Enfield before his money ran out. Myddelton turned to a former customer, James I, who became his partner in the project with a half share in the profits. By 1613 the New River Head in Finsbury, just north of the City, was reached.

Great tragedies lay ahead for London. In 1665 the still inadequate water supply and lack of sanitation brought the dreaded Plague to the overcrowded city, and before it ran its course 100,000 inhabitants died. The Great Fire less than a year later came as if to cleanse the stricken city. From a baker's shop on Pudding Lane, Eastcheap, the flames raged through the streets for five days, reaching as far west as the Temple.

Samuel Pepys watched it start from the attic of his house in Seething Lane near the Tower. Under the Lord Mayor's direction, houses were pulled down to stop the fire spreading, but most people were too busy removing their belongings to the churches or to boats on the river to help. Pepys hurriedly dug a pit in his garden to save his wine and "parmazan" cheese. He saw "St Paul's church with all the roof fallen", and watched the fire crossing the Bridge to Southwark.

After the fire, 13,000 houses and 87 parish churches lay in ruins, but rebuilding was immediately the main topic of discussion.

One architect's dream: Christopher Wren, Surveyor General to the Crown, returned from Paris, his mind filled with new ideas. London, too, he thought, should have *rond-points*, vistas and streets laid out in a grid pattern. However, the people wanted homes quickly and shopkeepers and traders wanted to carry on their businesses, so Wren's best ideas were never to be realised. Expedience dictated that the new should rise on the sites of the old, with one prudent difference: new buildings were constructed in brick, not wood.

Wren turned his inventive powers to rebuilding 50 of the damaged churches in the City. His achievements lie in the individuality of their soaring towers and steeples which rise above the rooftops. In 1675 work began on a new St Paul's Cathedral, his acknowledged masterpiece.

By 1700 City men were beginning to commute from fashionable suburbs like St James's, and from Soho and Mayfair in the west and Holborn and Clerkenwell in the north. Only a quarter of the regional population (674,000) lived in the old City.

Woolnoth, St George, Bloomsbury and Christchurch, Spitalfields.

Ripples of growth: House building spread through the green fields beyond Soho towards Hyde Park and across the Tyburn road. As the ripple of this 18th-century building ring moved outwards, the older centre was coming to the end of its useful life. The need for better communications, now becoming a priority, brought demands for another river crossing. Westminster Bridge was completed in 1751, but nearly 20 years passed before the City had its own second bridge at Blackfriars.

Whitehall was now beginning to take on

A tax was raised in 1710 to provide "fifty new churches in and about the cities of London and Westminster and Suburbs thereof" but only a handful were built. Gibbs built St Mary-le-Strand and St Martin-in-the-Fields, but it was Hawksmoor, Wren's right-hand man, who expressed his art most profoundly and nobly in St Anne's, Limehouse, St George-in-the-East, St Mary

Left, the Great Fire, which killed 100,000 Londoners, captured by an unknown artist. **Right**, *The Frozen Thames*, by Abram Hondius, shows that London's climate used to be considerably colder.

its 20th-century character. The palace of kings was replaced by the palaces of government, with office blocks for the Admiralty and Treasury, and William Kent's faintly incongruous barracks for the Horse Guards.

As the century proceeded the work of two Scottish men had far-reaching effects. From their very separate corners, heavyweight William Chambers and lightweight Robert Adam came out fighting for the title of most influential architect. Adam's Adelphi, begun in 1768, and Chambers' Somerset House of 1776, both set between the Strand and the river, aptly contrast their styles.

SPLENDOUR AND SWEATSHOPS

By 1800 London was poised on the brink of a population explosion without parallel anywhere in the world. In the next 35 years it was to double in size – and the railways were yet to come.

While Britain was at war with France, work on public buildings necessarily withered, but housing statistics swelled with the increases in civil servants. Paddington and Marylebone, Camberwell and Kensington, Bethnal Green and Hackney, Knightsbridge and Chelsea forged their identities and hastened to join hands in the family of London. It was certainly becoming an affluent family, prompting the Emperor of Russia on a visit in 1814 to ask "Where are your poor?"

Growing pains: The Emperor, however, had not been east of the Tower. Unlike the West End, the East End suffered ribbon building along the roads to Essex. Whitechapel High Street was "pestered with cottages", and Wapping with mean tenements. It was an area vulnerable to the impact of new developments in commerce following the Industrial Revolution. Canals had already linked the Thames with the industrial Midlands. Docks cruelly dismembered the riverside parishes. In 1825, 1,250 houses were swept away for St Katherine's Dock alone. The inhabitants were compressed, sardine style, into accommodation nearby. The character of the modern East End was in the making. "Sweat shops" and the labour to go with them multiplied in this fertile soil of ruthless competition, poverty and immigration.

The Thames was still the natural gateway to London, and the East End the natural landfall for the foreigner. In 1687 alone, 13,500 new Londoners arrived from the Continent in flight from persecution. The Huguenots settled in Spitalfields, planting mulberry trees in their gardens to feed the silkworms that produced the silk to feed the

looms in their attics. These were the elite of immigrants. The Polish and Russian Jews that came to Whitechapel were less privileged, producing clothing, boots and shoes and cheap furniture in living and working conditions that coined a word of unknown origin: "slum".

By the 1830s the Industrial Revolution was making its impact on the Thames below Wapping. The marshy pools of the Isle of Dogs, long dedicated to the rural pursuits of

duck shooting and hunting, were deepened to make the West and East India Docks. Wharves and shipyards lined the banks of the river itself in Blackwall, Deptford and Greenwich. The workers doubled the population and whole new parishes were formed. London was now the centre of Britain's industry; its trades literally "housed" in the older areas outside the City. Coachmakers gathered in Covent Garden's Long Acre; furniture makers in the straggling Tottenham Court Road. Vauxhall, Battersea and Wandsworth came up smelling of soap, paint, chemicals and varnish.

Left, an oil painting by Phoebus Leven, 1864, shows Covent Garden market as a centre of trade and gossip. **Right**, Gustav Doré chronicled the growth of the capital's slums.

With all this activity London's air was dense with smog – although this word had not yet been coined. Earliest photographs of London's streets show them disappearing into a "fog" after a couple of hundred yards, even on a good day.

Dickens was obsessed by this fog. *Bleak House* opens with probably his most famous piece of descriptive writing: "Fog everywhere. Fog up the river, where it flows among green aits and meadows; fog down the river, where it rolls defiled among the tiers of shipping, and the waterside pollutions of a great and dirty city."

The marks of prosperity: The growth of political, cultural and commercial importance of London as the "World Metropolis". The genius whose inspired proposals for a garden city linked by a new road to the Prince Regent's Carlton House met with such ready acceptance was John Nash.

His ideas were allowed to materialise only in part. Just eight villas were built, half a circus at Park Crescent, and the Regent's Canal, brought in for picturesque effect, was banished to the outer perimeter. The famous stucco terraces, palaces whose closer inspection of both design and workmanship can be a disappointment, are undeniably superb scenery. Their appreciation need not

residential London to the north and west was reflecting not only the new prosperity, but the recognition by dukes and speculators of the enormous potential of their estates so close to the centre. The big houses were razed and the streets and squares of Portland and Portman, Berners and Bedford, Southampton and Somers rose in their places in the rather severe pattern associated nowadays with Georgian London.

One estate, old Marylebone Park, shaped like a balloon with a string stretching down to the Strand, reverted to the Crown in 1811. Its development was to display the growing

be destroyed by the knowledge that today's renewed domes are only fibreglass deep.

Nash's Regent Street, completed in 1823, carved an inspired path between Soho and Mayfair that defined and isolated the character of both areas effectively.

A quarter turn brought the new street to Piccadilly and on line for Carlton House. Unfortunately it was replaced by Carlton House Terrace when Buckingham House was upgraded to a Palace. There followed a re-planned St James's Park, improvements in the Strand, and the creation of a new open space, Trafalgar Square.

The pity is that Nash's work at Buckingham Palace lies buried beneath the facades of later and lesser architects. The saying goes: "But is not our Nash too, a very great master? He found us all brick, and leaves us all plaster." An architect's most telling epitaph?

Congestion and crime: London, in the second quarter of the 19th century, used newfound power and a vast amount of public money to grapple with the problems of its own making. The City was becoming very congested, so bridges were built at Waterloo and Hammersmith. London Bridge was rebuilt and foot passengers given a tunnel under the Thames at Wapping.

Londoners were on the move. In 1829 Mr Shillibeer introduced them to the omnibus, and the first steam train arrived with the London & Greenwich Railway of 1838. Terminal stations followed at Euston, King's Cross and Paddington by 1853; at Blackfriars, Charing Cross and St Pancras by 1871. The tracks elbowed their way through built-up areas to the fringes of the city and destroyed thousands of homes en route. At the same time, Londoners gave up "living over the shop" and travelled out to dormitories in ever more distant suburbs.

The city was about to embark on a programme of renewal that was to bring the

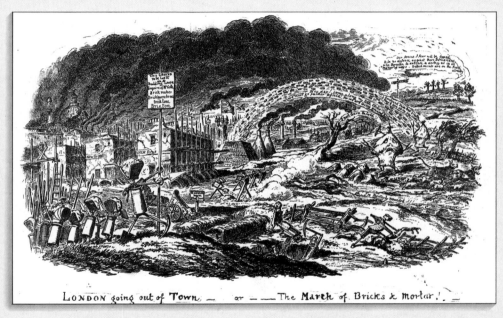

LONDON going out of Town — or — The March of Bricks & Mortar!

Courts of law and prisons responded to rising crime, while gentlemen's clubs responded to the Regency passion for gambling. In Bloomsbury's Gower Street, London University was born, and the market came to Covent Garden. Great collections were housed in the British Museum and National Gallery, and a lesser one in Sir John Soane's exquisite building at Dulwich.

Left, Regent Street, an integral part of Nash's grand design for London. Above, *The March of Bricks and Mortar*, depicted by the celebrated cartoonist George Cruickshank.

most significant changes since the rebuilding that followed the Great Fire.

The Great Exhibition of 1851: "All London is astir, and some part of all the world." So John Ruskin wrote in his dairy on the morning Queen Victoria opened the Great International Exhibition in Hyde Park. Paxton's palace of iron and glass, fathered by the station roofs of Euston, King's Cross and Bunning's Coal Exchange, grew from a doodle on blotting paper.

The lightweight, light-admittting structure was made for speedy erection and perfectly suited to its purpose of displaying

Britain's skills and achievements to the world. Transported to south London three years later, it gave its name to a new Victorian suburb, Crystal Palace – although the building itself has long gone.

With money taken at the turnstiles of the Great Exhibition, Prince Albert, Queen Victoria's husband, realised his great ambition: a centre of learning. Temples to the arts and sciences blossomed in Kensington's nursery gardens. The Victoria and Albert Museum were followed by the Queen's tribute to her Regent: the Royal Albert Memorial (the Albert Hall in 1871), museums, colleges and a large block of flats.

At Westminster, work was proceeding after the destruction by fire of the Houses of Parliament in 1834 – caused, ironically enough, by an overheated furnace. Barry and Pugin's gothic extravaganza rose, phoenix-like from the ashes; the House of Lords by 1847, the Commons and Big Ben by 1858 and the Victoria Tower by 1860. Shortly afterwards, it was discovered that, because of defective sewers, the whole place was a sitting on a cesspool!

A familiar face: By this time, the "sights" of London had dropped into place. The British Museum gave a home to the Elgin Marbles, and Trafalgar Square gave a hero's welcome to Nelson's column. The City Corporation, meanwhile, was making determined efforts to unlock the congested streets, cutting swathes through Holborn's houses and cemeteries for the viaduct to bridge the Fleet valley. Fleet Street, the Strand and Whitehall were by-passed by the grand boulevard of the Victoria Embankment, and Cheapside by Queen Victoria Street.

Further upstream, the Chelsea Embankment savaged the artists' riverside village. The Tower suffered, too, when a new river crossing opened in 1894 and had the gall to take its name: Tower Bridge. Steel dressed up in stone, but an acknowledged engineering feat, Tower Bridge has become a symbol for London, rivalling St Paul's.

By 1859 another problem had arisen, serious enough to cause the adjournment of the House of Commons: the unbearable stench from the Thames. Londoners still depended largely on the river for drinking water, and at the same time disposed of all their sewage in the river. Outbreaks of cholera were common until the City Engineer, Joseph Bazalgette, devised a scheme to take the sewage well downstream to Barking and release it into the river after treatment. His scheme, which involved creating the embankments, was in operation by 1875 and is still the basis of the modern drainage system.

Slums and suburbs: London was also at last waking up to the problems presented by a polarised community. East was East, poverty and overcrowding, and West was West, affluence and spacious living. The twain met where pockets of slums in older areas co-

existed with the city's greatest treasures, like Tom-All-Alone's next to Southwark Cathedral. Charles Dickens described the resort of down-and-outs and penny-a-nighters in *Bleak House*. Jo, the crossing sweeper, lived in Tom-All-Alone's, as one of "a crowd of foul existence that crawls in and out of gaps in walls and boards; and coils itself to sleep, in maggot numbers where the rain drips in".

Public conscience was aroused by the writings of Dickens and Henry Mayhew, stimulating political action and private philanthrophy.

The railways did some of their work for

them. The hovels of Shoreditch were destroyed for a terminus at Bishopsgate in 1843. St Pancras Station dispatched the squalor of Agar Town, which Dickens called "an English Connemara" because of its Irish population. Soon London's clerks and lower paid workers began colonising the new world at the city's edge, opened by the first suburban railway, the Metropolitan, in 1863.

The road builders did even better. St Giles's "Rookery" disappeared beneath New Oxford Street and Shaftesbury Avenue, and much of Wapping High Street was taken for road widening. The insanitary dwellings of Clare Market and Drury Lane were to

for the working classes of London along with the later Guinness Trust, made a positive and lasting contribution to the relieve the suffering of London's poor. Even today, the Peabody Trust continues to provide housing for the poor in many areas of central London.

Less lasting was a cathedral of a market hall that Baroness Burdett-Coutts built, in mistaken zeal, for the deprived inhabitants of Bethnal Green. Not surprisingly, it never paid its way.

The example of these public-spirited people was followed by wider powers for local authorities to deal with overcrowding and derelict property. Greater changes were im-

survive until the Aldwych development in 1900. Some slums persisted, such as the homes of immigrant communities like the Jews in Whitechapel, the Lascars in the West India Dock Road, and the Chinese community in Limehouse.

It was left to an American philanthropist, George Peabody, not just to destroy the wretched, insanitary hovels, but to provide a decent alternative. Peabody Trust dwellings

Left, the streets became increasingly congested.
Above, the world's first Underground railway was powered by steam.

minent. The City's square mile was separated from the 117 sq. miles (303 sq. km) of the new County of London, and in 1889 London's government was vested in London County Council, housed in the newly built County Hall, across the river from the home of the central government at Westminster.

Come the beginning of the 20th century, the city was throbbing with life, pulling the strings of "puppet states" within the Empire and unloading the Empire's fortunes across its wharves. London's docklands became known as the warehouse of the world.

Then came modern history.

Twice in its long history London has risen from the flames. On the first occasion, in 1666, it was a moment of carelessness in Farryner's bakeshop which led to the Great Fire. On the second, 275 years later, it was the bombs and rockets of the Third Reich which killed 29,000 Londoners and changed the face of the City.

Bomb damage: St Paul's Cathedral straddles the two eras. Perhaps the most famous home front photograph of World War II shows Sir Christopher Wren's great dome looming out of a swirl of smoke and ash. Wren's church, which is known to be at least the fifth to occupy the ancient site, was built on the charred ruins left by the Great Fire. Even then, there was a sense that St Paul's had a symbolic importance to the City that Samuel Pepys's diary movingly described as devastated by its losses. There is a story that, when Wren asked a workman to fetch him a stone in order to mark the precise centre of the cleared site, the man returned with a fragment of an old tombstone. On it was inscribed the single word *Resurgam*, "I will arise again".

In more recent years, St Paul's has become a symbol of a rather different sort, a bulwark rather than a phoenix. All around it, on the sites that were blazing in the famous wartime photograph, have sprung up some of the less happy examples of modern architecture in the capital. The more conservative of the clerks and clerics who walk through the charmless concrete precincts of Paternoster Square like to say that the modern town planners and architects have done more damage to London's landscape than the Luftwaffe did.

Policy change: Forty years after the war's end and two decades since the planners' worst excesses, there is a move back to "traditional" values in city architecture and planning. The adage "small is beautiful" had

never before seemed appropriate. The tendency to see London as a whole, rather than as a massive jigsaw of parts, meant that "policy" often won over common sense. So far, the process has been only defensive; a spate of renovations and refittings in place of the old demolish-and-build. In architecture, more than in most professions, you have to live with your mistakes for a very long time.

There is another architectural symbol of the modern metropolis which is more com-

plex. Along the busy spine of Holborn, High Holborn and New Oxford Streets is Centre Point, 350 vertical feet (107 metres) of offices, built in 1965 and largely unoccupied until the 1980s. Property prices and ground rents in central London were so high by its completion that it wasn't economical for many years to lease it out. At night, the words "Centre Point" in lights glow over the city from its vantage point at the junction of Oxford Street, Charing Cross Road and Tottenham Court Road. At the precise heart of London, a potent image of the architects' dilemma and fate, buildings conceived from

Left, England declared war on Germany on 3 September 1939. **Right**, newsvendors are still very much a feature of street life.

the outside and so only ever known from the outside, absolutely inescapable but unloved.

Skyscrapers: Curiously, Centre Point is an unrepresentative symbol of the new London. Of all the European cities devastated during the war, London is the least skyscrapered. With so much bombsite available in the centre and with only the rather notional boundary of the Green Belt on the periphery, there was still more than enough scope for the planners to spread outwards rather than upwards. The effect has been to highlight the few genuine skyscrapers, which are instantly recognisable on the horizon of the contemporary skyline.

giant IPC magazine publishers). Today, most of the high-rise building is residential and is well away from the city centre.

Suburban high-rise: With much of the traditional East End homes and industry destroyed in the Blitz, the planners decided to turn the old residential street on end and move it out to Essex or across the river to Peckham and Camberwell. The "vertical street" was an elegant phrase and idea that worked well on paper, but turned into a messy tragedy in actual practice. The fatal 1960s collapse of a residential tower block at Ronan Point in Hackney merely underlined a nagging doubt that was beginning to de-

Looking across London from the 1964 Post Office Tower (now the London Telecom Tower, closed to visitors in order to deter terrorist bombings) there is little of that "rising tide" effect that afflicts both New York and Tokyo and makes both cities a claustrophobic experience. The Telecom Tower is no longer the city's tallest building; that honour first went to the moodily black tower of the National Westminster Bank in Bishopsgate, EC2. This, in turn, has been superseded by Canary Wharf. There is a knot of "media towers" on the South Bank (housing London Weekend Television and the

velop about the technical and social problems of high-rise living. Though the high blocks built on the devastated Barbican site (now the Barbican Centre) attracted considerable social prestige, high-rise living became increasingly associated with poor-quality housing and a welter of social problems. It was all too easy to concentrate the poor and less well adjusted into multi-storey flats or sardine-tin estates.

City sprawl: For many people, the lure of one's own home was great and the biggest residential shift of the post-war years was to the new private estates and ribbon developments mushrooming in London's suburbs. The post-war houses of north London are often reminiscent of the Pete Seeger song *Little Boxes:* "all made out of ticky-tacky/ And they all look the same."

Housing in all forms has seen many changes. In 1910 only about 10 percent of all dwellings in the country were owned by the people who lived in them. By contrast, today only 10 percent are now privately rented, and the past couple of decades have seen the extensive refurbishment of Victorian terraces, dividing and sub-dividing houses into a multiplication of apartments. The result has been the gradual forcing of the old,

recent years by the arrival of computer-led trains and communications centres. The truth is that the development of Docklands has seen the destruction of some old properties, but it has also seen the creation of many new ones, and the developers have been forced to sell some of their houses at "affordable prices" to the residents of the area. The high premium of houses in this area allowed some of the more unscrupulous locals to buy affordable housing and resell it instantly at a much higher market price. The arrival of sky-high interest rates at the end of the 1980s have done much to restore realistc property values.

traditional Londoner further and further out into the suburbs, where house prices are – sometimes – cheaper. Inner London has been increasingly converted, and colonised by the new Londoner, who has migrated into the city from far corners of the country.

This colonisation has been accused of destroying London life, and nowhere more so than in Docklands, where the local environment of Eastenders has been transformed in

Left, during World War II, Underground stations also functioned as air raid shelters. **Above**, urban sprawl surrounds the Oval cricket ground.

Docklands has also provided a venue for the architects, who, frustrated by decades of conversions, have gone to town and created a new city of myriad shapes and sizes along the dozens of miles of waterfront.

Local rule: There has always been tension in London, as in any great city, between localism and corporate municipal values. With a resident population of 6.8 million and a working and visiting population that is far higher than that, Greater London is like a small country with the traditional conflict between national and local government. Since 1888 and until it became the Greater

THE BOBBY

The urban policeman—popularly known as a bobby—is almost a London landmark in his or her right, as much pointed at as Big Ben and almost as often photographed.

The British bobby has an avuncular image which is at odds with the city police of most other countries. He does not carry a gun or wear dark glasses; somewhere within his clothing are a truncheon (baton), a puny whistle and a pair of handcuffs. This lack of personal arsenal reflects the fact that London is not a dangerous city, considering its size.

In 1991-2 there were 185 murders in the metropolitan area, compared to more than 2,000 in New York City, although there are some differences in definition of murder between the two centres. Minor assaults are much more common, with Oxford Circus Underground station being the worst, particularly for pickpockets and bag snatchers.

The police have a good record for solving the more serious crimes. Of 1991-2's 185 murders, 163 were solved, representing a clear-up rate of 88 percent. However, the rate overall for the 945,300 notifiable offences committed in the city that year was well below that at 16 percent.

One of the largest categories affecting the visitor is the incidence of street robbery, at 22,500 in 1991-2 and increasing. On the other hand, the incidence of rape has been gradually decreasing.

Today there are more than 28,000 officers in the Metropolitan police department (Met). The force was started in 1829, but the original "Peelers", as they were called then, were such a welcome novelty that they spent much of their time chasing out-of-town criminals for a fee from wealthy landlords. In the 19th century the force was often supplemented by "special constables" for particularly dangerous occasions and gatherings such as the Chartist demonstration of 1848, which was policed by 4,000 regular policeman and 17,000 specials.

Today there are 1,500 specials in the Met, and despite being unpaid volunteer part-time officers they have the same uniform and the same powers as a regular bobby. This type of force is unique to the UK.

In addition to the Met, the City has its own distinct force of 1,000 officers, which functions within the confines of the financial square mile. City officers are distinguished by red and white markings and a combed helmet.

Basic qualifications for the force are being a British citizen of good character, being able to swim 100 metres and having good eyesight. There may also be an aptitude test. The Met has recently abolished minimum height qualifications, but the City force still sets high standards: male officers must be over 5' 11" tall.

A police officer does not have the right to go on strike and his brief extends beyond just the prevention of crime to the community to helping the public in emergencies and in difficulties.

For most visitors to London a policeman will be a source of advice and information. Athough the policy of community policing (friendly bobbies on bicycles) has been a key objective of the Met in recent years, the force has often been in conflict with London's resident ethnic communities.

The city's largest policing event for the Met is the Notting Hill Carnival, using 10,500 officers. Unfortunately, confrontations with the city's West Indian community have become regular.

Particularly contentious have been the "sus" laws—the stopping and searching of someone on the street on "reasonable suspicion that an offence has been or is being committed". They became law in 1986.

Adding to the tension is the fact that out of 1,147 members who joined the Met in 1991-2 only 6.6 percent belonged to an ethnic minority—a tiny proportion considering the mixture that constitutes London.

Despite the force's often contrary claims, the image of the police, particularly to visitors (a Londoner's view of the Metropolitan officer differs according to his ethnic origin, his neighbourhood in the city, and his social class) has always been a good one, helped by the media. Television programmes in particular have promoted the image of the fundamentally caring but rather over-worked hero of the street.

London Council (GLC) in 1965, the London County Council (LCC) oversaw all the planning policy and urban amenities within its 117 sq. miles (302 sq. km) of authority.

In the immediate post-war years, not even a mood of optimism (compounded of two parts relief, one part genuine forward looking) could ignore the fact that the social and political tide had turned. Central government was more powerful than ever before, but under Labour governments the commitment to planned municipal progress was not what it had been. The private speculators were to have their day; a uniformly, authority-planned city was out of favour.

planned society was something that the GLC never quite overcame. When it was abolished in 1986, as part of a government programme to streamline city bureaucracy by restoring final authority to the borough councils, the first signs of change came on the very day of abolition when workmen removed the "GLC" prefix from all the South Bank Centre signs. Abolition was one of the great political controversies of the decade, but has been superseded in the 1990s by the "poll tax" debate; some Labour-controlled London councils even took the Government to court over its imposition of the new local tax (levied on all adults rather than,

The LCC's great post-war achievement and symbol was the Royal Festival Hall, centrepiece of the current South Bank Centre and of the arts complex that includes the Queen Elizabeth Hall, National Theatre and National Film Theatre. The building may have looked promising in the firework's glare of the 1951 Festival of Britain for which it was built, but looks increasingly out of place in the 1990s. A facelift is planned.

Planned society: Popular suspicion of a

Landmarks: community mural in Hackney, and the ageing but still futuristic Telecom Tower.

as previously, only property owners).

Without the central control of the GLC, London reverted to its village sub-structure, based around its 33 boroughs. Outsiders are surprised to hear locals in Wandsworth or Lewisham, Blackheath or Southall, talk of "London" as if it were a separate place. It was the GLC's job to make the diverse communities work as one unit, to the advantage of all. On its reconstitution in 1965, it inherited massive social problems not of its own making and most of them not susceptible to central planning. Moreover, the actual trends were opposite to the political agenda.

Political issues became wider, but people's lives were once again being concentrated more and more on specific communities, either geographical, ethnic or social, with their own circumstances and problems.

Such decentralisation was brought to the fore once again in the late 1980s, with the threat to the future of the Inner London Education Authority (Ilea), the governing body which catered to all London's educational needs, from primary to adult. London boroughs are being given the opportunity to opt out of Ilea and run their own schools, adult classes and centres for problem children, and it seems that enough might do so to

leads to tension. In place of neighbourliness and co-operation, there grew a curious, mixture of hostility and intense tribalism. The "social problems" discussed in the media after the tragic Broadwater Farm estate rioting in 1986 in which a policeman was killed, were little more than an expression of that paradoxical mix. Once again, people became highly territorial.

A further instance of this concentration is the growth of new custom-built shopping centres in place of old local shops and pubs. People are being forced to travel further and further from home in order to shop, eat and drink. To cap paradox with irony, transpor-

bring about the collapse of the old system. Ilea was very much associated with the GLC in the past, and that association is probably the reason for its problems today.

Estate problems: One tried, but equally controversial, alternative to the high-rise approach to public housing was small but densely concentrated estates, often quite separate from the surrounding streets, with raised walkways and split-level entrances. These estates were a bid to restore the old community spirit of the East End streets, but such a spirit takes generations to build up. Random concentrations of people merely

tation is getting more problematic, and the average speed of London traffic has declined from 12 to 8 mph (13 kph). Even so, there is no wooing Londoners away from the private car. The giant Brent Cross shopping centre in NW4, for example, serves an astonishing two million people, the vast majority of whom arrive by car. Similar warehouse shopping centres have also been created in south London.

History's process: If it's hard to escape the sense of history in any important city, it's particularly hard in London. Science fiction writers like to fantasise about what would have happened if England had been invaded and conquered in 1942; would Piccadilly have become "Adolf Hilterstrasse" and Trafalgar Square "Hindenbergplatz"? Street signs are still the best fossil trace of a city's past. It's possible, even without a knowledge of architectural style, to date rows of streets by their names: Scutari, Therapia and Mundania Roads in Forest Hill declare their origins in the Crimean War; in Shepherd's Bush, the signs say Bloemfontein, Mafeking and Ladysmith, suggesting Victorian struggles overseas. Today in Brixton a park is named after a jazz drummer, Max Roach. An industrial estate is dedicated to the black

woman on the street, have spread upwards. Though the architects and planners are largely in retreat, they've also never been busier. Thames-side has a new ribbon development as the old disused warehouses and wharves of a past industrial age are demolished or renovated, both in Docklands and in upmarket areas such as Chelsea, Battersea and Fulham.

Rebirth: There are questions about turning the Smithfield Meat Market into another shopping and tourist centre along the lines of Covent Garden. The planners have not been sated and there is considerable controversy over plans to redevelop an area most people

American revolutionary Angela Davis, and there are several Nelson Mandela streets, squares and houses.

Change continues and brings with it the predictable mixture of enthusiasm and fear. The Prince of Wales, who made his first impact on the city's architectural community by referring to the proposed National Gallery extension as a "carbuncle", has since led the way in condemning the more outrageous projects. Suspicions about modern architecture, long held by the man and

Sitting pretty in Chelsea: pensioners and punks.

regard as complete. In the City, the exciting, post-modern Lloyd's building off Fenchurch Street, is loved by visitors but disliked by those who have to work in it.

Many of London's older buildings have spent much of the past few years encased in tarpaulins, shrouded in plastic or hidden behind lurid murals. Visitors could be forgiven for wondering whether they were viewing some new type of bizarre modern art project: "London, the wrapped city".

It's never finished, this process of change, and that is why, as Dr Johnson found, it is impossible to be tired of London.

Saris and sarongs; mosques and mandirs; calypso and chopsticks; turbans and tandooris. Somewhere within London there is something of everything and someone from everywhere.

Over a quarter of the central London's population was not born in the UK. The nation's non-white population may be just 4.4 percent, but it reaches 20 percent in inner London. The city is a cultural melting pot, which residents tend to take for granted.

Asians were the first immigrants to come to Britain in any number, and as many as 10,000 people of Indian origin were residents by 1579 – the year when missionary Thomas Stephens became the first Briton to set foot in India.

Immigrants: The ethnic influence stretches out as far as Heathrow. The airport was built by construction workers from Punjab, India. At the height of the 1950s post-war boom, London was starved of semi-skilled labour. A retired major in the British Indian Army hit upon the idea of importing sturdy Sikhs to bolster Heathrow's workforce.

After the Sikhs came the West Indians to run London's buses and the Underground railway network. In the prosperous textile mills of Yorkshire and Lancashire, the Pakistanis kept the machines rolling around the clock. As the corners of the British empire collapsed, the immigrants holding British passports claimed their rights to continue living in Great Britain. Many of them settled in ghettos around the city which are now communities in their own right.

The largest non-white ethnic groups are the Indians (689,000) followed by West Indians (500,000), Pakistanis (406,000), Chinese (122,000), Africans (102,000) and other smaller groups. Today, with the East African Asians, the Bangladeshis and the Vietnamese boat people, Britain's Asian

Preceding pages: minorities have injected new culture into the city. **Left**, traffic warden of Caribbean origin. **Right**, the Regent's Park mosque, gathering place for London's Muslims.

population of over one million is by far the largest in Europe.

There are plenty of sub-sections within the major groups: Sikhs, complete with Kirpans (small swords) and unshorn hair live in Southall, not far from Heathrow; the Bangladeshis dominate the rag trade in the less affluent East End of London, which was once the home of Russian and Jewish tailors and bootmakers; and the entrepreneurial Patels, the original dukanwallahs, with their

open-all-hours corner stores are just about everywhere. Many respond to the call of the muezzin in the Regent's Park Mosque.

A home away from home: The Patels (which in Gujarati means a village chief) made the best of three worlds. Born in job-starved India and angered by the rampant caste system, they gladly responded when the British, at the height of the Raj, asked for volunteers to work in East Africa on the coastal railways. There they learned English to deal with their bosses, mastered Swahili to get on with their African "boys", and scrupulously retained their own language, customs and culture. When African nationalism struck in the 1960s, they fled from Kenya, Uganda and Tanzania to what they regarded as their final home: Great Britain. In the capital they settled in the north London suburb of Brent, which became known as Little Gujarat. Brent was also the home of many newcomers. Today, its schools list 200 languages as the mother tongues of their students, ranging from Sinhalese to Serbo-Croatian, Cantonese to Canarese.

The largest number of immigrants to London come from the Republic of Ireland. After the Blitz, they helped lay the city's massive railway network and rebuild the

Domestic help: About half a million foreigners, mainly refugees and displaced persons from Europe, entered Britain after the war. In the 1960s, the British Ministry of Labour lured Spaniards and Portuguese with work permits. The final wave of immigrants started in the 1970s with workers coming from countries such as the Philippines, Morocco and Latin America. They came to work for hospitals and hotels, filling positions in catering and domestic work.

Domestic work was the order of the day for the young African slaves brought back to England in the 1570s. In Elizabethan England, there were black entertainers at court.

capital. Kilburn and Camden are high-density Irish areas.

Poles who fought with Britain against Nazi Germany as pilots and aircraft mechanics migrated along with the Italians, who brought their pasta and candle-lit religious festivals to Islington. The Greek Cypriots run most of the Greek restaurants, and all are part and parcel of modern London. In summer, when the countries of the Middle East become too hot for comfort, London attracts many Arabs, who spend much of their time enjoying the coolness of the parks and the breadth of shopping opportunities.

Black people were used as payment for the return of 89 English prisoners from Spain and Portugal. Adorned with pearls and silver bobbin lace, black people often paraded in the Lord Mayor's Pageant.

Although the numbers involved were very small, the blacks were noticeable enough to attract the disfavour of Queen Elizabeth, who in 1601 issued a proclamation stating that she was "highly discontented to understand the great numbers of negars and Blackamoores which (as she is informed) are crept into this realm." However, her banishment of all blacks was not very effective.

Two hundred years ago, ahead of the rest of the world, William Wilberforce, a London-dweller, formed the anti-slavery society. It still functions today.

Colour bar: While London boasts of being an ethnic showcase and a multi-cultural society, it has very few administrators or top civil servants from what it euphemistically calls the "New Commonwealth". Americans, used to seeing blacks, Hispanics and Amerasians as their mayors, state governors, ambassadors to the UN, or even presidential contenders, are astonished by the lack of varied races in the higher echelons of Whitehall or other key government departments.

Doyle made his character Sherlock Holmes describe London as "that great cesspool into which all the loungers of the empire are drained". Many Londoners still feel the same way about the new arrivals.

London has not proved a place of opportunity for many of the immigrants unless they are prepared to make sacrifices. As newsagents the Patels work enormously hard, starting at 5 a.m. with the delivery of the morning newspapers and working well into the evening. Outside of the central area of the city, a non-Asian newsagent is a rarity.

Minority influence: The influx of such a vast variety of people has revolutionised London.

You can pass through Fleet Street, the City of London or the Inns of Court without meeting a top editor, business tycoon or a leading Queen's Counsel from the settlers' communities. Many blame discrimination, but others cite the language barrier, weak academic qualifications, and the relatively advanced age at which the ethnic professionals attain their skills.

Attitudes are slow to change. Conan

Left, the police attempt (here successfully) to bridge the culture gap. **Above**, Sikh priests lead a temple procession in Southall.

People who ate nothing more exciting than fish and chips for their Saturday night out, are now familiar with shammi kebabs, bhindi bhaji and vegetables fried in chicken's blood and oyster sauce.

A new race-relations industry has grown up to fight for the rights of the minorities, including the right of Muslim girls to wear their traditional long trousers to school instead of short skirts, and the right of motorcycling Sikhs to wear turbans instead of required helmets.

London's authorities are keenly aware of the danger of ethnic rioting, which claimed its first police death in 1986. However, the rioters maintain that the police have a racist approach, and civilian racists continue to fire-bomb ethnic homes and attack women and children on their way to school. But minorities do sometimes fight back, even the Indians. In 1989, race relations were sorely tested by the publication of Salman Rushdie's *Satanic Verses* and the consequent death threat from the Muslim world. Rushdie was forced into hiding and his publishers, Viking Penguin, were given round-the-clock police protection.

Until the general election of 1987, there were no ethnic minority members of Parlia-

ment. In that election Diane Abbott (Caribbean origin), Bernie Grant (born in Guyana) and Paul Boateng (born in Ghana) all won seats, representing the Labour Party in London. One other minority member was elected from outside the capital, making a total of four. Abbott sits in the very same row once occupied by Enoch Powell, the fiery Conservative MP who called for the repatriation of Commonwealth immigrants.

Carnival: Anyone in London during the last weekend of August should not miss the Notting Hill carnival. The entire West Indian population takes to the streets in celebration

and the event is Europe's biggest open-air ethnic festival. In February, the Chinese community in Soho's Gerrard Street ushers in the Chinese New Year with dragon-dancers and street parades.

If aromatic crispy duck served with pancakes and spring onions, or roast pork and bean curd with shrimp sauce, are not to your palate, there are Armenian, Tunisian, Malaysian, Lebanese, Thai, Russian, Japanese and even Ethiopian restaurants all in the centre of London. Indian, Chinese, or Greek take-out food is as much a feature of life here as is beer and chips. Indeed, it can be difficult to find English restaurants.

Street bazaar: Petticoat Lane market, a stone's throw from the Liverpool Street railway station, is the nearest thing to an oriental bazaar this side of the Suez Canal. Hundreds of stalls do a roaring business every Sunday selling everything from cut-price French food processors to Taiwanese word processors, handloom Indian batik dresses to intricately hand-woven Pakistani carpets, featuring the Pope or the peacock.

Petticoat Lane attracts Arabs in flowing djabelas and Indian women in shimmering six-yard silk saris, which cover the entire body save the waist. According to Indian males, the waist is considered to be the sexiest part of the anatomy.

Indoors, ethnic interests are also well served in London's plethora of museums and galleries. The Commonwealth Institute on Kensington High Street offers insights into life in developing countries, with stunning model recreations of village environments. It covers 49 Commonwealth nations. The Museum of Mankind (Burlington Gardens) spreads its net of exhibitions even wider.

London extends a welcome to every type of visitor. Marx and Mahatma Gandhi studied here. Charles de Gaulle lived in exile here. Paul Theroux and V. S. Naipaul work here. People from every corner have settled here, and people from all over the world visit here. Even Harrods, the distinctively English store, sells 40 percent of its merchandise to overseas tourists.

Left, young Londoners at Brixton market. Right, Soho has a thriving Chinese community.

Being a cockney is as much a state of mind as it is a turn of phrase, and it is not exclusively genetic. The original definition of a cockney – born within the sound of Bow Bells, a church in the city – would nowadays exclude most Londoners. The population of the city is tiny, and the sound of the bells doesn't penetrate far these days.

A cockney no longer needs to be white and Anglo-Saxon; there are West Indian, Jewish and Pakistani cockneys. Nor does he necessarily have to be a Londoner; the high cost of living has driven many out and neighbouring towns like Stevenage have large cockney populations. So what then makes a cockney? A sense of humour, certain traditions, being a member of an identifiable urban group, and a distinctive language.

Cockney rhyming slang supposedly originated amongst barrow boys who didn't want their customers to understand what they said to each other. Rhyming slang is not a shorthand language; "deaf and dumb" means bum, "apples and pears" means stairs, "north and south" means mouth. Nor is it a language that stands still, despite the popular understanding. Today's cockneys are constantly recreating their slang and different groups of friends have a different language. Thus "bugs bunny" means money to one group one month and "Alan Whicker" means a nicker (£1) the next.

Sticking together: Cockneys are concentrated in the East End of London; thus *Eastenders*, a popular TV soap opera, is set in a cockney milieu. They are generally reckoned to be shrewd, streetwise people, who prefer to work for themselves – although this doesn't mean they work hard. They value freedom more than wealth. They stick together and a cockney stallholder in Petticoat Lane market will sell something at the "real" price to another cockney – provided no other customers notice. Many of their deals are "dodgy"; whilst they would

__Left__ and __right__: today's cockney is still the king of London's street markets.

never steal from each other, a clever burglary makes a cockney a hero amongst his peers.

Pubs play a large part in the community and each community jealously guards its pub and its patch. A good pub landlord arranges group excursions; dads bring their dressed-up sons to the pub on a Sunday morning, and members of a group of regulars at one pub do not go to drink in another unless they particularly want a fight.

Cockneys drink "Forsyte saga" or lager;

they eat pie and mash with green parsley sauce and seafood. "A cockney wedding with no eels is a poxy wedding," says one.

The aristocracy of the cockneys are the pearly kings and queens, so-called because of their clothing, which is embroidered with mother-of-pearl buttons.

A true cockney is never short of a joke or a jibe. The quick humour is almost a part of the culture. Ask a cockney taxi driver if he was born within the sound of Bow Bells and he will probably say something like "Yes, pal, but my mother had the radio on loud at the time."

THE CABBIE

There are plenty of cliché characters in London: Beefeaters, Chelsea Pensioners, red-jacketed Horseguards, and even a few spiky-haired punks. However, the average Londoner doesn't stumble across a Beefeater all that often and he's probably never taken a photo of a Horseguard. But visitors and Londoners alike do regularly meet one city character: the taxi driver.

Taxi drivers, or cabbies, are true Londoners. They know London, and are essential to its life, running through the city's veins in their little black cells.

The Knowledge: A London taxi driver is completely immersed in his profession. He takes pride in it, knowing that nowhere else in the world does a taxi driver need to know so much in order to win a licence to work. Would-be drivers must register with the Public Carriage Office and then spend up to four years learning London in minute detail ("doing the Knowledge" as it's called), travelling the streets of the metropolis on two wheels, whatever the weather, and working out a multitude of routes from a clipboard mounted on the handlebars.

"The Knowledge" sounds like a philosophical absolute, and in a way it is. Once qualified, the London cabbie is his own boss, a condition that spells heaven to many British people. It is hardly surprising, therefore, that "being a taxi driver" is a cabbie's favourite topic of conversation.

In the past few years there has been such a large increase of qualified London cabbies that the drivers fear there may not be enough work to go around. There are now 20,700 drivers working in London, of which about 10,400 are owner-drivers. The others either hire vehicles from the big fleets or work night shifts in someone else's cab. In all, there are 15,622 vehicles.

The common cab, known technically as the FX4, was launched in 1959 and is still

going strong, despite the arrival of the new Metrocab, which looks like a square hearse and has yet to equal the FX4's popularity with cabbie or customer.

Safety rules: Each driver and each cab is licensed by the Public Carriage Office, and there are strict regulations controlling both, primarily to insure the safety of the passenger. The cabs must be in perfect working order (they are checked once a year, and are expected to have a working life of around 10 years), and they must be clean. Once having acquired "The Knowledge," the driver must also pass a special driving test.

Legislation regarding taxis – or Hackney Carriages as they are officially called – has existed for 300 years, on the presumption that a driver with a licence would be less likely to assault his passengers. It states that the taxi driver is obliged to take a passenger wherever he wishes to go within the Metropolitan Police District or City of London, provided the journey doesn't exceed six miles. He is also obliged to go by the most direct route; direct, meaning in distance and/

<u>Left</u>, "Being his own boss" is every cabbie's dream. <u>Right</u>, eternally cheerful, eternally talkative, many a visitor's one and only Londoner.

or time. If a driver says, "I'll just go this way to avoid Oxford Street", it means that he is taking a route that he believes, given the traffic conditions, will take the least time.

The most common complaint from passengers is that drivers take roundabout routes. In reality this is unlikely, since it is not in a cabbie's interest to keep a passenger (or a "fare") in the cab a moment longer than is necessary. It is more profitable for drivers to get rid of one passenger and pick up another, resulting in another hire fee. A more just complaint is that increasingly taxis travel around (particularly late at night) with their "For Hire" lights on, but pick and

holds, despite the extensive public transport networks. The result of all this is jams, and the result of jams is an eternally-ticking meter and an eternally growing fare. Expert cab travellers contend that the average cabbie (if such a person exists) is no longer keen to follow back streets and short cuts, but for the sake of a quiet life is happy to sit in the city's main arteries and quietly earn his living by going nowhere.

A class apart: Taxi driving in London is still very much a male profession. Only 60 drivers are women, though the number is rapidly increasing. It is also very much a white, working-class occupation, and traditionally

choose their passengers, saying to those they refuse, "Sorry, I'm heading east", meaning that they are only interested in work that takes them part of their way home. Many will make excuses to avoid having to leave the city centre.

On the other side of the coin are the taxi users who complain that taxis do not detour as often as they used to. The residents of every city complain bitterly about congestion and traffic and London is no exception. Private car ownership in the UK has tripled since the early 1960s, and 70 percent of London households are car-owning house-

a large percentage of drivers are Jewish.

In practice, taxi drivers are a class unto themselves. In many ways they have a uniquely levelling attitude to the English class system. They know that they are as good as anybody because they have the opportunity to compare themselves to all types of people passing through their cabs. They meet people from all walks of life and of all nationalities – more than the Foreign Secretary does, probably. And they meet more British people than the Home Secretary.

Some years ago, BBC Television's *Mastermind* competition, whose entrants are usually librarians, teachers and retired civil servants, was won by a London taxi driver.

Tips for the traveller: From a practical point of view, here are a few hints on travelling by London taxis. First, throughout the city and especially outside hotels and stations there are taxi ranks where taxis wait for passengers. At Heathrow airport there is also a separate rank for taxis operating a cab-share scheme: passengers pay a standard fare for a trip into central London (the amount depending on how many other people share the cab).

Within London it is fairly easy to hail a cab by shouting or waving. It is usually worth hailing taxis on the opposite side of the road just for a quick demonstration of how London taxis can, in the common parlance, "turn on a sixpence", and of how the drivers are impervious to the sound of screeching tyres and elbows on horns all around them.

These are the easy bits; the difficult choice confronts you after settling into your seat. Do you try to strike up a conversation?

Most London taxi drivers, particularly the older ones, love to talk. London social gatherings are a forum for anecdotes about taxi drivers (and not Beefeaters or Horseguards). The reason is not because the drivers can negotiate the rabbit warren under the Barbican Centre; it's because, given the chance, cabbies never stop talking. Traffic, foreign policy, famous people they have chauffeured, where to eat in the Canary Islands, why the wife has walked out on them, are all topics of conversation.

Having a two-way conversation is almost out of the question. For one thing, the passenger can only see the back of the driver's head (whereas the cabbie can see the passenger in his rear-view mirror), and for another, the driver can't hear much because of the engine. What tends to happen is that he shouts a monologue over his shoulder through the statutory six-inch gap in the glass partition, while the passenger makes feeble (and ignored) attempts to join in. Most cabs carry a notice that reads "Thank you for not smoking". A cartoon in the satirical mag-

azine *Private Eye* adapted this notice so that it read "Thank you for not interrupting".

When the conversation or journey (whichever is the longest) is over, there is the matter of paying the fare. Displayed on a meter, it is shown usually as two separate amounts: an amount for the trip (calculated on a combination of distance and time) plus a second amount for any "extras" (additional passengers, travelling at certain times of day or at weekends.)

Drivers don't expect enormous tips (in cabbie lore, tips supposedly stands for "To Insure Prompt Service"), though they claim they are taxed on an expectation of receiving 15 percent above the fare. They prefer a rounding-up of the fare by about 10 to 15 percent to the nearest 50p or £1 and they will sometimes huff about having to give change, as it takes up their time. It is worth having the money ready. One reason taxi drivers prefer carrying men rather than women is that women are supposed to spend more time in the cab than men because they have to find the money in their handbags.

Cabs and minicabs: The London taxi is an institution that is also a brilliant working proposition. It is emphatically a trade and not a public service. Economic pressures on the cabbie and regulations for the protection of the passenger mean that the public is efficiently served – even more so since so many taxis have become radio-controlled.

"Minicab" firms are another matter entirely, and it is worth emphasising here that minicabs have absolutely nothing in common with London taxis, although they are successfully opposing the black cabs' monopoly on picking up people in the street. A minicab is often simply a private car, and some minicabs are not only unlicensed as Hackney Carriages but also not adequately insured. Minicabs are cheaper than taxis for long distances, but there is no cast-iron guarantee of safety from the minicab firm.

Moreover, the minicab driver can be useless to a stranger to London. There is nothing worse than settling into the back seat, warily eyeing a rusty hole in the floor under your feet, and saying "Oxford Street, please" and having the driver ask brightly, "Oxford Street? Where's that?"

Left, the traditional black cab literally and figuratively in the centre of the City.

In the early 1980s there was great consternation about the state of the theatre in London. Suddenly the media started to use the term "dark" in its specific theatrical sense: "Why are so many of our theatres dark?" they asked. Shows closed; there was even gossip about the unstoppable *Mousetrap*, (first staged in 1952, and now the longest running play in the world). The theatres were all dressed up, but they had nowhere to go.

By 1985 the theatre made a comeback and the Society of West End Theatre Managers recorded its best ever year. In 1986, when the supposed mainstay of London theatre, the American tourist, stayed away for fear of Libyan terrorism and Chernobyl fall-out, the theatre did extremely well. Since then, attendance has steadily increased, reaching nearly 11 million by the beginning of the 1990s. Tourists comprise more than 40 percent of the average audience.

Some believe the theatre has saved itself at a terrible moral price, by becoming the musicals capital of the world. Where managements might have invested in new work by budding playwrights, now they only back blockbuster musicals which sell out months ahead. *Jesus Christ Superstar*, a case in point, took in £7 million in London, and has since been produced in 37 other countries. Its successors are *Cats*, *Les Misérables*, *Phantom of the Opera* and *Miss Saigon*.

Traditionalists claim that, while theatres as enterprises are doing well, the range and overall quality of productions are suffering. But there is plenty of new drama on Shaftesbury Avenue too, although it tends to get submerged by the musicals' hype.

Cast an eye down the listings in *Time Out* magazine and there is certainly enough range and quality for the most demanding taste, including classics at the National Theatre and the Barbican, huge, well-mounted musicals in the larger West End theatres, new writing at the Royal Court and Bush, experimental work and alternative comedy at the fringe theatres, and the fashionable playwrights (fewer now, admittedly) in Shaftesbury Avenue.

Fringe forest: Moreover, in addition to the 50 central theatres there are around 60 recognised fringe venues in the City, with productions ranging from standard Shakespeare on a low budget to the latest shows by minority groups keen to put across political or social

messages. There is even one fringe group which is so fringe that it doesn't have a venue, but will come and perform in your own front room. *Time Out* can be relied on for good weekly information, with potted reviews, ticket prices and so on – although not even native Londoners understand some of the more arcane allusions in the text.

Choosing what to see is difficult. Every theatre is emblazoned with quotations from press reviews, but these can be misleading. The London theatre critics, though honourable men, do not have the power to make or break a production. Which is just as well,

Left, Shaftesbury Avenue is the heart of the theatre district. **Right**, *Cats* helped London to lead the world in staging popular musicals.

because sometimes they are wildly at variance with public taste. The RSC's *Nicholas Nickleby*, which went on to a couple of revivals and a New York transfer, received grudging, lukewarm reviews when it first opened. And *Les Misérables*, now playing all over the world, got only a couple of good reviews from the national press.

Theatre's historical past: Theatre has an enormously long tradition in London. The first theatre opened its doors in 1576. There were several side-swipes at social issues in those early productions. In the *Roaring Girl* of 1611, playwright Thomas Dekker dwelt at some length on the awfulness of London's traffic jams.

Accordingly, visiting the London theatre is redolent of the past. Each has some grand historical association: the Phoenix with Noel Coward, the Royal Court with the heady days of Angry Young Men, the Arts with *Waiting for Godot,* the Savoy with Gilbert and Sullivan, Drury Lane (confusingly not actually *in* Drury Lane) with Edmund Kean, the Criterion with Rattigan's *French Without Tears*. Some are associated with sensational events: outside the Adelphi in 1897, the tragedian William Terriss was stabbed to death; and inside the Garrick the ghost of a former manager is supposed to appear.

A project on Bankside (on the southern end of London Bridge) has been recreating the Globe theatre of 1599, in which Shakespeare had shares and often performed in his own plays; it is due for completion in 1994. Nearby is the Bear Gardens Museum, devoted to Elizabethan and Jacobean theatre.

Equally insightful is Stage by Stage, a company run by actors and actresses who function as guides, which provides tours by arrangement backstage of selected West End theatres.

Most of the present buildings were built in the 50-year period 1880–1930, though thankfully many have now been renovated. There have been some spectacular improvements in recent years. Canadian entrepreneur Ed Mirvish bought the Old Vic (near Waterloo station) and paid £2.5 million to

Les Misérables became a massive success despite poor press reviews.

refurbish it. The Maybox Group did a similarly wonderful job on the ailing Whitehall Theatre, restoring it to its art deco splendour.

It's a trend that seems likely to continue, as theatres that until recently were languishing as television studios or even as disused radio show theatres are being re-commissioned as venues for theatres.

Ticket-hunting: With all this growth, is it easier to get a ticket? Well, it depends. Despite the prevalent notion that everything in London is so successful it's sold out, most shows are available. It is the more expensive tickets – generally for musicals, where prices go as high as £25 – that are hardest to obtain.

price. The cheapest performances are matinees, but understudies may then replace the leading players.

Dealing with touts (or scalpers) is another matter entirely. Tickets are offered outside the theatre for anything up to 10 times their face value. Ticket tout prices for a last performance of Michael Crawford in *Phantom of the Opera* in 1987 reached £1,000. There is nothing illegal in this, but it is obviously good sense to ask the face value of the ticket on offer, and the exact position of the seat.

It is important to know the terminology of English theatre geography. What in America

Unlike New York, where most of the ticket-buying is done through agencies, in London tickets can be purchased at the box office, cutting out the fee (sometimes extortionate) of the middle-man. There are, however, a number of good, reliable ticket agencies, who sometimes have more to offer than the theatre itself. A day or so before the performance, they return their tickets to the box office. These tickets are then sold to students, pensioners and the unwaged.

On the day of the performance, unsold tickets are also available from a booth in Leicester Square selling at around half-

is called the "Orchestra" (the seats at the lowest level) is in England called the Stalls; then in ascending order come the "Dress Circle" (or "Royal Circle"), then the "Upper Circle" (or "Grand Circle"). The "Gods" refers to the very top, and the seats are not recommended to anyone with vertigo or hearing impediments.

One of the most important features of London theatre is the presence within it of two major subsidised companies: the National Theatre and the Royal Shakespeare Company, both of which seem to stagger from one financial crisis to the next. In terms of audiences, both are highly successful and originate productions which transfer into the the mainstream theatre of the West End.

The National, on the South Bank, is the more congenial building, at least, from the inside. It holds the record for the longest interval, one hour, necessary for a very complicated scene change. The Barbican, which houses the RSC, opened in 1982 and has a splendid main auditorium, but the bars and concourses are curiously dingy and impersonal. It also boasts the small-scale auditorium The Pit, which according to legend was hastily converted from a rehearsal room before anyone noticed it had no ventilation.

and anecdote in equal measure: "Why are the seats in the Olivier theatre lilac-coloured? Because that was Lord Olivier's favourite colour." Almost every National production is worth seeing.

There is open-air theatre in Regent's Park (always Shakespeare), and less frequently in Holland Park, Covent Garden and St Martin's in the Fields. For the more adventurous late night comedy cabaret has its own sub-culture in London. Riverside Studios in Crisp Road, W6, attracts experimental plays and overseas visiting companies, and the basement Soho Poly Theatre, 16 Riding House Street, encourages new writing.

Nevertheless the Pit has seen some of the most exciting productions in London.

National Theatre: Meanwhile the National, with its three auditoria, has a stronger sense of a working organism than the Barbican. National Theatre audiences arrive early to enjoy a drink. Barbican audiences dive in at the last moment, having had pre-show drinks in neighbouring pubs.

The theatre also runs a very interesting backstage tour, which imparts information

The South Bank arts complex brightens the Thames as well as London's cultural life.

Finally, any visitor interested in theatre ought to see the Theatre Museum in Covent Garden and visit French's Theatre Bookshop in Fitzroy Square.

Cinema: The Great British Public is not a keen film-going public, and many of the large movie-houses of previous decades are now bingo halls. The cinemas themselves divide broadly into two sections, the independents (repertory cinemas) and the West End screens, which belong to the three or four major chains. Leicester Square and the immediate environs is the focus of London's commercial cinema.

London

0   250 yards
     250 m

Inner Circle

Open Air
Theatre

Inner Circle

Bedford
College

Mme.
Tussaud's **(27)**

To Paddington Station

(26)

Academy
of Music

Outer Circle

Walk Rd.

Circle

Albany St.

Outer

Stanhope St.

Circle

Hampstead Rd.

To Hampstead and
S Camden Town

Eversholt St.

St. Pancras Station

King's Cross Station

Euston
Station

Euston
Rd.

Euston Rd.

Mabledon Pl.

Judd St.

Argyll St.

Swinton St

Gray's Inn

Square

Coram

Fields

Euston Tower

Holy Trinity

Harley St.

Portland Pl.

Devonshire

Marylebone Rd.

Weymouth

New St.

Wimpole St.

Cavendish Place

BBC

Cleveland St.

Titchfield St.

Fitzroy St.

Post Office
Tower

Charlotte St.

Gower St.

University
College

Tavistock

(34)

University

(36)

British
Museum **(35)**

BLOOMSBURY

Southampton Row

Guilford St.

Lamb's Conduit St.

Millman St.

Red Lion

Wallace
Collection

Regent St.

St.

Rathbone St.

Court Rd.

Russell St.

Great

Montague St.

Oxford St.

ST. GILES

Selfridges

Oxford St.

(29)

MAYFAIR

Brook St.

North Audley St.

Park

Park St.

Park St.

Park Lane

Hyde
Park

To Harrods and Brompton Oratory

To Notting Hill Gate
and Portobello Road

Roosevelt
Memorial

Grosvenor St.

New Bond Street Old Bond Street

Palladium

(28)

Regent St.

SOHO

(32)

Wardour St.

Greek St.

Shaftesbury Av.

Charing Cross Rd.

(30)

(33)

Museum
of Mankind

Royal
Academy

Piccadilly

Piccadilly
Circus

Haymarket

National Portrait
Gallery

(3)

National
Gallery **(2)**

(7)

(6)

Leicester
Square

(4)

St. Martin-
in-the-
Fields

(5)

Royal
Opera House

Convent
Garden

Somerset
House

Str

C

Freemasons
Hall

Kingsway

(31)

St. James's St.

Square

(9)

(10)

Marlborough
House

ICA

Trafalgar
Square **(1)**

(8)

Whitehall

Admiralty

Northumberland Av.

Mall

Charing
Cross
Station

Cleopatra's
Needle

Quee
Elizabeth Ha

5

Achilles

Apsley House

Knightsbridge

Wellington
Arch

(25)

Grosvenor Place

Constitution Hill

Green
Park

St. James's Palace

(16)

Lancaster
House

(11)

Piccadilly

St. James's

(15)

Park

The

Government Offices

(19)

Banqueting
House

(20)

Embankment

Victoria

Royal Festival
Hall

(53)

County
Hall

Buckingham
Palace

(12)

Palace

Gardens

(14)

Queen's
Gallery

Queen Victoria
Memorial

Birdcage Walk

Wellington
Barracks

New
Scotland
Yard

Gt. George St.

Victoria St.

Westminster
Abbey **(17)**

(18)

Westminster
Bridge

Houses of
Parliament

Thames

St. Tho
Hospita

Belgrave Place

(24)

BELGRAVIA

To Chelsea
and King's Road

Ecclestone St.

Belgrave Square

Buckingham Palace Rd.

Royal Mews

(13)

Victoria
Station

(22)

Victoria St.

Peter St.

Westminster
Cathedral **(21)**

(23)

Millbank

Lambeth
Bridge

Lambeth Pl. Rd.

Lambeth
Palace

Lambeth P

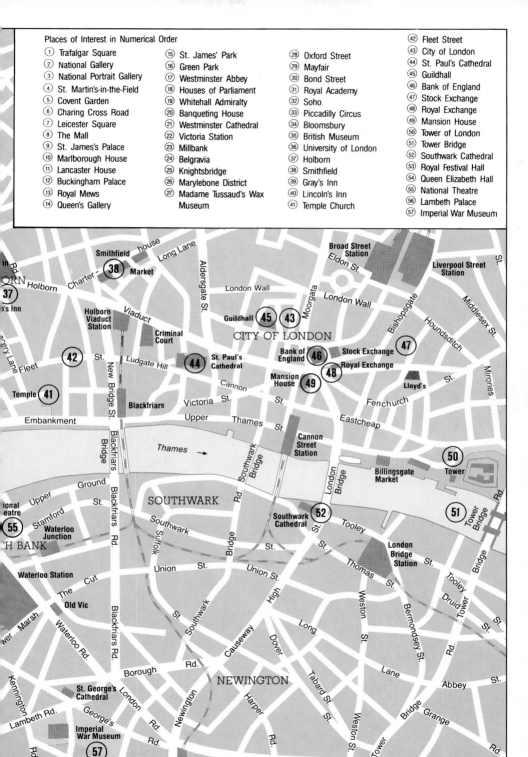

Places of Interest in Numerical Order

1. Trafalgar Square
2. National Gallery
3. National Portrait Gallery
4. St. Martin's-in-the-Field
5. Covent Garden
6. Charing Cross Road
7. Leicester Square
8. The Mall
9. St. James's Palace
10. Marlborough House
11. Lancaster House
12. Buckingham Palace
13. Royal Mews
14. Queen's Gallery
15. St. James' Park
16. Green Park
17. Westminster Abbey
18. Houses of Parliament
19. Whitehall Admiralty
20. Banqueting House
21. Westminster Cathedral
22. Victoria Station
23. Millbank
24. Belgravia
25. Knightsbridge
26. Marylebone District
27. Madame Tussaud's Wax Museum
28. Oxford Street
29. Mayfair
30. Bond Street
31. Royal Academy
32. Soho
33. Piccadilly Circus
34. Bloomsbury
35. British Museum
36. University of London
37. Holborn
38. Smithfield
39. Gray's Inn
40. Lincoln's Inn
41. Temple Church
42. Fleet Street
43. City of London
44. St. Paul's Cathedral
45. Guildhall
46. Bank of England
47. Stock Exchange
48. Royal Exchange
49. Mansion House
50. Tower of London
51. Tower Bridge
52. Southwark Cathedral
53. Royal Festival Hall
54. Queen Elizabeth Hall
55. National Theatre
56. Lambeth Palace
57. Imperial War Museum

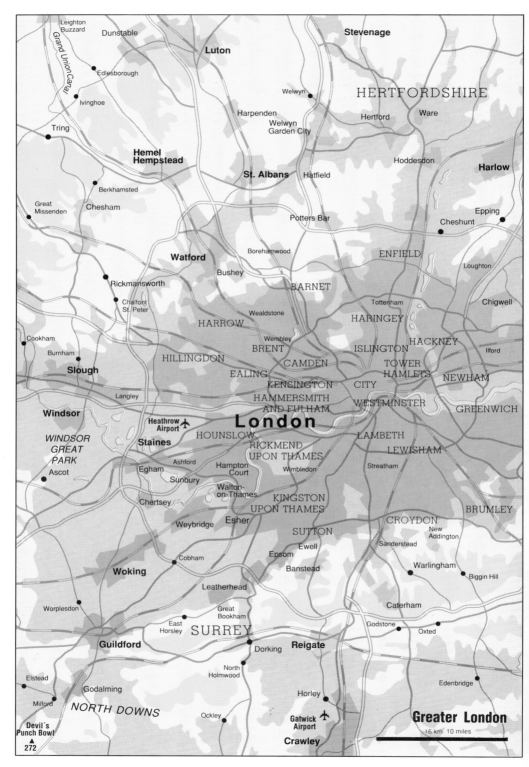

Leighton
Buzzard
Dunstable
Luton
Stevenage
Grand Union Canal
Edlesborough
Welwyn
HERTFORDSHIRE
Ivinghoe
Harpenden
Welwyn
Garden City
Hertford
Ware
Tring
**Hemel
Hempstead**
Hoddesdon
Harlow
Berkhamsted
St. Albans
Hatfield
Epping
Great
Missenden
Chesham
Cheshunt
Potters Bar
Watford
Borehamwood
ENFIELD
Loughton
Rickmansworth
Bushey
Chalfont
St. Peter
Wealdstone
BARNET
Tottenham
Chigwell
Cookham
HARROW
HARINGEY
Burnham
Wembley
HACKNEY
Ilford
HILLINGDON
BRENT
ISLINGTON
Slough
Langley
EALING
CAMDEN
**TOWER
HAMLETS**
NEWHAM
KENSINGTON
CITY
Windsor
**HAMMERSMITH
AND FULHAM**
WESTMINSTER
GREENWICH
Heathrow
Airport
London
**WINDSOR
GREAT
PARK**
Staines
HOUNSLOW
LAMBETH
Ascot
Ashford
Hampton
Court
Wimbledon
LEWISHAM
**RICKMEND
UPON THAMES**
Streatham
Egham
Sunbury
Walton-
on-Thames
Chertsey
**KINGSTON
UPON THAMES**
CROYDON
BRUMLEY
Weybridge
Esher
New
Addington
SUTTON
Sanderstead
Cobham
Ewell
Woking
Epsom
Warlingham
Banstead
Biggin Hill
Leatherhead
Worplesdon
Caterham
Great
Bookham
East
Horsley
SURREY
Godstone
Oxted
Guildford
Dorking
Reigate
Elstead
North
Holmwood
Edenbridge
Godalming
Milford
Horley
NORTH DOWNS
Ockley
Gatwick
Airport
Devil's
Punch Bowl
▲
272
Crawley

Greater London

16 km 10 miles

For a cosmopolitan city, London is very parochial. Each neighbourhood, each street corner, is proud of its own identity. South Londoners talk of going to the centre as "going up to town". West Londoners would not be seen dead in the East End (which they believe dangerous and dirty), and Eastenders think central London is full of tourists and high prices.

Central London – the London covered in this book – is the shared London of all these groups and of half the rest of the world as well. Symbols of London, the Beefeaters, the bobbies, the cabbies, the cockneys, the pageantry, the Royal Family, the Houses of Parliament, all are here, along with the stock market, motorcycle messengers, dirty air, and traffic that moves at an average speed citywide of 8 miles an hour.

London has a bit of everything. Today the population of the 625 sq. miles (162 sq. km) stands at 6.7 million; it measures 60 miles (100 km) across from south to north and plays host to 19 million visitors a year.

To help make sense of this city, we have divided it nine ways. The West End features all the qualities of the centre of the city, the theatres, the shopping and the street culture; Official London centres around Palaces and Prime Ministers; the chapter on Parks reveals just how green London is; Posh London dwells on Porsches and designer living in the West; Village London spotlights the neighbourhoods and the people that make them; Wigs and Pens unites the past and present of Fleet Street and London's legal centre; the chapter on the City portrays the financial power of the square mile; Docklands and the River tells the story of trading growth, decay and renewal; and finally London's surroundings are described in Day Trips – which can be taken if ever, as Dr Johnson said no man should, you get tired of London.

As a visitor, you may be one of the 72 percent who visit the Tower of London, or even the 92 percent who make their way to Piccadilly Circus. But you will probably also be one of the millions who find some small, distinctive corner of the city to be enthusiastic about.

Preceding pages: Piccadilly Circus, resisting all attempts to make it tidy, tops the league of most often visited London sights.

THE WEST END

There is a central and nodal part of London which... is symptomatic and symbolical of the whole chaotic and magnificent business."
– J. C. Squire, *A London Reverie*

Like so many places in Britain, the West End of London is not so much a precise location but rather a loose description of the region which extends from Temple Bar along the River Thames to Chelsea and Knightsbridge in the west and to Bloomsbury and the Marylebone Road in the north.

Within its broadest boundaries lie the most fashionable residential and commercial areas of London: the home of the best shops and the most exclusive hotels, of leading theatres and nightlife, and of many famous museums, galleries and palaces. Here is the centre of British government, law, learning, fashion and entertainment. For simplicity's sake we have bounded the West End by Hyde Park Corner to the west and Aldwych to the east. There is as much variety within this area as in the pages of the *Encyclopaedia Britannica*.

Glittering facades: The giant neon hoardings and jostling crowds of **Piccadilly Circus** hold promise of all types of worldy delights. Here is the acclaimed heart of London's theatre land, cinemas, nightclubs, pubs and restaurants. All crammed together in a few narrow bustling streets and tiny squares that make up **Soho**.

The first illuminated advertising sign appeared in Piccadilly Circus in 1890 to capture a new imagination. A few years later the statue of Eros, Greek god of love, was erected in honour of the Seventh Earl of Shaftesbury who drove the broad thoroughfare (which bears his name) through the highly squalid slum.

Now the homeless mingle with the tourists on the steps surrounding Eros. Piccadilly Circus and the rest of Soho

have seen big changes in the past few years, and more are coming. The rent boys who once hung out near the stairways and walkways leading to the Underground station are gone along with the drug peddlers as the local council strives to clean up the area.

Soho has always been popular with foreigners. Flemish weavers, Protestant Huguenots, Greeks, Italians, Belgians, Swiss, Chinese and Russian Jews have sought refuge here. Their influence is still felt in the patisseries, delicatessens and fabric shops which survive.

Four hundred years ago Soho was an area of open fields. Its name is thought to come from an ancient hunting cry. In the centre of **Soho Square** is a statue of Charles II and an ancient-looking building that disguises a ventilation shaft.

Soho quickly became fashionable with artists and writers. A host of historic characters, from Dylan Thomas to Thomas Gainsborough, Casanova to Oscar Wilde, are associated with the area. The restaurant at 41 Beak Street

Left, a wall of badges reflects the popularity of Britain's pop culture. **Right**, beadles, doormen and footmen maintain the dignity of the city centre.

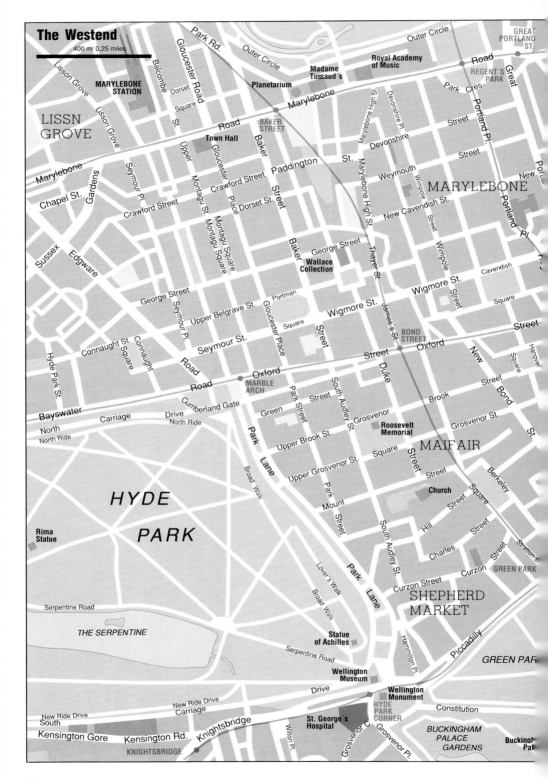

The Westend

400 m/ 0,25 miles

LISSN GROVE

MARYLEBONE STATION

Lisson Grove
Lisson Grove
Balcombe
Dorset Square
St.
Gloucester Road
Park Rd.
Outer Circle

Planetarium
Madame Tussaud´s
Royal Academy of Music
Outer Circle

GREAT PORTLAND ST.

REGENT´S PARK

Marylebone

BAKER STREET

Town Hall
Upper
Gloucester Street
Crawford Street
Crawford Street
Paddington
Baker
Street

Road
Road
Marylebone

Marylebone
Chapel St.
Gardens
Seymour Pl.
Montagu St.
Montagu Square
Dorset St.
Devonshire Pl.
Marylebone High St.
Devonshire
Weymouth
St.
Paddington
Park Cres.
Portland Pl.
Street
Street
New Portland Pl.

MARYLEBONE

New Cavendish St.
Wimpole
Wimpole
Street
Street

Sussex
Edgware
Crawford Street
Montagu Place
Dorset St.
George Street
Wallace Collection
Baker
Street
Thayer St.
Cavendish Square

Wallace Collection

Wigmore St.
Wigmore St.

George Street
Seymour Pl.
Upper Belgrave St.
Gloucester Place
Portman Square
Wigmore St.
James´s St.
BOND STREET
Oxford
Street
Hanover Square

Connaught St.
Connaught Square
Connaught
Seymour St.
Road
Oxford
Street
Duke
Oxford
New Bond St.
Brook
Street

Hyde Park St.
Bayswater
North
North Ride
Carriage
Cumberland Gate
Drive
North Ride
MARBLE ARCH
Green
Park Street
Street
South Audley St.
Grosvenor
Roosevelt Memorial
Grosvenor St.

MAIFAIR

Upper Brook St.
Square
Street
Street
Berkeley
Square

HYDE
PARK

Broad Walk
Park Lane
Upper Grosvenor St.
Park Street
Mount
Street
Church
Street
Hill
Street

Rima Statue

South Audley St.
Hill
Charles
Street
Curzon

GREEN PARK

Lover´s Walk
Broad Walk
Park Lane
Curzon Street
Curzon Street

SHEPHERD MARKET

Serpentine Road

THE SERPENTINE

Hammilton Pl.
Piccadilly

GREEN PAR

Statue of Achilles
Serpentine Road

Wellington Museum

Drive
Wellington Monument
HYDE PARK CORNER
Constitution

New Ride Drive
Carriage
New Ride Drive
South
Kensington Gore
Kensington Rd.
Knightsbridge
Wilton Pl.
St. George´s Hospital
Grosvenor C
Grosvenor Pl.
BUCKINGHAM PALACE GARDENS
Buckingh
Pal

KNIGHTSBRIDGE

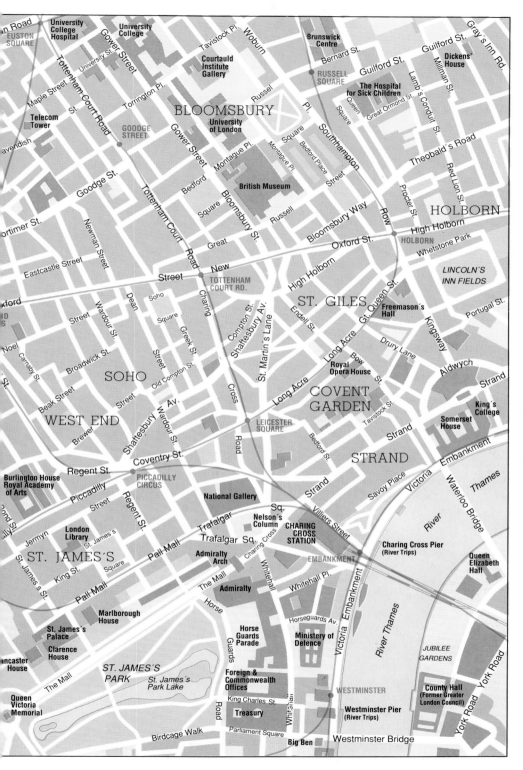

EUSTON SQUARE
University College Hospital
University College
Tavistock Pl.
Woburn
Brunswick Centre
Bernard St.
Guilford St.
Gray's Inn Rd.
Guilford St.
Dickens' House
Millman St.

Gower Street
Courtauld Institute Gallery
RUSSELL SQUARE
Guilford St.
Lamb's Conduit St.

Maple Street
Telecom Tower
Tottenham Court Road
University St.
Torrington Pl.
Torrington Pl.
Russel
BLOOMSBURY
Southampton
The Hospital for Sick Children
Great Ormond St.
Queen
Square
Theobald's Road
Red Lion St.

avendish
GOODGE STREET
Gower Street
Montague Pl.
Bedford Place
Street
Procter St.
HOLBORN

ortimer St.
Goodge St.
Tottenham Court Road
Bedford Square
Bloomsbury St.
Montague Pl.
Square
British Museum
Russell
Bloomsbury Way
Row
High Holborn
HOLBORN
Whetstone Park

Newman Street
Great
New
Oxford St.
High Holborn

Eastcastle Street
Street
TOTTENHAM COURT RD.
LINCOLN'S INN FIELDS

xford
Dean
Soho
Charing
High Holborn
ST. GILES
Gt. Queen St.
Freemason's Hall
Portugal St.

Noel
Wardour St.
Street
Square
Compton St.
Shaftesbury Av.
St. Martin's Lane
Endell St.
Long Acre
Drury Lane
Kingsway

Carnaby St.
Broadwick St.
Greek St.
Old Compton St.
Cross
Long Acre
Bow
Royal Opera House
Aldwych
Strand

SOHO
Beak Street
Street
Shaftesbury
Av.
Wardour St.
COVENT GARDEN
King's College
Strand

WEST END
Brewer
Road
LEICESTER SQUARE
Bedford St.
Tavistock St.
Strand
Somerset House

Coventry St.
STRAND

Burlington House Royal Academy of Arts
Regent St.
PICCADILLY CIRCUS
Strand
Savoy Place
Victoria
Embankment
Thames

ond St.
Piccadilly
Street
Regent St.
National Gallery
Sq.
Villiers Street
River
Waterloo Bridge

lly
London Library
St. James's
Trafalgar
Nelson's Column
Trafalgar Sq.
CHARING CROSS STATION
Charing Cross Pier (River Trips)
Queen Elizabeth Hall

Jermyn
King St.
Square
Pall Mall
Admiralty Arch
Charing Cross
EMBANKMENT

ST. JAMES'S
St. James's S St.
Pall Mall
The Mall
Admiralty
Whitehall
Whitehall Pl.
Victoria Embankment
River Thames

Marlborough House
Horse
Horse Guards Parade
Horseguards Av.
JUBILEE GARDENS
York Road

ancaster House
St. James's Palace
Clarence House
ST. JAMES'S PARK
St. James's Park Lake
Guards
Ministry of Defence
WESTMINSTER
County Hall (Former Greater London Council)

The Mall
Foreign & Commonwealth Offices
King Charles St.
Whitehall

Queen Victoria Memorial
Birdcage Walk
Parliament Square
Treasury
Road
Westminster Pier (River Trips)
Big Ben
Westminster Bridge
York Road

was the home of Antonio Canaletto, the Venetian painter, from 1749 to 1751. In 1926 John Logie Baird transmitted the first flickering television images in the attic of a house, at 22 Frith Street, next door to the house where Mozart stayed as a boy. Another dining place, **Leoni's Quo Vadis,** is in the house at 26 Dean Street where Karl Marx wrote *Das Kapital* between 1851 and 1856. The original Leoni, who ran the restaurant with his family from 1926 until his death in 1969, found a hidden library of Marx's research materials. The family still runs the restaurant and if you ask nicely, they will show you where the clan Marx resided in the house.

An outbreak of cholera in the mid-19th century drove out most of Soho's wealthier residents and led to the conditions which spurred Lord Shaftesbury to start his clean up.

Club variety: In spite of being forced to resort to the sacrilege of a disco upstairs, **Ronnie Scott's** legendary jazz club is still going strong at 46–49 Frith Street.

Its wide fame ensures a queue of people outside the door nearly every night, especially after the pubs shut at 11 p.m.

The London club scene is always changing. For every multi-million pound extravaganza such as the **Hippodrome**, on the corner of Charing Cross Road, or the **Empire Ballroom**, in Leicester Square, there are hundreds of others. These truly upmarket clubs call for immaculate dress and a fistful of fivers. The would-be clientele is vetted at the door and, once inside, finds the crowd young and desperately trendy.

These clubs are not to be confused with the St James's clubs and certainly not with those other Soho clubs featuring topless bars and striptease, where a bottle of "Champagne" could set you back £100 and many of the girls are available for extra-curricular activities. **Raymond's Revuebar,** ("Now for a sensational 33rd year") remains the king of the strip joints, its lavish showgirl numbers almost respectable now in spite of their plush vulgarity.

Sleaze survives in Soho despite the dire warnings of the fundamentally minded.

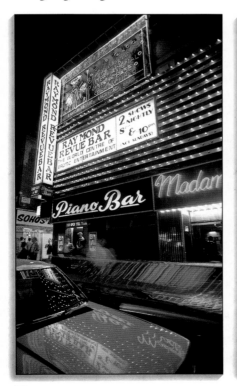

Soho has long revelled in its sinful reputation, but determined campaigning by the surprisingly active local residents following Lord Shaftesbury's lead has closed most of the sex shops and strip clubs. In 1983 there were 174 sex-related establishments. Very few are left. The proliferation of book shops and seedy striptease shows was first replaced by nude encounter bars and later by peep shows.

Nevertheless, the backstreets of Soho can be a fairly godless zone. Indeed, its parish church, **St Anne's**, was gutted after being bombed in 1941 and was never rebuilt. Street-walking has been illegal since 1959 and for a while the girls worked behind closed doors. Now they are back on the streets, flushed out by increased competition. Telephone boxes throughout the West End are inundated with small ads flaunting all manner of sexual endeavour.

In the pedestrian precinct of **Gerrard Street** (home of Chinese grocers, restaurants and stores), kitschy Chinese street furniture, lamps and archways designate this as London's **Chinatown**. The oriental cuisine here is excellent.

Antiseptic experience: Nowhere are the recent changes in Soho more obvious than in Piccadilly Circus itself. The massive vault of the ultra-modern shopping arcade **Trocadero Centre**, with its glass walkways, potted plants, waterfalls and cafés, lies hidden behind the facade of its Georgian predecessor. London long resisted the temptation of such places, but the Trocadero (the city's fifth most visited tourist site) has now been joined next door by the **London Pavilion**, a shopping development offering an equally antiseptic air.

At the Trocadero you can wonder at the **Guinness World of Records** ("You've read the book, now see the show"), gaze in awe at the holograms of **Light Fantastic** and witness the "spectacular, five-screen entertainment" of the **London Experience** (a feat of endurance with sound and smoke effects), designed to provide history and an in-

The best of London's restaurants are seldom British.

troduction to the real London. Needless to say, it doesn't. For that you have to step outside.

Old Compton Street, with its food stores and clothes shops and neon-lit clubs and bars, is much more like the true Soho. A few of the celebrated delicatessens and continental food stores which once dominated the street live on, but many are replaced by restaurants and clubs. Wheeler's still dispenses a mean oyster, and the French House and the Soho Brasserie even offer a little trendy chic in the mad whirl.

Wardour Street, once known as the only street in the world which was shady on both sides, is the headquarters of Britain's once formidable film industry. Soho is also the home of the capital's advertising and recording industries. Recently it has also become a centre for fashion boutiques and clothes designers.

Meanwhile the clothing, fruit and vegetable traders of **Berwick Street Market** continue to do business in the draughty street, and as a group they probably represent the most dense concentration of cockneys in central London outside the taxi cafés.

Leicester Square, home of the big cinemas, has been given a wash-and-brush-up in recent years. Many gather outside the Swiss Centre to watch the clock chime. The starlings that frequent the square (an estimated 250,000 of them) may not be so easy to shift. An attempt to drive them out by placing speakers emitting ultra-high-frequency sounds in the trees failed.

Trafalgar Square: This suitably vast square laid out to commemorate Nelson's momentous naval victory of 1805 is a vivid reflection of Britain at the height of its power, when its armies and civil servants ruled more than a quarter of the planet. Capped by the 167-ft (50-metre) Corinthian column and 12-ft (3.6-metre) statue of the great man himself, the square is the point where all roads seemingly emanate to all parts of the country. It has long been the site of

The Trafalgar Square cleanup removed half a ton of pigeons' droppings from the top of Nelson's Column.

massive public gatherings and of countless demonstrations and celebrations.

The capital's pigeons, a mangy crew spoilt rotten by the tourists, have little respect for such magnificence. More than half a ton of pigeon droppings were removed from Nelson's Column in the latest clean-up. In the southwest corner, **Admiralty Arch** marks the start of **The Mall**, the royal red road leading to Buckingham Palace. On the north side, overlooking the square, stands the imposing neo-classical facade of the **National Gallery**, home to works of Rembrandt, Rubens, El Greco and Van Gogh, and the city's most popular tourist attraction after the Tower of London. The planned building of a glass tower on the western side of the gallery was withdrawn after the Prince of Wales described it as a "monstrous carbuncle on the face of a much-loved friend". The new Sainsbury wing has proved more acceptable.

One work removed from public view was the gallery's biggest attraction, the 480-year-old Leonardo da Vinci cartoon of *The Virgin Mary and Child*, which was damaged when a gunman blasted a one-inch hole in the fragile chalk and charcoal; the cartoon is now back, its repair almost invisible. Such madness is nothing new. Behind the National Gallery, in the **National Portrait Gallery,** a controversial painting of the Princess of Wales was slashed soon after its unveiling.

Across the road, the church of **St Martin's-in-the-Fields** is the oldest building in Trafalgar Square. It is the burial ground of Nell Gwynn, mistress of Charles II and, a little ironically, the parish church of the royal family. Its crypts, now a youth centre, were a famous air raid shelter in the bombing Blitz during World War II.

There are oddities in the square. The round stone lamp-post on the southeast corner is actually the smallest police station in England. Its lamp is said to have come from Nelson's *Victory*. Legend also has it that the French crown

jewels are buried beneath the square, placed there by Madame du Barry, mistress of the deposed Louis XV, when the site was part of the old royal mews.

Every Christmas a 70-ft (20-metre) Norwegian spruce is erected in the square, a gift from the city of Oslo in recognition of the protection given to members of the Norwegian royal family in World War II.

Major political protests were banned from Trafalgar Square during its £2.5 million facelift, the first since its construction in the 1830s. Landseer's lions have been polished, the huge paving stones re-laid, and the fountains renovated. The idea was that bollards would create avenues along which the police could move swiftly to deal with excitable crowds; but in April 1990 a demonstration against the government's new community charge (the "poll tax", since replaced by the Council Tax) developed into a second battle of Trafalgar, causing widespread damage to nearby shops and restaurants.

But the pigeons still come back for more.

Fashion link: The mundane architecture of modern buildings in **The Strand**, the main thoroughfare connecting the West End with the City, cannot hide the fact that it was once one of the most fashionable streets in London. Here you can dine on roast beef at Simpson's, opened in 1848, or take high tea at the relaunched famous J. Lyons tea house.

London's official hub, the point where all mileages from the capital are recorded, is marked by a bronze plaque in the pavement behind the equestrian statue of Charles I facing down Whitehall. The statue itself stands on the site of the first of 13 crosses set up by Edward I in 1291 to mark the stages in the funeral procession of his queen, Eleanor of Castile, from Nottinghamshire to Westminster Abbey.

In Tudor and Stuart times, The Strand was bordered by the mansions of the aristocracy whose gardens flowed down to the Thames. The restored **Water Gate** in the park next door to the Embankment Underground station once marked the river entrance to **York House**, birthplace of Francis Bacon and home of the dukes of Buckingham.

Benjamin Franklin made his home in Craven Street and Rudyard Kipling in Villiers Street, where the old Players' Theatre music hall ran under the railway arches for more than 40 years. After temporary accommodation elsewhere, it is now back in its new "old" home. Destitute Londoners doss down for the night under the railway bridge.

The **Adelphi Theatre** in the Strand was opened in the early 19th century and it was quickly followed by others. Richard D'Oyly Carte, sponsor of Gilbert and Sullivan operas at the **Savoy Theatre**, also financed the building of the **Savoy Hotel**, which opened in 1889 as one of the first in London with private bathrooms, electric lights and lifts (elevators).

From the footpath the Savoy is almost unnoticeable, but then it is ostentatious enough to have its own private road and

Covent Garden: a busker's auditorium and a flower seller's market.

to demand that vehicles drive on the right-hand side. Past the silver art deco front of the rebuilt theatre, through the revolving doors and into the vast foyer, another world unfolds in the huge lounge overlooking the private gardens and the river.

D'Oyly Carte himself is commemorated in a stained-glass window in the Queen's Chapel of the Savoy, behind the hotel. It is a truly ancient looking stone building which was originally constructed in the 16th century.

Below the chapel, the British Broadcasting Company started its first daily radio broadcasts in 1923. The first public broadcasting station in Britain was established in the previous year by the Marconi Wireless Telegraph Company in the crescent of the **Aldwych** on the opposite side of the Strand, near where the BBC studios at Bush House now stand.

Pleasure garden: Named after a convent whose fields once occupied the site, **Covent Garden** was for centuries until 1974 the principal market in London for vegetables, fruit and flowers. Since the early 1980s the area has seen a remarkable transformation. Numerous restaurants and cafés, shops and showrooms, now occupy the old warehouses in the narrow streets and alleyways surrounding the market square.

Many of the streets around Covent Garden have been cordoned off with pedestrian pathways. Dinky gift stores and card and poster shops proliferate. **Neal's Yard**, at Earlham Street, with its apothecary and bakery and natural food shops, is gathered around a tiny square full of potted trees.

The beautiful old buildings of the market itself are now lined with stalls, boutiques, bars and restaurants. This square was originally laid out with colonnaded town houses designed by Inigo Jones. A small market was established as early as 1661. The terraces and arcades have long since disappeared, although the recast arcade on the north side, where the **Rock Garden** dis-

Inigo Jones's market piazza is a mecca for the fashion-conscious, and friend.

PUBS

Much has been said and written about public houses (as *The Times* still insists on describing pubs), especially by some of London's literary forefathers, many of whom were particularly partial to a pint or two.

Suffice it to say here that, like most other things in a city this size, it is impossible to generalise about the 5,438 pubs in London. Some have live music, some stage striptease, some are genteel and some rough, a large number are Victorian (a strange product of such a morally critical age) and some were opened last week. Every Londoner has his or her own favourite, the choice of which will depend as much on the people that frequent it as on the decor.

The Punch and Judy in Covent Garden is typical of pubs in the central entertainment area; it is packed and vibrant with young people who come to meet their friends and stay all evening.

Not so in the City, however, where not all pubs are as quaint as Ye Olde Cheshire Cheese (frequented by Dr. Johnson) in an alleyway at 145 Fleet Street. Everywhere is packed at lunchtime in the City but after 9 p.m. most pubs are closed, and many don't open at all at on the weekend.

In the East End the pub retains some of its country role as the centre of a community and a good

landlord knows the names of all his regulars and even organises weekend excursions. Pubs like the Duke of Edinburgh in Wanstead welcome everyone: the family, children and all.

The King's Head in Islington is one of several theatre pubs. Here a variety of plays are put on against a background of clinking glasses and ringing tills. The audience's attention is divided and tends to wander between the performing actor and serving bartender.

From Richmond to Greenwich the banks of the Thames are lined with pubs, many of which open directly onto the river's towpath. The Dove in Hammersmith is one such (and is jam-packed with people on a balmy summer's evening) and is the venue where the patriotic anthem *Rule Britannia* was composed.

London has several pubs that date from the 17th century, and many retain a 17th-century atmosphere. One of the best examples is The George in Southwark, the only original galleried coaching inn in London. Rebuilt in 1676, it has remained largely unchanged since. The galleries were once the entrance to the inn's rooms.

A fine example of the explosion of pubs during the Victorian era (distinctive for their engraved mirrors, grand central bars and dark velvet upholstery) is the Duke of Cumberland in Fulham, complete with Grecian urns.

The traditional drink in a pub is English beer (ale or bitter). The genuine article is drawn up by hand pump and served at the temperature of the cellar; chilling literally kills it, as beer continues to ferment in the barrel. Chilled foreign beers (without the flavour of hops), described in England as "lager", are extensively served in pubs.

Most pubs used to brew their own beer on the premises but very few still do so; one of these has the longest name in London: The Ferret and Firkin in the Balloon up the Creek, in Lots Road, Chelsea. As a rule pubs are owned by large brewing companies and sell only company brands, which is why some enthusiasts travel for miles to find the beer they like.

A relative newcomer to the evening leisure scene is the wine bar, which has an atmosphere that falls half way between pub and restaurant. Some, like the Criterion Brasserie on Piccadilly Circus, attract a fashionable clientele but they lack the traditional cosiness of old London pubs.

Pub opening hours have recently been liberalised to open all day from 11 a.m. to 11 p.m. Monday to Saturday; the Sunday hours of 11 a.m. to 3 p.m. and 5.30 p.m. to 11 p.m. remained unchanged. Despite opponents' predictions of large-scale drunkenness and debauchery, the move hasn't changed the pub scene very much at all. Cynics would argue that it has simply given landlords the opportunity to recoup losses caused by the trend towards drinking less. But why did they ever close in the afternoon in the first place? The restriction was imposed in World War I to stop munitions workers getting tiddly, and, in true English tradition, nobody got around to changing it for more than 70 years.

penses equal helpings of American-style hamburgers and live rock music.

The portico of **St Paul's**, the actors' church, used as a backdrop in the film *My Fair Lady* and also designed by Inigo Jones, dominates the western end of the square. The vaults and grounds of this church are said to contain the remains of more famous people than any other church except Westminster Abbey, although all the headstones have long been removed.

Polling for the two Members of Parliament for Westminister used to take place outside the church until the secret ballot was introduced in 1872. These so-called "hustings" were often riotous affairs, and the Covent Garden husting of 1818 resulted in the dissolution of Parliament.

The old flower market, in the southeast corner of the square, now contains the **London Transport Museum,** which has a big collection of horse-drawn coaches, buses, trams, trains, rail carriages, and some working displays.

Next door to it is the new **Theatre Museum**, entered from Russell Street.

The original Theatre Royal opened in **Drury Lane** in 1663 and 70 years later another theatre was built on the site of what became the Royal Opera House, the prestigious headquarters for opera and ballet in Britain.

Opposite its white Corinthian portico is Bow Street police station, home of the scarlet-waistcoated Bow Street Runners**,** the prototype policemen. On the corner is the courthouse where Henry Fielding, the novelist, wrote part of *Tom Jones* while serving as a magistrate.

Street performers: In his diary, Samuel Pepys recorded details of the first Punch and Judy show, which was held in the market square, and the event is marked every June by the **Busking Festival**. Buskers are seen everywhere in London these days, but in Covent Garden they are part of the establishment. Would-be performers undergo rigorous auditions and restrictions, keeping the standards in general high, unlike those in the Un-

A stringent audition for Covent Garden performers.

derground tunnels where the echoing acoustics often do much to improve the quality of a questionable performance.

At the other end of the spectrum, the gargantuan 2,098-seat **Royal Opera House** is home to the Royal Ballet and the Royal Opera. Plans have recently been approved for development of the existing site to provide, among other things, a new enlarged stage and orchestra pit, facilities for the Royal Ballet to establish a permanent home in Covent Garden, and a magnificent new foyer space from the shell of the Floral Hall. Tickets are costly, but 65 cheaper amphitheatre seats and 45 standing places can be purchased from 10 a.m. on the day of a performance.

Covent Garden meets Soho at **Charing Cross Road**, where dozens of bookshops lend fame to an otherwise undistinguished street. Here is **Foyle's**, with more than four million volumes on just about any subject stored higgledy-piggledy on every floor. **Zwemmer's** is known for its fine art books. Antique and second-hand book shops abound in the area.

Clubs of influence: West of Trafalgar Square, along elegant **Pall Mall**, St James's is the epitome of aristocratic London. Its exclusive clubs mingle with the grand homes of royalty. And the area has been the haunt of men of influence since the 17th century.

It's rather reassuring to learn that, for the most part, the clubs enjoy a reputation for dull food and boring, snobbish company. However, they do usually have excellent wine cellars.

Club members are known to be amongst the more reactionary in the country. In 1889, a workers' demonstration moved along Pall Mall and had nailbrushes and shoes thrown at them from the Reform Club.

It's said that bishops and Fellows of the Royal Society join the **Athenaeum**, the foremost literary club, while actors and publishers opt for the **Garrick**. Diplomats, politicians and spies prefer to opt for **Brooks'**, the **Traveller's**,

The rare, the exotic and the cheap are piled cheek by jowl in Charing Cross Road's bookshops.

Boodles or **White's**. Journalists gather at the **Groucho Club** in Soho.

The **Reform Club** in Pall Mall, the leading liberal club, was the setting for Phileas Fogg's wager that he could travel around the world in 80 days. The most famous club of all in its time was **Crockford's**, "a notorious gambling hell" founded by a fishmonger from Temple Bar.

Almost all of London's clubs are the near exclusive preserve of men. Their continuing influence in the social, commercial and political life of the capital cannot be underestimated. Dukes join the **Turf Club**, while top Tories dine together at the **Carlton**, which was bombed by the IRA in 1990.

In **Waterloo Place**, at the bottom end of Regent Street, the bronze statue of Frederick, the Grand Old Duke of York (as in, "He had 10,000 men ..."), overlooks the Mall and St James's Park from atop its 124-ft (37-metre) column. The duke, however, is of dubious repute. The cost of his monument was met by extracting a day's wages from every man in the armed services. The joke was that his statue was placed so high to enable him to avoid his creditors.

Royal terrace: Running in both directions from either side of the Duke of York's Steps is the Georgian opulence of **Carlton House Terrace**, once the home of the aristocracy and now mainly of government departments. It was designed by John Nash, on the site of Carlton House, the former residence of George IV. Nash was also responsible for the grand plan to connect the royal home to the Prince Regent's new property north of Marylebone Road, via the broad sweep of Regent Street.

Prime Minister W. E. Gladstone lived in a house on the left of Carlton House Terrace from 1856 until 1875. Next door, the **Institute of Contemporary Arts** (usually referred to as the ICA), with gallery, cinema and theatre, resides somewhat incongruously in the restored Nash House; incongruously because the ICA, despite rather a pre-

Bastions of culture: the Royal Opera House and an exclusive gentleman's club.

tentious sounding name, usually has a remarkable eclectic, unrestrained diet of modern work, often on the borderlines of art, which it mixes with well-known classics. On the right are the headquarters of **The Royal Society**. Founded in 1660, it is one of the most influential and important scientific bodies in the world.

Nell Gwynne, the former orange seller and mistress to the king, lived for 15 years until her death in 1687 in a house on the site of No. 79 Pall Mall.

There is little to indicate the entrance to **Marlborough House**, designed by Sir Christopher Wren and the home of Queen Mary, consort of George V, until her death in 1953. Now it is a Commonwealth conference and research centre.

One building that is unmistakable, if only for its unprepossessing exterior, is **St James's Palace**, built by Henry VIII in about 1540. It was never popular with the royals who preferred the palace at Whitehall until it burnt down in 1698.

Little remains of the original Tudor

palace, which was built on the site of a leper hospital run by St James the Less. The state apartments are not open to the public and the chief relic, the **Gate-house** or **Clock Tower**, is best viewed from the street. Further on are more royal residences: **York House** and **Clarence House**, home of the Queen Mother, and **Lancaster House** where Chopin once gave a piano recital for Queen Victoria.

Henry Jermyn, first Earl of St Alban, laid out the fashionable area around **St James's Square** in about 1660. The Dukes of Norfolk had a town house in the square from 1723 until 1938. The same building was used by General Eisenhower to launch the invasions of North Africa and northwest Europe in World War II.

In the northeast corner of the central gardens, small bouquets of flowers are still placed at the foot of the memorial to WPC Yvonne Fletcher, Britain's smallest woman police officer. She was fatally shot during demonstrations outside the former Libyan People's Bureau in April 1984.

The traditional frontages on **St James's Street** compete for attention with the striking lines of the offices of *The Economist* and, opposite, the futuristic design of No. 66, all granite, steel and curved glass.

By contrast, **Berry Bros and Rudd**, at 3 St James's Street, is straight out of a Dickens novel. **James Lock and Co.**, at No. 6, is the birthplace of the bowler hat. A few doors up, **Lobb's** shod the feet of Queen Victoria, among a host of others. A record is permanently stored of every customer's foot.

Jermyn Street is another street of fashionable shops, restaurants and hotels and clubs. At its eastern end is the **Haymarket,** running south from Piccadilly Circus, which is home of **Burberry's** – makers of the beige overcoats that all Americans adore – the **Theatre Royal** and **Her Majesty's**.

Arcadia: London's oldest enclosed shopping arcade, the **Royal Opera Ar-**

Chic cigars at Davidoff in St James's Street.

82

cade, was once a part of Her Majesty's Theatre, the biggest in the country until it burnt down and was transferred across the road.

Behind the imposing Rennaisance-style facade of **Burlington House** on **Piccadilly**, there is a handsome court-yard beyond which the **Royal Academy of Arts.** The Academy stages big, thematic exhibitions all year round and is famous for its summer exhibition of members' work, a massive collection of paintings ranging from the sublime to the ridiculous. In 1987 one of the exhibits was painted by a little-known artist, the royal Prince of Wales.

Around the corner in Burlington Street is the excellent and stimulating **Museum of Mankind**. It is the ethnography department of the British Museum and displays items from the anthropological collection.

The **Burlington Arcade** was built in 1819, a Regency promenade of tiny but exclusive shops, still patrolled by its famous Beadles. In their top-hats and livery, these former soldiers of the 10th Hussars ensure good behaviour, with "no undue whistling, humming or hurrying". Only a Beadle knows what constitutes undue humming.

London has several highly decorative shopping arcades dating from Victorian and later times. Almost opposite is the **Piccadilly Arcade,** best known for its glass and china ware. The graceful, bow-fronted Regency windows belie the fact that it was built in 1910.

Fortnum and Mason's, grocers to the Queen, has a food hall to rival Harrods in its presentation. Here even the shop assistants wear tails, which might help to explain why men's pullovers sell for a minimum of about £200. Still, the changing of the guard on the clock face at the front every hour is worth waiting for.

Further along Piccadilly, "Tea at the **Ritz**", once an institution for people of so-called refinement, is now reserved for residents and invited guests after becoming overrun by hordes of eager

tourists. The casino, probably the classiest in London, might prove less difficult to get into. The ever-so-elegant Louis XVI dining room overlooking Green Park is open to all – or anyone willing to pay the price.

Exclusive quarter: The region bounded by Piccadilly and Park Lane, Oxford and Regent Streets, has been synonymous with wealth and power since the early 18th century, when it was first laid out by the Grosvenor family, dukes of Westminster. **Mayfair** takes its name from the fair which was held annually on the site of what is now Shepherd Market. In the best British tradition, it clings to its exclusivity, although many of the magnificent Georgian homes of business barons and princes of property are now overrun with hotels, apartments, offices, shops and showrooms.

The high street of Mayfair is **Bond Street**, divided into Old Bond Street at its southern end leading north to New Bond Street. Here are London's most exclusive couturiers and designer bou-

tiques, jewellery shops, antique stores and art galleries.

The headquarters of **Sotheby's**, the world famous auctioneers, founded in 1744 and now owned by Americans, is at No. 34. Admission is free, as long as you look reasonably presentable in the eyes of the management. In 1987 Sotheby's set a world record of £24,750,000 for the sale of Van Gogh's work, *Sunflowers*, since superseded by rivals Christie's, who sold Van Gogh's *Portrait of Dr Gachet* for $82.5 million.

Here too is **Savile Row**, home of gentlemen's outfitters, where even "off-the-peg" suits are priced from a minimum of about £400. The sky's the limit as far as prices for tailor-made suits are concerned.

Face places: The **Embassy Club,** at 7 Bond Street, has long regarded itself as being a class above most other London nightspots. A plaque near the entrance commemorates the visits of Edward VII and Mrs Wallis Simpson in the 1930s. In the 1950s it was the haunt of Princess Margaret. The joke since has been that only royalty can afford the prices.

The most exclusive Mayfair night-clubs are almost impossible to get into, unless of course you happen to be a member or, better still, a "face". Prince Charles was to be found at **Annabel's** in Berkeley Square on the night before his wedding in 1981. Sarah Ferguson was there in police uniform with the Princess of Wales on the night before her wedding to Prince Andrew, who was once refused admittance because he wasn't wearing a tie.

Upstairs is the **Clermont Club**, the high society gambling den, where Lord Lucan lost heavily in 1974 and then disappeared after the mysterious murder of his nanny and the attempted murder of his wife.

Shepherd Market, a tiny pedestrian enclave landed incongruously amidst the grand town houses and exclusive hotels, was established by Mayfair's planners to supply the daily needs of the local residents. Even today there are

Sotheby's art auctioneers, setting the pace for world art prices.

stores selling fish, fruit and vegetables, hardware and building materials. A multitude of restaurants includes a "workingman's café". There are also specialist shops, one selling hand-tooled model soldiers, another old and rare recordings from show business and the classics.

At night Shepherd Market is notorious for its street walkers. Monica Coghlan, a prostitute, claimed she was picked up there by Jeffrey Archer, the prominent Tory and best-selling author, who was eventually awarded £500,000 for defamation charges against a newspaper that published her claim.

American tradition: The Americans have always laid claim to a large part of Mayfair, ever since John Adams, the first United States minister to Britain and later the nation's president, took up residence at 9 Grosvenor Square in 1785. In 1790, 31 of the 47 households in the square belonged to titled families.

Grosvenor Square is now dominated by the enormous American eagle surmounting the US embassy on the western side. The cost of the statue of Franklin D. Roosevelt in the gardens was met by grateful British citizens after World War II. The required £40,000 was raised in less than 24 hours. A little over 20 years later, it was lucky to survive massive anti-Vietnam War demonstrations.

Brook Street, running from the northeast corner of the square to Bond Street, is the home of **Claridge's Hotel**, one of London's premier luxury hotels. Handel wrote the *Messiah*, amongst other things, at the much-altered No. 25 where he lived for 35 years until his death in 1759. Here also is the **Savile Club**, the 120-year-old literary establishment, where the members recently voted on the thorny topic of whether or not to allow lay guests at its breakfast table and "mixed-sex lunches" on Saturday afternoons.

Nightingales no longer sing in **Berkeley Square** (if they ever did), and although some of its original buildings

Bond Street bargains are strictly for the wealthy.

remain, this once highly aristocratic square is much spoilt by ugly-looking office buildings. The exclusive Berkeley Square Ball was discontinued in 1989 because of the dreadful behaviour of the guests.

Lord Clive of India committed suicide at No. 45. The Earl of Shelburne, the prime minister who conceded the independence of the United States in 1783, lived on the site of Lansdowne House, which was pulled down in 1985 to make way for yet another office block. And **Berkeley Square House** is built on the site of the house where Queen Elizabeth II was born in 1926.

Park Lane, running from Hyde Park Corner to Marble Arch, forms the western boundary of Mayfair. Its once magnificent homes are largely replaced by modern hotels and apartment buildings. These include the **Hilton Hotel** and the **Dorchester Hotel**, headquarters of General Eisenhower in World War II, and long popular with film stars visiting London. It is now Arab-owned.

To the north, the residence of the Grosvenor family (owners of the 300-acre estate covering Mayfair and Park Lane) was knocked down in 1928 to make way for the **Grosvenor House Hotel**. The Great Room of the hotel is still London's largest banqueting hall.

Of the original houses in Park Lane, few remain. Benjamin Disraeli, Prime Minister of Great Britain, lived from 1839 to 1872 at No. 93.

A chain of stores: A stone slab on a traffic island opposite Marble Arch at the head of **Oxford Street**, London's principal shopping thoroughfare, marks the spot where a triangular gallows known as the Tyburn Tree stood permanently from 1571 to 1759.

It's estimated that up to 50,000 people met their maker at Tyburn between 1196 and 1783. Oxford Street itself, an old Roman road, was once known as Tyburn Street, the route by which the condemned were transported to the gallows from Newgate prison or the Tower. The site of London's main place

On a normal day it's hard work – but at Christmas Oxford Street is a shopper's nightmare.

of execution took its name from Tyburn Brook, which flowed into the Westbourne River at what is now the Serpentine in Hyde Park.

The **Tyburn River** runs underground through sewerage pipes from Hampstead, under Oxford Street near the HMV record shop, then parallel to Bond Street, around Berkeley Square and west to Buckingham Palace where it is diverted to feed Rosamond's Pond in St James's Park.

In 1850, the **Marble Arch**, designed by John Nash and said to be based on the Arch of Constantine in Rome, was placed at Tyburn after being removed from the front of Buckingham Palace because it was too narrow for the wheels of the State coaches.

The crowds still flock to **Oxford Street**, drawn by the big department stores. At Christmas time, the celebrated lights are turned on and the thoroughfare gets even more crowded.

Meeting points: At Oxford Circus, **Regent Street** continues north, part of Nash's scheme to connect the Prince Regent's home at Carlton House with his newly-acquired property at Regent's Park. Here the Ladies Lavatory company opened its first public facilities in 1884 for the benefit of shoppers in the area.

Among several famous restaurants in Regent's Street are **Veeraswamy's**, London's first Indian restaurant, and the **Café Royal**, which was used by artists such as Oscar Wilde, Whistler and Aubrey Beardsley. Private boxing matches, it is reputed, still occasionally take place in the upstairs rooms.

Further along, the Christmas decorations go up in mid-October in the overflowing floors of **Hamley's**, the world's biggest toy store, founded in 1760. It is quite a contrast to the heavily-timbered, mock-Tudor style of **Liberty's**, around the corner in **Great Marlborough Street**. Built in 1924 but founded in the 19th century by Mr Liberty, patron of the arts and expert in foreign silks, the distinctive Liberty

shop to ▪atch the ▪imate: mith & on, ▪nbrella ▪ecialists.

designs continue Mrs L's tradition.

Other stores include jewellers such as **Mappin and Webb** and **Garrards**, which maintains the Crown Jewels kept in the Tower of London. The **London Diamond Centre** has a big collection of precious stones, some of which are for sale, and exhibition areas.

Carnaby Street, on the eastern side of Regent Street leading to Oxford Street, was once the site of a pesthouse and leper colony. For a few brief years in the 1960s, it became the centre of so-called "Swinging London". As quickly as it came into fashion it fell out again. Laid out as a pedestrian precinct, it is now the home of cheap clothing and souvenir shops catering to tourists.

Marylebone: The district of London stretching from Oxford Street to Marylebone Road to the north and to Bloomsbury and Holborn in the east is the West End's biggest residential quarter. **Marylebone** (pronounced "Marry-le-bun") was formed with the development of a new road running from Pad-

dington to Islington through the parish of St Mary-le-bourne to relieve congestion in Oxford Street. Soon afterwards the Adam brothers conceived Portland Place as a home for the rich, and 30 years later Nash included it in his grand design to connect Regent's Park with St James's. The plan was never realised.

The Adam houses in **Portland Place** are now gradually giving way to more modern structures. Several embassies and a number of institutes and learned societies are found here. At its southern end rises the imposing but nondescript mass of **Broadcasting House**, headquarters of the British Broadcasting Corporation, where the first public television transmission was made in 1932.

In **Langham Place**, which curves around to connect Portland Place with Regent Street, the circular **All Souls' Church** with its pointed spire was built by Nash to round off the northern end of Regent Street.

To the east stands the distinctive **Telecom Tower,** which rises more than

Back to back, Liberty's and Carnaby Street present very different shopping opportunities.

600 ft (180 metres). The revolving restaurant at the top was closed in 1975 after an IRA bomb attack.

To the west of Great Portland Street is **Harley Street**, the specialist physicians' quarter. Drugs are big business here. So big in fact that in June 1987 the police raided an £800-a-week holiday appartment building and seized 50 kilos of cocaine worth £10 million, one of the biggest drugs raids in Britain's history.

Collections and imitations: In Manchester Square is **Hertford House**, home of the **Wallace Collection**, a staggering display of art wealth collected mainly by the third and fourth Marquesses of Hertford in the mid-19th century. Thankfully the Wallace Collection is generally free of the crowds which invade places such as **Madame Tussaud's** and the **Planetarium** on the Marylebone Road near Baker Street.

The good Madame has been one of London's most popular attractions ever since her wax figures arrived after the French Revolution. The crowds still flock to this make-believe world of kings and queens, celebrities, sporting heroes and politicians – though the standard of waxworks is variable. The adjacent Planetarium has excellent laser light shows as well as exhibits.

At **Baker Street**, the Underground's District line platforms were the terminus for the Bakerloo railway. It was London's first underground railway line, which ran to Waterloo south of the Thames. The brickwork on the platforms has been restored.

Holmes' home: Baker Street connects Marylebone Road with Oxford Street. The address in Baker Street where Sir Arthur Conan Doyle deposited *Sherlock Holmes* is in fact occupied by a bank, with someone working full-time to deal with the volume of letters Holmes receives. Those relating to alleged crimes are referred to the Metropolitan Police. Not far away is the **Sherlock Holmes Museum**, which also claims the famous address – and would rather like the letters, too.

Park Crescent, part of Nash's scheme to link Regent's Park with St James's.

OFFICIAL LONDON

The city of Westminster lies a mile or so upstream from the City of London. Once separate communities, today they are both at the centre of London's modern metropolis and are generally referred to as Westminster and the City.

For centuries Westminster was the focus of government and the monarchy, just as the City was Britain's trading and financial centre. Their fickle and sometimes stormy relationship has figured largely in British history. Occasionally in the past, this conflict of interests has turned to violence as in the 17th-century civil war.

Westminster houses the nation's policy making civil servants; the nation's spies; Prime Minister and her cabinet, and the Queen and her family. Additionally, many of their predecessors are buried in Westminster Abbey.

Westminster owes its existence to the last of the Saxon kings, Edward the Confessor, who built a great abbey and a palace on this marshy spot upstream from the City 1,000 years ago.

Officialdom street: Official London really begins just south of **Trafalgar Square**, where a bronze statue of a little man on horseback points towards the heart of Westminster. Le Sueur's 1633 sculpture of King Charles I is the oldest of many excellent equestrian statues in London.

It has a chequered history. King Charles lost the civil war with parliament and was beheaded in 1642. The statue was sold to a scrap dealer, who promised to melt it down for souvenirs, but actually hid it until the monarchy was restored. In 1675 it was placed on a marble plinth facing straight down the broad and unmistakeably official thoroughfare called **Whitehall**.

Nowadays to the British, Whitehall epitomises government, officialdom and "red tape". Apart from a few shops and a theatre, most of the buildings are ministries and government offices. On a winter Sunday morning the street has a haunting melancholy atmosphere; windswept and deserted. During summer weekdays tourists outnumber and outcolour the rather drab civil servants.

Beyond the Whitehall Theatre are the offices of the the the Armed Forces Commander-in-Chief, known as the **Horse Guards**. Outside this colonnaded building are mounted sentries in fancy uniforms, white gloves, plumes and helmets. These are soldiers of the Life Guards or Royal Horse Guards, guarding the site of the main gateway to the ancient **Palace of Whitehall** used by King Henry VIII in the 16th century, and still regarded as the official entrance to the palaces. There is a guard-changing ceremony here at 11 a.m.

Through the archway of Horse Guards and opening out onto St James' park is the huge **Horse Guards Parade** where in June the Queen's birthday is honoured by a splendid ceremony called the **Trooping of the Colour**.

Preceding pages: sunset reflection in Parliament's windows. **Left**, on duty for the cameras, a dismounted Horseguard. **Right**, Big Ben, London's favourite landmark.

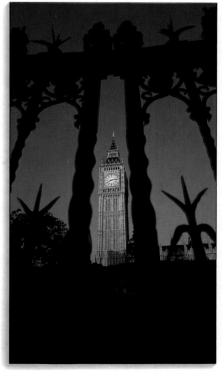

Opposite Horse Guards, on the other side of Whitehall, is the magnificent renaissance style **Banqueting House** built by Inigo Jones, the 17th-century English architect who introduced this Italian style of architecture into England. It is the only surviving fragment of Whitehall palace. Inside this huge hall, the ceiling is divided into nine large panels filled with almost overpoweringly rich baroque figure paintings by the Flemish painter Rubens. Shortly after he finished this work, he became at the king's behest Sir Peter Paul Rubens.

The **Cenotaph**, the national war memorial, rather unspectacularly breaks the monotony of Whitehall. On Remembrance Sunday every November this shrine is the focal point of a service attended by the Queen and the nation's leaders to remember the dead of the two great wars.

Downing Street is little more than a short terrace of four 18th-century houses in dull brown brick, unfortunately now sealed off behind a heavy gate to prevent a terrorist attack. Number 10 is the official residence of the Prime Minister, and the venue for high level government discussions and cabinet meetings. The plain black painted door and simple net-curtained windows suggest nothing of its stylish, well-proportioned rooms and the important state business which goes on inside. Prime ministers have lived here since the 18th century when King George II offered the house to his prime minister. The other houses are used as official residences for other senior members of government.

Across Whitehall are the grey characterless office blocks which house the Ministries of Defence and Technology. Beyond the Cenotaph, Whitehall becomes **Parliament Street**. The great stolid buildings on the same side as the Horse Guards house the Foreign and Commonwealth Offices and, after King Charles Street, the Treasury. A sign on the corner points the way to the **Cabinet War Rooms**. These are an interesting

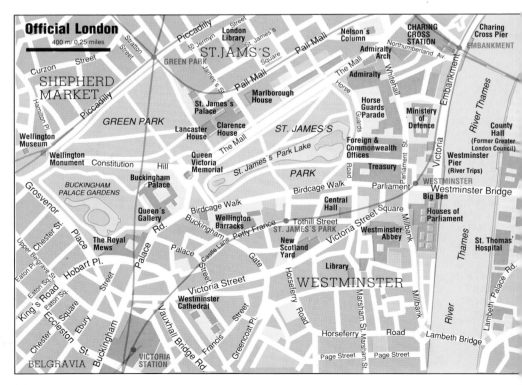

relic of World War II: bombproof underground rooms used by the government. The rooms include the combined office-bedroom used by Sir Winston Churchill.

Lined with landmarks: Parliament Street empties out into **Parliament Square**, with its tall trees and lawns lined with statues of illustrious statesmen. This, the country's first official roundabout, is surrounded by national landmarks.

The clocktower of the Houses of Parliament has become a symbol of London. Its elaborately fretted stone sides rise up nearly 330 ft (100 metres) to a richly gilded spire above the clock. Its 13-ton hour bell was supposedly nicknamed **Big Ben** after a rather fat government official called Sir Benjamin Hall who was commissioner of works when the bell was installed. During World War II the well-known chimes of Big Ben heralded the BBC's radio news from London. Since then the sound of the bell and the view of the clocktower

have become symbolic of the British parliament, of patriotism and of television and radio news broadcasts.

Beyond the clocktower is the graceful **Westminster Bridge** with excellent views up and down river. Wordsworth wrote of the view: "Earth has not anything to show more fair." Just downstream from the bridge is **Westminster Pier**, the starting point of most of the boat trips on the Thames. On the other end of the bridge, the prominent building in Portland stone is **County Hall**, the former headquarters of the now defunct Greater London Council.

The oldest part of the Houses of Parliament, **Westminster Hall**, is beyond the forest of ornamental railings protecting the corner entrance, New Palace Yard. The Statue of Oliver Cromwell stands guard against the side of the ancient hall.

Begun in 1078, Westminster Hall is one of the oldest and most historic buildings in London. The thick buttressed walls are spanned with a unique

Keeping up with the neighbours: the prime minister's doorman and (right) Her Majesty's footman.

and magnificent hammer beamed oak roof. This hall has witnessed many crucial events in British history; coronation celebrations, lyings-in-state and treason trials. Amongst those condemned to death were Sir Thomas More, who fell foul of King Henry VIII, King Charles I, accused of treason against parliament, and the 17th-century revolutionary Guy Fawkes, who tried to blow up the buildings. The story of the discovery of this bomb plot is still lightheartedly celebrated every November 5th with firework displays all over Britain.

However, in 1835 a disastrous fire destroyed most of the ancient rambling Palace of Westminster. Westminster Hall and a small crypt chapel survived. Parliament grabbed at the opportunity to build itself a nice comfortable purpose-built meeting place. The present **Houses of Parliament** were built in an exuberant gothic style by Sir Charles Barry and Augustus Pugin – or rather, according to their gospel. Unfortunately, the House of Commons (on the

left side of the central spire, whilst the House of Lords is on the right) was virtually obliterated in a bombing raid on 10 May 1941.

Corridors of power: Outwardly little has changed over 130 years. The houses have distinctive but simple rectangular outlines which are embellished with gilded spires and towers, mullioned windows and intricate stone carving and statues. Under the immense **Victoria Tower**, which marks the west end of the building is the grand entrance used by the Queen when opening a new session of government. Most of this tower is used to store the old records of parliament. A Union Jack (the British national flag) flies from the tower when parliament is in session. Night sittings are indicated by a light shining over the clocktower.

The building covers 8 acres (3.2 hectares); there are 11 open courtyards and over 1,100 rooms. Apart from the ceremonial state rooms and the two main debating chambers, the House of Lords

Royalty watching has become a national pastime.

and the House of Commons, there are libraries, dining rooms and tea rooms and also offices and secretarial facilities for government ministers, opposition leaders and ordinary members of parliament. Underneath **St Stephen's Hall** is the ancient crypt chapel. Members can take their marriage vows and even have their children baptised here if they wish.

There is nothing spartan about the buildings at all. Many of the walls are covered with heroic Victorian paintings and the woodwork is carved in an intricate gothic fashion. The construction symbolises some of the contradictions which are evident in British democracy and character: strong, traditional and class-conscious, with an ambivalence to change; diligent yet comfort-loving.

Watching a session of either house from the public galleries usually involves waiting in a long queue. Some of the flavour can be gained from television coverage of the proceedings, which began in 1989.

At the far end of the government complex are the **Victoria Tower Gardens**, which contain memorials to Emmeline Pankhurst and her daughter, who were instrumental in winning votes for women.

Official art: From **Millbank** a short street leads into one of London's most unobtrusive but notable concert halls, **St John's Smith Square**. Originally a badly war-damaged 18th-century church, it now has excellent acoustics and a reputation for high quality classical music, which is often broadcast on the radio. In the crypt is a good wine-bar cum restaurant.

Further down Millbank, beyond Lambeth Bridge, is the **Tate Gallery,** Britain's top gallery of British painting, sculpture and foreign art of the 19th and 20th century. The collection is so large that only one-sixth is on show at any one time. Among the outstanding British paintings are attractive portraits by Gainsborough, intensely dramatic and impressionistic seascapes and landscapes by Turner (now housed in an

Guardsmen parade for the Trooping of the Colour ceremony.

PARLIAMENT

The Houses of Parliament consist of the House of Commons and the House of Lords. The Commons, the House of locally elected Members of Parliament (MPs), wield virtually all the power but inhabit only half the building.

Jutting out towards Parliament Square is Westminster Hall, with offices, Committee rooms, dining rooms and libraries of the Commons stretching behind it to the river. Right in the centre is the debating chamber of the House of Commons.

To the right of Westminster Hall is the domain of the Lords. Senior judges, bishops and archbishops, dukes, marquesses, earls, viscounts and barons all make their contribution to the legislational system here.

Most of the members of this chamber govern by birthright. As descendants of the previous ruling classes they still have a say in government. Their role is generally one of blocking the measures proposed by the lower house (the House of Commons), although they can only block a bill a certain number of times before it becomes law. Apart from the religious element in the Lords, a considerable number of members are life peers who are ennobled as a reward for duties done to the nation. Many previous members of the Commons are rewarded for years of good service – or summarily removed to the Upper House to get them out of the way – by a life peerage. The House of Lords is not as politically aligned as is the Commons, and nor is it as conservative as might be supposed.

There are 651 elected MPs. The Commons chamber seats only about 450. Generally seating is not a problem since MPs attend sessions only when they wish. In the rectangular chamber, the governing party sits on one side, facing the opposition. Cabinet ministers sit on the front bench, with the "shadow cabinet" opposite.

Major parties represented are the Conservatives, Labour, the Liberal Democrats, and the Scottish Nationalists. General Elections are run on the basis of local rather than proportional representation. Therefore a party's presence in the House may not reflect its overall national standing. In the 1992 election the Conservative Party won 333 seats (51 percent) but only 42 per cent of the national vote.

A party, however, needs an overall majority in the House to push through its bills – unless opposition MPs also agree with the principles at stake. The procedure of lawmaking is so complex that a bill usually takes over six months to be enacted. If it is still incomplete at the end of the parliamentary year, it is dropped.

For particularly contentious issues the government is forced on occasions to pack the house; MPs are recalled from holidays or even from their beds if they are ill in order to ensure the smooth passage of a difficult bill. The government's Whips are the party members who bring members into line on such issues. Should the government – the ruling party – ever be defeated on a major issue, implying a substantial rebellion within its own ranks, there is a real danger of it being drummed out of the house, and a snap general election would then be called.

There are various techniques employed by the opposition to delay enactment of a bill. One is "filibustering", which entails continuous talking all day and night to prevent a bill being brought to the vote.

The press is at liberty to report on Parliament and both houses are now televised, although in a limited way (cameramen are forbidden to show MPs gently snoozing, for instance). In addition, a select group of journalists known as lobby correspondents have informal discussions with MPs and the prime minister's press secretary. Information thus gleaned is attributed to "sources close to the Prime Minister".

Parliament meets from October to July. In November, the governing party's plans for the year are announced in the Queen's Speech at the State Opening, which takes place in the chamber of the Lords. From the Strangers' Gallery, the public can watch the House of Commons at work on most days. The House meets at 2.30 p.m. and cabinet ministers answer questions for an hour. Prime Minister's question time (3.15 p.m.–3.30 p.m. on Tuesdays and Thursdays) usually attracts a full house.

extension of their own), and views of the English countryside by Constable.

The 19th-century French Impressionists are well represented in the gallery and so are a wide variety of 20th-century British and foreign painters and sculptors. They range from Picasso and Dali to Jackson Pollock, Mark Rothko and Henry Moore. The Tate also stages free lectures and film shows.

Back in Parliament Square close to Westminster Abbey is **St Margaret's Church**, which is used by members of the House of Commons for official services and for high society weddings. Buried here is Sir Walter Raleigh, sea-captain and a courtier of the first Queen Elizabeth. He is reputed to have been the first to bring back tobacco and the potato from America.

Opposite the end of the Houses of Parliament is the medieval moated **Jewel Tower** of the old palace of Westminster. The crown jewels used to be kept here, but were moved to the greater security of the Tower of London.

National shrine: The most historic religious building in the country is **Westminster Abbey**. It is also an outstanding piece of gothic architecture, which is probably more striking from the detail on the inside than from its outward aspects.

Much of the present abbey, the third on the site, was built in the 13th-century early English gothic style by King Henry III. In the 16th century, King Henry VII added on the remarkable chapel at the eastern end of the sanctuary in the late gothic perpendicular style. In the 17th century, Hawksmoor designed the towers at the main west entrance.

Until the 16th century the abbey was an important monastery. In addition to their religious duties, the monks translated and copied important books and manuscripts. They also ran a school to teach reading and writing in English and Latin, starting a long tradition of quality formal education on this side of the square. Henry VIII dissolved the

Recognisable security for the Royals.

monasteries when he quarrelled with the Pope but Westminster Abbey continued to be used as royal church for coronations and burials. All but two of the reigning monarchs from William the Conqueror onwards have been crowned here.

The Abbey has always had a special place in national life because of its royal connections. Eminent figures in public life are honoured in this national shrine. Large areas of the interior have the cluttered and confused appearance of an overcrowded sculpture museum.

The nave boasts a fine example of graceful early gothic vaulting, with tiers of arches on either side and an impressive choir screen, behind which is the choir and sanctuary. In the south transept is **Poets' Corner**. Chaucer and Tennyson are buried here, but Shakespeare, Milton, Keats and countless others only have a monument.

Chapel detail: Behind the sanctuary are magnificent and ornate royal chapels and tombs. The entrance is on the

western side of the nave and there is an entry fee. The **Chapel of Edward the Confessor** is the earliest, containing the tomb of the founder of the abbey himself, and that of Henry III, the man who rebuilt it in its present form.

The now ancient **Coronation Chair** is kept in this chapel, and it encloses the **Stone of Scone**, a block of reddish sandstone. It was first used by the Scots for their own coronations, before being carried off by Edward I in 1297 for the same use in England. In 1950 the stone was stolen by Scottish nationalists and replaced a year later.

One of the most refined and daring pieces of late gothic architecture is the **Chapel of Henry VII**. With its carved stalls, brilliantly patterned banners and above all the exquisite fan-vaulting of the roof, it is a breathtaking sight. Looking at its apparently delicate structure, it's difficult to believe that it withstood the blast of a bomb dropped nearby during World War II.

In the cloisters, the first section is often bustling with people buying or making brass rubbings. Beyond them is the **Chapter House** where early in the morning the medieval monks gathered to listen to their abbot. The inlaid decorated floor tiles are amongst the best preserved medieval tiles.

The **Undercroft Museum** in the main cloisters has a collection of effigies and other relics. Here passageways lead to **Westminster School**, founded by Elizabeth I when the monk's school was closed. It is still one of the most highly-regarded private schools.

Hidden nearby is the tiny but delightful **Little Cloister**; the main cloisters lead to **Dean's Yard**, which used to be part of the Abbey gardens.

A canyon of offices: The west door of the abbey opens onto **Victoria Street**, important commercially but since its rebuilding a long grey canyon of undistinguished office blocks, with the domed building of Methodist Central Hall guarding its opening. Some distance down this uninteresting street is **West-**

Boadicea's statue, described by one critic as an "armoured milk-float". <u>Right,</u> Westminster Abbey has hosted almost every coronation since 1066.

ROYALTY

Almost every day of the year a member of the Royal Family appears in public somewhere in London, pursued by battalions of royalty-watchers, professional and amateur. As patrons of various societies, the members of the family are in constant demand to open buildings, give prizes, and visit hospitals. The Court Circular, published daily in major national newspapers, details all their engagements, while the tabloid press relishes their disengagements.

There are easier ways to see the Royal Family. On the second Saturday in June, for example, when the Queen's birthday is officially celebrated, she travels by carriage to Horse Guards Parade for the ceremony of Trooping the Colour. In November she travels by state coach to Westminster for the State Opening of Parliament, escorted along the Mall by the Household Cavalry and greeted by a fanfare of trumpets. This is the only time in the year when she wears the monarch's traditional robes and crown. In the same month she attends the Service of Remembrance at the Cenotaph in Whitehall. And a member of the Royal Family always takes the salute at the Royal Tournament, a military show held in July at Earl's Court.

The Queen herself plays only a small part in government, though the scale of this interest is largely unmeasured. A great deal is implied from sentences in the press that read "sources close to the prime minister said..." Similarly, "the palace is understood to disapprove of..." carries great implications. At the opening of each parliament the Queen reads a prepared speech which announces the government of the time's proposed plan for that parliamentary season, whether she agrees with the measures within it or not. And while she appears in public relatively frequently, her only other major utterance is her televised speech to the nation at Christmas time, which usually carries some caring message rather than anything that might be construed as political.

Outside the UK her interests are sometimes more obvious, as demonstrated in the Fijian coup, where she sent personal messages to the deposed governor and the Fijian people. Prince Charles, on the other hand, takes a far more active role, sometimes steering a controversial course which is often interpreted as either criticising or endorsing the moves of government.

Several shops in London have royal warrants, identified by a Royal crest. These honours are granted by senior members of the Royal Family who use the shops regularly (Princess Diana is reputed to make surprise shopping visits to the boutiques of Beauchamp Place in Knightsbridge). The Queen buys perfume, for example, from J Floris (Jermyn Street) and Prince Philip has his hair cut by Truefitt and Hill, Bond Street.

The family is known for its love of horses, and several members go every year in June to Epsom in Surrey for the Derby, the most prestigious flat race of the year. They also go to Royal Ascot, a four-day meeting later in June at a racecourse owned by the Queen in Berkshire. Women wear spectacular hats at Ascot and frequently attract more attention than the horses. A racehorse owner herself, the Queen's daughter Princess Anne has made her name as a jockey.

At the Windsor Horse Show in May, Prince Philip competes in four-horse carriage racing. Prince Charles has often played polo at his home ground, the Guards' Polo Club at Smith's Lawn near Windsor.

The Queen usually spends Ascot week, Christmas and April at Windsor, January at Sandringham (Norfolk), early July at Holyrood House (Edinburgh) and September at Balmoral (Aberdeenshire in Scotland).

Kensington Palace is the London home of Princess Diana, Princess Margaret, the Duke and Duchess of Gloucester and Prince and Princess Michael of Kent. The Queen Mother lives in London at Clarence House, which is behind St. James's Palace, where the Duke and Duchess of Kent have an apartment. Prince Charles also stays here when in London.

Princess Anne, recently remarried, lives in a flat in Dolphin Square. Prince Andrew and Prince Edward reside at Buckingham Palace. Unfortunately for the visitor, it is rare to see a member of the Royal Family appear in a palace window.

minster **Cathedral**, the most important Catholic church in London. With its bold red and white brickwork, it looks like a gigantic layer cake. Built at the end of the 19th century in an outlandish Italian-Byzantine style that is unique in London, it provides a welcome break from the unrelenting street. The striped tower is 330 ft (100 metres) high and incorporates a lift for public use. The views from the gallery at the top are superb. The interior of the cathedral is spacious, sumptuous and impressive. Many of the chapels are enriched with multicoloured marble cladding on the walls.

Broadway leads off from the north side of Victoria Street. At the far end is St James's Underground station, incorporated in the towering building of London Transport headquarters.

Around the corner from Broadway, in Petty France, is the **Main Passport Office.** Also nearby is **Queen Anne's Gate**, a small and quiet street which has managed to preserve much of its 18th-century atmosphere. It's worth a detour to see the original carved door canopies, although all but one have now been painted over. MI5, the British Secret Service, supposedly occupies one of these houses.

At the far end of Victoria street is the **Victoria railway station**, the point where new arrivals in the country first set foot to ground, and get swept off their feet by a tide of hurrying commuters. The station has the busiest tourist information office in the capital.

Royal quarters: The delicately named **Birdcage Walk** (there was once an aviary here) is a rather indelicate road which diverges from Parliament Square towards Buckingham Palace.

The road divides St James's Park from the drilling ground of the **Wellington Barracks**, the home of the Royal Grenadier Guards and the Coldstream Guards. Here the **Guards' Chapel and Museum** are on the site of a former chapel which was hit by a bomb at the end of World War II, killing

121 members of a church congregation.

Buckingham Palace has been the main London home of the royal family since the time of Queen Victoria. It was begun in the 17th-century for a Duke of Buckingham but has been altered many times since. There are no public tours of the palace but the **Queen's Gallery** and the **Royal Mews** are open (both in Buckingham Palace Road). The gallery houses a changing selection of the royal art collection; the mews have an assortment of royal cars and coaches. The **Gold State Coach** was built for George III in 1762 and is still used by the Queen on major state occasions.

Royal guards: Only the invited get further into the palace, although one intruder did penetrate as far as the Queen's bedroom one night in 1982. She talked to him quietly whilst managing to summon palace security.

In the summer, Royal Garden Parties are held here. Guests are invited because of some worthy contribution made to the nation, but very few of the hundreds get to shake the Queen's hand. In keeping with many events in the London society "season" of high-class social events, these garden parties – which take place, rain or shine, in the palace's 40-acre garden – have long been a quaint way of keeping the right sort of unmarried in each others' company; guests are requested not to bring their married sons and daughters.

If the Queen is in residence, the royal standard flies from the centre flag-pole. On great occasions the family appears on the first-floor balcony to wave to the crowds outside the gates. Most of the visitors who crowd the railings outside come to see the **Changing of the Guard**, which takes place at 11.30 every morning (alternate mornings in winter) outside the palace.

The New Guard and the Old Guard meet in the forecourt of the palace and exchange symbolic keys to the accompaniment of regimental music. The Irish Guards are distinctive for their bearskin hats, (now made from syn-

A guest at a royal garden party poses for anyone who wants a picture.

thetic materials). Behind the scenes are more sophisticated protection measures: there is a large nuclear shelter underneath the palace.

The **Queen Victoria Memorial**, in front of the palace, was built in 1901. It encompasses many symbolic figures which in essence glorify the achievements of the British empire and its builders. The actual monument became the centre of a massive reconstruction about 1913 following the renovation of the palace.

The **Mall**, leading to Trafalgar Square, was considerably altered into the impressive wide tree-lined avenue we see today. At the far end **Admiralty Arch** was constructed to lead the processional way.

Royal lining: The Mall is lined with a succession of grand buildings and historic houses reflecting different styles and periods. Many have been used as royal residences. **Clarence House** is the home of Queen Elizabeth the Queen Mother, the brick tudor **St James's Palace** was the home of Henry VIII and is now used by palace and government officials. Next door, the two white painted classical facades of **Carlton House Terrace** were built by John Nash, who was responsible for many of the grander parts of central London.

Here also is the **Institute of Contemporary Arts.** In this incongruous setting are a gallery, bookshop and film theatre devoted to the changing scene of living art and design in London.

Opposite is an example of wartime architecture. The large reinforced concrete structure on the corner of the park is a bomb-proof shelter built for the Admiralty, which was nicknamed the Citadel, or Lenin's Tomb.

Admiralty Arch is only three decades older, but considerably more aesthetically pleasing. It is also functional: behind those ubiquitous net curtained windows above the arches themselves are more government offices which are part of the old Admiralty Building, which adjoins Whitehall.

Horseguards progress up a snow-covered Mall.

LONDON'S PARKS

A city literally breathes through its open spaces. The trees produce oxygen, and the buildings and traffic relax their hold to reveal a wider sky. Amongst the list of clichés about London's heart should be another: London's parks are its lungs.

The city is well provided with breathing space. In all there are 387 parks in Greater London of more than 20 acres (8 hectares) each, and there are countless other smaller ones.

Inevitably these parks are planted with history. A 200-year-old tree in one of the central parks probably started life surrounded by countryside; now it is wreathed by traffic fumes.

Usually the great parks have royal connections, dating from the days when they were the private turf of the monarchy. In a sense the growth of British democracy is reflected in the gradual handing over of these spaces to the public. This process is also clearly demonstrated in the increase in rights to use of common land over the centuries. London's commons, like the Houses of Parliament that guarantee the park's continuation and survival, belong to the people. While no one herds sheep on them any more, the populace go there as proprietors, not mere guests.

For centuries these open spaces have been the scene of demonstrations and destruction. The trees have recently been hardest hit. Dutch Elm disease killed more than 20 million trees countrywide in the 1960s and '70s.

The 100 miles-an-hour gales of 15 October 1987 cut a devastating swathe across south and southeast England. London's parks suffered serious damage, with tragic losses in specialist gardens such as those at Kew. Irreplaceable trees brought back by 18th and 19th-century explorers and botanists were destroyed.

Trees fell in their thousands during the storm, and thousands more had to be cut down in the ensuing weeks because they were feared to be unsafe. The chief superintendent of works at Hyde Park woke to find her husband's Daimler car pinned flat by a huge elm. Fortunately most drivers were in bed at the time of the storm and only 16 people died in the gales, which is a tiny proportion of those who could have suffered had the storm raged during waking hours.

In Greenwich an oak tree which is supposed to have shaded Henry VIII managed to survive, though 200 of its neighbours crashed to the ground.

Hunting and gathering: The Domesday Book of 1086 records the area of **Hyde Park** as being inhabited by wild bulls and boars. Covering 350 acres (140 hectares), it is the best known of the great royal parks. It was first owned by the monks of Westminster Abbey and later by Henry VIII who used it for hunting. It was opened to the public in the 1600s and then sold off in chunks by Oliver Cromwell, who managed to ac-

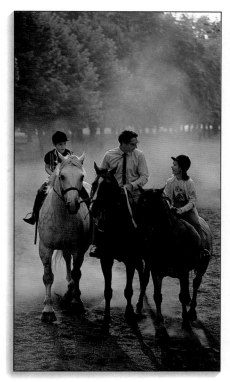

cidentally shoot himself in the leg whilst within its area. When the monarchy was restored the park was reopened in its entirety to the public.

The Serpentine, which attracts hardy swimmers all year round, was created in the 1730s as a royal boating pond. Mary Shelley, the poet's wife, drowned herself there in 1816. In 1814 the lake was the site of a spectacular re-enactment of Nelson's victory at the battle of Trafalgar. Generally the park is known for quieter pursuits: William III's Route du Roi (**Rotten Row**) is where the well-heeled canter their horses. Today it occasionally hosts international winter sports events.

Hyde Park has always been known for great gatherings. In 1851 six million people visited the Great Exhibition, which was housed in a massive Crystal Palace built over some of the more magnificent trees. In the late 1960s carnivals and concerts played there with the Rolling Stones and Blind Faith performing. More recently, the Queen and Prince Philip were guests of honour at the world's biggest picnic, given by St John's Ambulance.

At the northeast end is **Speaker's Corner**, the ancient site of the Tyburn gallows. Condemned men were allowed to speak freely at this point, and the tradition has extended to everyone. On Sunday morning Speaker's Corner is packed with soapbox orators arguing everything from vegetarianism and abstinence to flat-earthism. Here, for example, left-wing MPs read aloud portions of the banned book *Spycatcher*. There are also professional hecklers who do their best to disrupt any speech with cutting remarks.

Statues and spies: If Hyde Park is sprawling and rather forbidding on any but sunny days, Kensington Gardens is more intimate and has a less troubled history than most of London's public places. The famous statue of J. M. Barrie's **Peter Pan** is here, as is the **Albert Memorial**, Queen Victoria's little souvenir of her dead husband, as

Historically, the parks have been the scene of great – and intimate – gatherings.

well as formal, carefully landscaped gardens. At the far end are **Kensington Palace** and "**Millionaire's Row**". The **Serpentine Art Gallery** is unique and usually stages surprisingly adventurous exhibitions, given its pastoral setting.

Moving eastward, and thus paradoxically toward the West End, **Green Park** sprawls in front of Buckingham Palace between Piccadilly and St James's. The name is supposed to derive from the fact that the area was originally flowerless, a burial ground for one of the nearby lazar-houses run by the church for London's lepers.

This was the place favoured by London's dandies for settling their disputes the old-fashioned way. Pistols rather than lawsuits were the weapons used. As if encouraged, the park also became favoured by footpads, the forerunners of the muggers.

Today the parks are regulated by a special constabulary, the parks' police, and are not likely to be particularly dangerous. The popular image of a London park is a place where mysterious men in long overcoats leave packages for each other in wastepaper bins, survey each other through holes cut in the middle of *The Times*, or even stab each other with poisonous umbrellas. The proximity of Whitehall means there may well be the odd spy or two in **St James's Park**, but they are more likely to be removing their shoes and socks to feel the grass between their toes than plotting a nation's downfall.

Royal front garden: St James's also has a leper connection, but unlike Green Park it is awash with flowers. The park curves around its elegant lake, with pelicans and black swans, against a backdrop of Whitehall's spires and towers. Originally established as the front garden of the various royal palaces, St James's was destroyed by Cromwell. It was later restored by John Nash and Capability Brown.

The bandstand is the venue for regular lunchtime concerts; however in 1982 a bomb was hidden inside it by the

Debate and counter-debate at Speakers' Corner.

Irish Republican Army, and detonated as a detachment of the Queen's Household Cavalry was passing. Four cavalrymen and seven horses were killed.

Everyone knows **Regent's Park** because of the zoo, but the park also boasts another splendid pond, on which it is possible to float gently in a boat with eyes shut, listening to the exotic cries from the zoo, and imagine oneself in a far-off land.

But Regent's Park also has an explosive history; in 1874 four people were suddenly torn away from their earthly surroundings when the barge Tilbury erupted in what became known as the Regent's Park Explosion.

The park has a fine sculpture by Barbara Hepworth. It also has an open-air summer theatre (Shakespeare only), and is surrounded by Nash's elegant Regency terraces, as a taste of what a lot of London could have been like if this architect had had his way.

Holland Park in W8 has a fine, up-market feel. The grounds of Holland House (largely destroyed by bombs in World War II) include beautiful formal gardens (the Rose, Dutch and Iris) and some unmissable sculpture, notably by Eric Gill.

Common ground: Size is not everything. At the opposite end of the scale from Hyde Park is the tiny but distinctive **Postman's Park** in EC1. A lunchtime refuge for shift workers from the General Post Office opposite, it is barely large enough to swing any of the cats that congregate there. Its main claim to fame is the sculptor G. F. Watts's tribute to men and women of courage, with a series of intriguing plaques praising their deeds.

For anyone who finds such walled-in spaces claustrophobic, **Hampstead Heath** at 790 acres (316 hectares) provides a massive alternative. Most famous of the commons, it commands a fine view of London and is also meant to have health-giving waters. Two ponds, one for men and one for women, are used for summer bathing. The bowl

Far from the madding shoppers.

112

beneath Kenwood House is the venue for firework-assisted summer concerts.

South of the river: Residents have always been quick to protect their rights to their common ground. In Peckham in south-east London 19th-century locals to **Peckham Rye** refused to allow the establishment of Wombwell's Wild Beast Show on the land. This was also the place where the young poet William Blake saw angels dancing in a tree. These days the beasts of Peckham Rye are Rottweilers chasing balls (or joggers), and the only visionaries are gluesniffers in the shrubbery.

Clapham Common is attractive for its simplicity. Here are held revivalist missions, fairs, circuses, and reggae festivals, unmarred by the violence that can affect the Notting Hill Carnival. The only building *on* the common is a pub, the **Windmill**, and drinkers cover the grass on a summer's evening.

On the road southeast into Kent is **Blackheath**, a high flat common crisscrossed by paths. In times past, it was a favourite place for highwaymen, but it has loftier associations. Henry VIII was welcomed here after a battle victory; James I first introduced golf to England here, and the heath was the gathering place for Jack Cade's 1450 rebellion against the crown. Here John Ball preached the famous sermon "When Adam dalf and Eve span / Who was then the gentleman?" that cost him his life.

Kew and Richmond: Few Londoners let a year go by without going to the **Royal Botanical Gardens** at Kew, which used to claim to have a specimen of every plant in existence until the 1987 storms did damage that will take at least 50 years to repair. The botanic garden started in 1759, and was contributed to by the Empire's campaigners, who started to send back plants from the New World. Kew is an exporter as well. It introduced the rubber tree to Malaysia, quinine to India and bread-fruit trees to the West Indies.

Its beauties are both in and out of doors. The various glass houses hum with the growth vibrations of so many plants. The palm house is beautifully warm in winter, and cricket which is played on the green outside the main gates during summer contributes to a rural village atmosphere. There are several distinctive buildings, including the Orangery (an exhibition area) and Kew Palace, where George III was locked away when he was thought to be mad.

Even more rural is **Richmond Park** (still within the Underground network), which is the largest of the royal parks. It was created as a hunting ground by Charles I in 1637. Here there are herds of red and fallow deer, horseback riding and long country walks, all within the Greater London area.

Many Londoners spend their first romantic weekends at Richmond Park, finding privacy away from their parents. Later the same couples come to Richmond with their first children and later still as pensioners in their cars, circling the park slowly on the perimeter roads.

Kew's hothouses protect the more sensitive species from the British climate.

POSH LONDON

"The mass of the London Population have a second hand look which is not to be detected in the mass of the Parisian population."

— Charles Dickens,
Uncommercial Traveller, 1861

The same would not be so today. The whole of London westwards from Hyde Park Corner down past Harrods to Earl's Court and back up the river to Sloane Square would be indignant at such a suggestion. This massive area is part of an extremely posh, smart city, which is inhabited by scores of English in their quasi-uniform of stripey shirts, sensible stockings, pearls, cravates, blazers and corduroys.

It is a region of large-housed villages, with pretty side streets and squares dotted throughout. Most period films shot in London are filmed here. Mews houses, the former stables behind large terraces which have been converted into small urban cottages set in their own quiet cul de sacs, are idyllic settings for the film makers.

Upstairs, Downstairs: Much of Posh London was developed in the Victorian era. These days the housing prices are the highest in London.

Hyde Park Corner used to stand at the fringe of London. Apsley House, a museum to the Duke of Wellington and still inhabited by today's Duke, boasts the address Number One, London. Today the green fields that once lay to the west of Number One are covered with mile upon mile of terraces, squares and parks. Here live the descendants of the exclusive people who orginally lived in Mayfair.

Hyde Park Corner has changed. Not so long ago there was a hospital on the roundabout, with a forlorn sign asking for quiet. The arch in the middle was designed by Decimus Burton in 1828, and houses a tiny police station. It is popularly known as the **Wellington Arch**, because of the statue of the Duke that used to stand on top of it. However, Burton disliked both the statue and its positioning and left money in his will to have it removed.

On the Piccadilly side stands the **Hard Rock Café**, still reckoned to serve the best burgers in town. Inside are Keith Moon's drums, guitars from Jimi Hendrix and Eric Clapton, and a signed photograph of John Lennon. Outside the queue for tables stretches down the pavement.

Exclusivity: At the time when most of the squares and terraces of **Belgravia** were built (1825), these areas (west of Hyde Park Corner) were intended to rival Mayfair. They were so exclusive that the residents employed watchmen to operate gates to keep out the mob.

From Knightsbridge the best entrance to Belgravia is via **Wilton Place**. The stucco terraces were developed by architect Thomas Cubitt, who gives his name to the modern construction com-

Preceding pages: a butler in Chelsea symbolises success; village London and Posh London meet in Chelsea. **Left**, elegant Belgravia. **Right,** Cubitt's terracing in Wilton Crescent.

pany known for its motorway bridges.

Belgrave Square has suffered the same fate as much of Mayfair. Most residences are occupied by embassies and various societies and associations. The square usually has a heavy police presence.

Eaton Square, to the south, is more residential. However many of its supposed residents live in other parts of the world and the houses are dark and obviously under-used. Chopin gave his first London recital here at No. 88.

Chelsea proper begins in **Sloane Square**, the home of the **Royal Court Theatre**. Here modern fashion meets traditional respectability. The atmospheric old theatre is a venue for modern fringe productions that sometimes transfer to the West End. Productions have to cope with the rumble and vibration from the Underground, which runs directly beneath.

The square was named after physician Sir Hans Sloane (1660–1753), whose personal collection formed the basis of what is now the British Museum. Sir Hans laid out much of this area of the city and his name crops up often on street plans. He also unwittingly gave his name to a typical young middle-class urbanite living in Chelsea: the Sloane Ranger. Diana Spencer was a typical Sloane Ranger before she married Prince Charles. She wore flat-heeled shoes, pearls, a navy blue sweater, baggy skirt and a quilted jacket. She also stood in the required slightly slouched position. What a change from the cover girl of today!

Fashion mirror: Sloane Rangers are found down **King's Road**, which stretches west from the square. Until 1829 this was a private royal road leading from Hampton Court to the Court of King James. King's Road rose to fame in the Swinging '60s, and was the mecca for the 1970s punk fashions. The shops have mirrored the changing fashions of recent years and few remain for any prolonged period. King's Road is still a good place for extreme hairstyles, al-

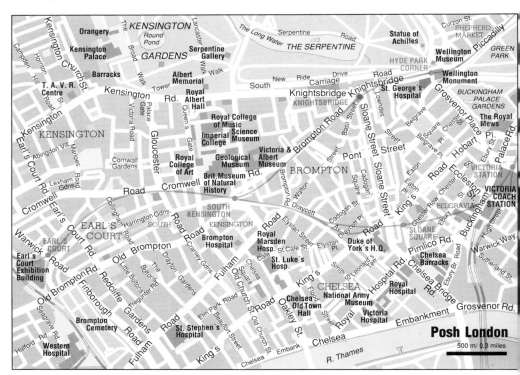

Posh London

500 m/ 0.3 miles

though the fashionable these days prefer Kensington.

A noticeboard in the newsagents opposite the massive middle class emporium **Peter Jones** reflects the diversity of the area: a diplomat advertises for a nanny, an "artistic oriental manager" advertises for accommodation, and someone wants to employ an "energetic sandwich maker".

Village Chelsea is never far from the road, in the side streets to the south and north. The prettily painted 18th and 19th-century terraces have a tradition of housing artists and intellectuals. Past residents include Turner, Rosetti, Whistler, Sargent, and Carlyle. Today, they have been supplanted by people who like to be noticed: actors, designers and musicians. Margaret Thatcher used to live in Flood Street.

Halfway down the road an impressive Victorian portico fronts an 18th-century building which was once a pheasantry, later a ballet school (Dame Margot Fonteyn was one of its star pupils) and now houses the Camino Rey restaurant.

Old Chelsea: On the left hand side of the road opposite **Sydney Street** stands the **Old Chelsea Town Hall**. The old borough of Royal Kensington, which was given its royal appellation in 1901 by Queen Victoria, was merged much against its wishes with Chelsea in 1965, and took over the administration of both. The Old Chelsea Town Hall continues to provide a cultural and social focus for residents. The Registry Office next door is well-known for society weddings. Here pop star Bob Geldof married Paula Yates, 150 years after Charles Dickens got married in St Luke's, a stunning gothic church half way up Sydney Street.

On either side of the Town Hall are two antique markets which are barely visible from the outside. Inside they are warrens of narrow passageways and tiny stalls. **Chenil Galleries** and **Antiquarius** contain hoards of English antiques and many stallholders are of the

he King's
oad mixes
raditional
nd stylish
hopping.

best English gentility. It is hard to believe that the whole world could house so many antique silver picture frames.

At the junction with Beaufort Street, the **Chelsea Pot** must be about the cheapest and most basic restaurant in central London. For those who have slogged all the way down the King's Road taking in its diversity there is one last haven before the return slog back to the Underground. The **Man in the Moon** pub has a spacious wood-pannelled interior and beautifully engraved windows.

Down Hospital Road: Amongst the leather mini-skirts and the ankle length furs on King's Road are uniformed old gents with the initials RH on their caps. These are Chelsea Pensioners, retired war veterans who have found a home in the **Royal Hospital**. It is a magnificent building inspired by the Hotel des Invalides in Paris and built by Wren in 1692 on Royal Hospital Road, which runs parallel with King's Road. Here 420 pensioners are boarded, lodged,

clothed, nursed and given a small allowance, including a pint of beer a day. The annual **Chelsea Flower Show**, the largest of its kind in the world, is held in the Royal Hospital's spacious gardens every May.

On either side of the hospital are **Ranelagh Gardens** (the daily walking ground for nannies for the well-to-do and their charges), and the **National Army Museum**. The Museum follows the history of the British Army from 1485 to 1915, indicating just how many invasions England has been involved in. Massive flamboyant paintings, some as long as 20 ft (6 metres), celebrate the greatest and worst moments.

Here is the skeleton of Napoleon's favourite horse, and here also are displays relating to the Indian Army and the colonial land forces, some of whom still have close links with the British Army. Many of the museum staff are former soldiers.

Behind a high wall further down the road is the **Chelsea Physic Garden**,

In full bloom: a Chelsea punk and a stall at the Chelsea Flower Show, the largest in the world.

which was founded in 1676 for the study of medicinal plants. The garden has regular open days in the summer, and contains an eccentric variety of rare trees and herbs, including poisonous specimens such as Mandrake and Deadly Nightshade.

At the foot of **Royal Hospital Road**, a statue of the essayist, Thomas Carlyle, watches the traffic grind by on the Embankment. Behind him a fine row of Queen Anne houses make up **Cheyne Walk**, still one of the most exclusive streets in the city. A host of famous people have lived here, including George Eliot, David Lloyd George, Hilaire Belloc, J. M. W. Turner, and even Paul Getty. Pre-Raphaelite artist Dante Gabriel Rossetti lived with the poet Swinburne in No. 16, and they kept peacocks in their back garden. The birds so disturbed the neighbours that nowadays every lease on the row prohibits tenants from keeping them.

Carlyle: Behind Cheyne Walk is a network of small, extremely pretty streets which are worth wandering around, even if you don't visit **Carlyle's House**, at No. 24 Cheyne Row. The house is preserved exactly as it was – even to the point of not having electricity – and is open to the public from Wednesday to Sunday in the summer. It is easy to imagine Mr. and Mrs. Carlyle sitting in their kitchen, although it may not have been a cosy scene. It was fortunate the Carlyles married each other, the saying goes; otherwise there would have been four miserable people in the world instead of two. Yet leading intellectuals of the time, including Dickens, Tennyson and Ruskin, used to come and visit Carlyle here.

Sir Hans Sloane's tomb is in **Chelsea Old Church,** a rather unattractive building which was painstakingly rebuilt after being destroyed by a landmine in 1941. The site was formerly occupied by a 12th-century Norman church. Henry VIII, who had a large house on the river where Cheyne Walk now is, supposedly married Jane

The Man in the Moon, a haven at the end of the King's Road.

NIGHT SITES

*"Ah, London! London! our delight,
Great flower that opens but at night."*
– Richard Le Gallienne, French poet

The geography of any major city seems to change at night as offices empty into pubs and trains drain the centre of workers and replace them with players.

The West End, a shopping and office centre by day, is the centre of London's night sites. Soho is still the most fashionable area, and is still the sex centre of London, although smut is on the retreat. Some of the best food and the trendiest clubs are here including Ronnie Scott's jazz club in Frith Street *(pictured)*. Other gathering spots for swingers include Kettners in Romilly Street and the Soho Brasserie in Old Compton Street. These are "gathering spots" because many of the Champagne drinkers go on to a nightclub such as Stringfellows in Upper St Martins' Lane. London's hippest clubs have all-powerful doorpersons who act as arbiters of taste, letting in those faces and fashions that fit, and excluding those who don't, irrespective of the weight of the wallet.

There was always a possibility, in the recent past, that one might spot a member of the royal family in one or other or these clubs. It was in a nightclub that Princess Anne's name became linked with a pop singer and Prince Andrew with a calendar girl. Unfortunately at the moment most of the key royals are now either just too old or much too young for nightclubbing.

The most successful and biggest discos in town are The Hippodrome (Cranbourne Street), The Limelight (Shaftesbury Avenue) and the famous gay disco Heaven (Villiers Street). Other nightclubs worth trying to get into are Tokyo Joe's in Piccadilly, Tramps in Jermyn Street and the White Elephant Club in Curzon Street.

Londoners themselves get a buzz from being in the company of the countless nationalities that throng Leicester Square, Piccadilly, Trafalgar Square, Covent Garden and even the Trocadero Centre. These are the best known central areas for evening promenading, although bar and restaurant prices will be high and often poor value. London may not have the climate for it, yet 84 percent of all overseas visitors describe their evening activities as "just walking around".

Further afield Chelsea's King's Road and Kensington High Street are similarly thronged on the weekend. Here are intimate and expensive restaurants, wine bars and clubs, with more of an emphasis on the local rather than the international. Local internationals – those who have settled, however transiently, in London – animate Earl's Court deep into the night, and side streets here offer the best to the most basic restaurants and pubs. Once a month (usually on the last Saturday), customised cars of all shapes and sizes cruise up and down the King's Road to the applause of crowds who assemble on the pavements outside the pubs.

The South Bank complex (on the southern end of Waterloo Bridge) may not be appealing to the eye, but it does offer a range of cultural choice from concerts through theatre to film and some of the best views of central London are from the north bank of the river.

Here, on the concrete promenade of the Jubilee Walkway on a summer's evening, busking jazz saxophonists make the place feel a little like New York, although the view of London on the north bank is decidedly unique just to this city. Many key buildings are visible from here (better views are from the upper floor of the Queen Elizabeth Hall or the National Theatre), from the Houses of Parliament and Westminster Abbey on the far left through the centre of London (Covent Garden is hidden behind the river frontage) to St. Paul's on the horizon to the extreme right. In summer, cruising restaurants cover and recover this stretch of the Thames (book at Westminster Pier).

For a glamorously old-fashioned evening, head for Mayfair and St. James's. Here you'll find discreet restaurants and exclusive nightclubs like Annabel's in Berkeley Square, appealing to an older, sophisticated crowd, who don't need to ask the price.

Seymour here, in secrecy, several days before the official ceremony.

On the south side of Cheyne Walk, just west of Battersea Bridge, is a colony of British Boat People – 58 moorings on the riverside which accommodate houseboats. The boats are homes to those who like the life afloat and the exclusive address, but who dislike paying inflated London house prices.

House boats are not cheap, however, and the prices hover around £100,000 for a 70-ft (21-metre) boat which doesn't even move; it's the moorings themselves which put the prices so high. Moreover, purchasers often have to find the sum in cash, as building societies and banks are unwilling to give mortgage loans on such properties.

Kangaroo alley: On the fringes of **Earl's Court**, the atmospheric **Brompton Cemetery** rambles untidily across several acres of land, littered with ramshackle tombs, some of which were designed by famous architects.

Harrods, where takings on a sale day can each £3 million.

George Borrow and Byron are buried here. Also here is the memorable valediction, "Have a good sleep, dear."

A little further up **Warwick Road** stands the **Earl's Court Exhibition Hall**, the venue for numerous impressive annual shows including the Boat Show and the Ideal Home Exhibition. The Earl's Court Underground was the first to have escalators in 1911, and a man with a wooden leg was employed to ride up and down to get people to trust the new-fangled thing.

Earl's Court is nicknamed "Kangaroo Alley" because of the large number of Australians passing through this area of West London. Accommodation is cheap, the restaurants range from the very basic to the very select, some of the shops stay open 24 hours a day, and the cosmopolitan, transitory population encourages prostitution.

Knightsbridge: The other main artery of Posh London begins at **Hyde Park Corner**, runs through Kensington, and turns eventually into the motorway that leads out to Heathrow airport. Tidal waves of traffic sweep in or out according to the time-of-day, repeatedly snagging on the chauffeur driven Rolls-Royces that bunch up outside the front doors of **Harrods**, the world's most famous department store.

The Harrods shopping bag is the bag to be seen with anywhere in the world. The store motto – *Omnia, Omnibus, Ubique*, "all things, for all people, everywhere" – means what it says. An endless list of peculiar and exotic requests includes sending a pound of sausages to a customer in the Mediterranean and a sauna to someone in the Middle East.

The Harrods sales are spectacular events. The store can take up to £3 million a day and the lifts travel approximately 100 miles (160 km) during sales. The most dignified of the English lose their dignity completely in the scramble to save hundreds of pounds. The more dedicated camp out for days on the street to be first ones in the door.

The store was started by Henry Charles Harrod when his grocery business opened in 1849, although the present building was opened in 1905. The Egyptian Al-Fayed brothers bought the store and other House of Fraser outlets for £615 million in 1983, and they paid in cash.

Select shopping: If Harrods is a little daunting there is no shortage of smaller scale shopping in Knightsbridge. **Knight's Arcade** and the **Brompton Arcade** are sumptuous but discreet. The villagey street **Beauchamp Place**, west of Harrods, is the stamping ground of the select, including the royals. Designers – both domestic and international – have little boutiques here.

Opposite Harrods is the Knightsbridge safe deposit centre, made infamous in 1987 by the biggest single robbery to take place in Great Britain. To this day the total of £30 million worth of lost cash and jewellery remains an estimate, as many depositors did not admit their losses.

Further on, Brompton Road veers left towards South Kensington and Earl's Court, which diverges at this point from Cromwell Road.

Cultural exchange: Proximity to the museum district has caused South Kensington to blossom around its fine art deco Underground station. The **Ismaili Centre** (1979), on the south side of Cromwell Road, is the closest and most recent of these cultural centres to the Underground station. It was built by the Aga Khan as a cultural centre for Shia Ismailis, for whose sect the Aga Khan is the greatest living prophet. The centre, which was designed by British architects although retaining some Moorish flavour, promotes Islamic art through the **Zamana Gallery**. The prayer hall is closed to the public and tourists.

A range of impressive facades dominate the Ismaili Centre from the other side of the Cromwell Road. To the right the **Brompton Oratory** is a massive wedding cake of a building, designed by a 29-year-old country-dwelling archi-

tect, Herbert Gribble, whose career took a sudden step upwards as a result. The nave is wider than St Paul's. The cathedral – which is officially called the London Oratory – used to host the principal Roman Catholic congregation in the city, but has since been supplanted by Westminster Cathedral, in Victoria Street. The building was opened in 1884, but only completely finished some years later.

Three museums: Next door to the Oratory is the **Victoria and Albert Museum**, the first in a series of buildings reflecting the enormous influence that Queen Victoria and her Prince had on the development of this quarter. Most of the Museum quarter stands on land bought with the proceeds from the Great Exhibition of 1851, when the massive Crystal Palace made of glass covered much of Hyde Park.

The museum is a massive storehouse of many cultures, and is exhaustive and exhausting in its detail. Next to it the **Natural History Museum** is probably

best known for its frontage and its dinosaur room, which can be hired for private parties.

The **Science Museum** (behind) traces the harnessing of power and all the associated industry and inventions, and has a wealth of working models which entertain anyone who has half a child's fascination for the world.

Cromwell Road: Dwarfed by all these towering monuments to the nation's and the world's development is a small green-painted wooden building which sits on piles of bricks in the middle of the road. This unprepossessing structure is actually another exclusive restaurant. It is for cab drivers only, and one of a few unobstrusive cabbie restaurants dotted throughout London.

On the corner of Queen's Gate Terrace, opposite the Natural History Museum, stands **Baden-Powell House**, with a statue of the man who created the Boy Scouts, Lord B-P himself, standing on watch outside. Inside there is a small exhibition area dedicated to this peculiar man, who was an actor, secret agent, horseman, artist, writer, sportsman, speaker and film maker. And he thought that all enterprising boys should be so too. Lord B-P was the author of such classics as *Lessons from the Varsity of Life*, *Rovering to Success*, *Life's Snags*, and *Paddle Your Own Canoe*.

Cromwell Road becomes decreasingly hospitable for pedestrians as it progresses; however a couple of further locations are notable. **Gloucester Road** has several large tourist hotels and a large number of short-term rental apartments and is consequently very cosmopolitan. It also harbours one of the best Indian restaurants in London (and Londoners are great aficionados of Indian cuisine), the **Bombay Brasserie**, which is located in Bailey's Hotel opposite the Underground station. Try to get a table in the conservatory.

Hidden on the north side of Cromwell Road west of Gloucester Road is the **Sainsbury's** megastore, one of the largest supermarkets in central London, and

Aspects of Victoriana: a pub in Gloucester Road and the Royal Albert Hall.

named "Millionaire's Row".

The proximity of the Royal Court turned Kensington into an exclusive village. Athough these days the **High Street** has a permanent identity crisis as to whether it is highly fashionable or old and traditional, the side streets have no doubt.

Kensington Square is an elegant mixture of architectural styles and only the latest of cars and flashiest indicate that this is the 20th century.

Market contrasts: In essence the **Kensington Market** on the High Street opposite Old Church Street is a village of its own kind. It is a labyrinth of stairs and pyschedelic walkways, with a mixture of Carnaby street fashion (leather jackets, printed T-shirts and torn jeans) and more interesting designer clothes, bondage materials, tattoo specialists and ear piercers. Over the road **Hyper Hyper** hides a more original warren behind an imposing facade. Here are individual modern fashions at reasonable prices. Further down the High Street are two large stores which have changed hands several times in the last few decades, victims of Kensington's identity crisis.

The **Roof Garden** restaurant, six storeys above street level on the second at 99 Derry Street, has a unique acre and a half of ornamental gardens which surrounds its exclusive restaurant. In order to cope with the additional weight created by the garden's deep soil and its rocky underlining, the building had to be reinforced.

The gardens, which date from 1938, are complete with a stream and wandering flamingoes, and are modelled variously on English Woodland, Tudor Rose and Spanish styles. The Roof Garden is owned by the creator of the Virgin empire, Richard Branson.

In the summer it is open daily for lunch, and only on Sundays in the winter. Amongst the creepers in the secluded Rose Garden, you can relax as the wash of the city's noise becomes a gentle shush of a backdrop.

South Kensington blossoms as a tourist haunt, thanks to the closeness of the major museums.

MUSEUMS

There's clearly a buoyant future in reflecting the past. Among a whole rash of new museums launched in the 1980s, for example, were the Museum of the Moving Image on the South Bank, Rock Circus at Piccadilly Circus, and the Design Museum at Butler's Wharf. The Imperial War Museum has also launched a Blitz Experience in its basement, and the Florence Nightingale Museum at St Thomas's Hospital traces the history of nursing.

They are building on an already strong foundation. The richness of London's museums and galleries reflects the wealth and power of the British Empire, especially during the 19th century, when explorers plundered the countries they discovered. They did so in order to pay for their trips and to be able to return home with something exotic to show.

Like the old aristocracy, Victorian business tycoons built or bought great houses and filled them with their rich art collections. Some hoped to enhance their position in fashionable society by offering their col-

lection to the nation at low cost. A number of such donations, which include books, sculptures and paintings, form the foundation of collections of the British Museum (started in 1759), the National Gallery (1824) and the Tate Gallery (1897). The last of London's four major collections, the Victoria and Albert Museum (V&A), was based on the purchase of thousands of objects from the Great Exhibition of 1851 which brought many of the world's treasures to London's doorstep.

While most great national collections in Europe are based on the private wealth of past kings and princes, and their old palaces turned into galleries, in Britain the Royal Family still has its own private collection. British national collections were built up by gifts from private individuals supplemented occasionally by money from parliament.

The British regard museums as a fundamental part of their cultural heritage, and their passions are revealed in their condemnation of any "fiddling" with the buildings: the extension to the National Gallery, the new wing of the Tate and the voluntary charge levied at the V&A were all subjects of immensely fervent debate among people who probably hadn't been to any of those institutions for years, if ever. A celebrated museum is always there, most Londoners reason, so a visit can wait until next week, next month, next year...

London's art collections are spread all over the metropolis; there are some 250 museums and galleries in the city. The major collections, however, are conveniently located in central London.

The British Museum, London's top free attraction with more than 3.8 million visitors a year, is bursting at the seams. Egyptian, Assyrian and Greek sculpture galleries here are excellent, with massive granite stone Pharoahs. The Rossetta stone, an unremarkable slab of black basalt, was the key to the decipherment of ancient Egyptian writing. Look for the lion hunting scene on the Assyrian relief carvings, and hunt out the Elgin Marbles while you can.

The National Gallery is especially strong on European painting from the 12th to the 19th century. Unlike the Tate, which only displays one-sixth of its total collection, the complete collection is on show at the National. The most famous include *The Baptism of Christ* by Piero della Francesca, a tranquil but powerful piece of figure painting; the 15th-century *Arnolfini Marriage* by Jan Van Eyck with its meticulous crisp detail; Titian's action-packed and rich coloured *Bacchus and Ariadne*; Rubens' de-

Ceramics in the V&A.

lightful portrait of Rembrandt, Constable's interpretation of the English countryside, Velazquez and Van Gogh, and one of Monet's richly impressionistic lily-pond paintings.

The Tate is the result of a generous gift from 19th-century sugar millionaire Henry Tate. It began as the national collection of British Art but has developed to house the national collection of Modern Art as well. Of the British artists, Hogarth (who satirised early 18th-century England), Reynolds (famous for his portraits), Gainsborough and Constable (distinctive landscape artists) and Turner (a dramatic seascape artist) are all well-represented. The modern collection starts with impressionism and embraces a large surrealist collection.

The seven miles of gallery space within the V&A takes over where the British Museum's leaves off – from medieval times to the 20th century. There are two distinct types of galleries; primary galleries on the ground floor show objects from the same period together, whereas the study collection galleries, located mainly on the upper floors, are for those interested in greater detail.

And when you're tired of the V&A you've got almost as many miles of gallery space in the Natural History Museum and Science Museum located just next door.

Beyond these major collections are a wealth of secondary museums and galleries. The Museum of London in the City opened in 1986 and houses some fascinating detail on old London and some very convincing models, including a simulation of the Fire of London.

Sir John Soane's museum in Lincoln's Inn Fields was once the home of architect/collector Sir John. Today it is crammed full of the beautiful and the curious and you have to ring the door bell to be admitted!

The clientele of the Photographer's Gallery in Great Newport Street show just how trendy the photographer's art is, and the premises, when compared to those of more conventional galleries, show that photography as an art still has a long way to go to before it becomes respectable and well-funded by the community.

Major venues for exhibition (as opposed to permanent collections) are the Hayward on the South Bank (the most avant-garde of the big galleries), the Royal Academy on Piccadilly (conventional and popular shows), and the Barbican Gallery in the Barbican Centre (a mixture of conventional and avant-garde).

The Central Hall, the Natural History Museum.

VILLAGE LONDON

At its widest point, from South Croydon to Potter's Bar, the metropolis of London is nearly 60 miles (100 km) across and, though the overall population has been in decline since World War II, London remains one of the world's most populous cities. Perhaps because it is so big, many of those who live within its confines hardly think of it as a unified city at all, but as a collection of largely independent villages or communities. While Londoners may commute many miles to work, they are likely to do their shopping and build their social lives on their home patch.

Divided city: The River Thames cuts through London, forming an effective physical and psychological block to free movement. While south Londoners stream across London Bridge to work in the City every day, they are more likely to go shopping in Croydon or Bromley than the West End.

Eastenders regard Central London as a flash, tourist quarter, where their money buys practically nothing. It has been said that the average Londoner would find it less traumatic to move from London to Melbourne or New York than to move his home across the river into central London.

The Londoners' strong sense of localised identity even shows in their speech. Language experts are able to pinpoint the part of the city a true born-and-bred Londoner comes from by his accent and his dialect.

Many of the "villages" of London were actually once true villages which were surrounded by open fields. Others are more accurately described as "communities", where the concentration of different ethnic groups have created their own environments over the years of immigration.

Central London has lost many of its most historic buildings to natural disasters like the Great Fire and to the onward march of voracious developers. However, a number of the old villages (notably Hampstead, Dulwich and Wimbledon) have managed to preserve their historical hearts, whilst housing estates and shopping centres spring up around them.

Some villages have been swamped by development. Croydon, once a village, now has pretensions to city status. If it were recognised as a separate entity, Croydon would rank as one of the 15 largest cities in the United Kingdom. Already it has a Manhattan-style high-rise town centre, which houses the head offices of major national and multinational corporations, superlative shopping facilities and good night life, including theatres and one of London's best concert halls.

While most visitors are busy with the tourist haunts of the City and West End, those who go further afield are rewarded with a glimpse of what the locals call "real London": the London where Londoners live.

Preceding pages: pubs are at the centre of community life. Left, minority communities loom large in many of London's villages. Right, villages like Hampstead were swallowed into the expanding metropolis.

Out of London's distinct urban villages and communities, we have chosen seven, carefully avoiding those in the central areas which are already covered in other sections of this book: villages like Soho, Bloomsbury, Chelsea, Kensington, Belgravia and Mayfair – all are described elsewhere.

Of the seven, all but Dulwich and Greenwich, which are served by British Rail, are on the Underground network. All are served by red buses.

Dulwich: One of the finest views of London's sprawl is from the clubhouse at Dulwich Golf Club. Yet the foreground is green and wooded, like the heart of the English countryside. With its leafy streets and Georgian, Victorian and Edwardian houses, its village school and spacious park, Dulwich is an oasis of quiet elegance. It was once chosen by Prime Minister Margaret Thatcher as a post-retirement retreat, when she bought a house in Dulwich Gate.

The district's unspoilt character is the result of a remarkable history. Dulwich is largely the creation of one man, Edward Alleyn, an Elizabethan actor-manager. In 1605 he bought land in the area and established the Estates Governors of God's Gift to administer a chapel, almshouses and a schoolroom for the poor.

Today, the estate has more than 15,000 homes, **Dulwich College**, **Alleyn's School** and **James Allen Girl's School**. The land has not changed hands for 300 years, and the last village farm disappeared only in 1954.

The Dulwich college silver was pawned during the Civil War to provide funds for the Royalist cause, but recovered fortunes and a bequest of valuable paintings (originally intended for the Polish National Gallery) to the college led to the opening of **Dulwich Picture Gallery**. The magnificent building was designed by Sir John Soane and opened in 1814. Included in the gallery are important works by Rubens,

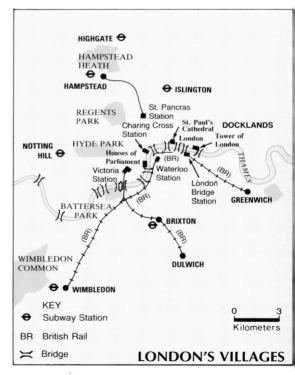

Leafy Dulwich.

138

Rembrandt, Van Dyck, Gainsborough, Murillo and others, some of which were stolen and later recovered in the 1960s.

At one end of Dulwich village the **Old Grammar School** was built to the plans of Charles Barry, who later designed the Houses of Parliament. His son, Charles Barry the Younger, was responsible for the superb Italianate edifice, reminiscent of Venice, which now houses Dulwich College. At the other end, **College Road** is the last toll road in London still in operation.

Dulwich Wells, located on the site of the present Grove Tavern, was a popular medicinal spa in the 18th century. Today, the **Crown and Greyhound**, known to locals as "The Dog", is the favoured watering hole. It is surrounded by pretty shops and grand houses and is close to the old burial ground which contains the tomb of Old Bridget, Queen of the Gypsies. **Gypsy Hill**, which is nearby, was the traditional meeting place of the nation's gypsy community until the end of last century.

The gypsies used to come down to the village to tell fortunes. One dear old fortune teller, they say, sat cross-legged on Dulwich green for so long that when she died they buried her sitting up.

At the corner of Calton Avenue and Court Lane, the site of the stocks which were used to punish local miscreants is marked by a plaque which reads: "It is a sport to a fool to do mischief. Thine own wickedness shall correct thee."

Greenwich: Until recently, the Thames was London's great transport artery, moving goods and people from one end of the City to the other. River trips for pleasure, such as that from Westminster down to Greenwich, were popular in Victorian days when Greenwich was a separate town.

Kings and queens also liked to retreat from the City to Greenwich, and in 1530 the former monastic lands of Greenwich became Crown property. The old Greenwich Palace was the birthplace of Henry VIII, and his daughters Mary I and Elizabeth I. The Palace was demol-

The National Maritime Museum at Greenwich.

ished in the 1660s.

Still standing, and now part of the Naval Museum, **Queen's House** was built in 1635 while the superbly proportioned **Royal Naval College** (designed by Christopher Wren) and the **Royal Observatory** were both built after the Restoration of the Monarchy. The naval college was originally a hospital for seamen to match the Royal Hospital in Chelsea, but is now the training ground for naval officers.

The best view of all three magnificent buildings is from the other side of the river. The 1,217-ft (365-metre) Victorian pedestrian tunnel (entrance next to the *Cutty Sark*) crosses under the river and fetches up in a pretty little park on the Isle of Dogs, on the edge of the massive urban development of Docklands.

The *Cutty Sark* (Scottish dialect meaning a piece of cloth) is an old tea-clipper sailing ship, now in dry dock and open to the public. Dwarfed by it is the tiny *Gypsy Moth*, in which Sir Francis

Chichester sailed single-handed around the world. The *Cutty* set a record by sailing 363 miles (581 km) in 24 hours; Chichester sailed 29,630 miles (47,408 km) in 226 days. Nearby, the town centre has several antiques shops and a covered antiques market, also a thriving community centre in the **Greenwich Theatre**, with a restaurant, art gallery and jazz club.

The **Naval Museum** traces the history both of the Royal Navy and the Merchant Navy. Among the exhibits is one that includes the tunic worn by Lord Nelson at the Battle of Trafalgar, complete with the hole made by the bullet which killed him.

Behind the museum, on the top of the hill in Greenwich Park is the **Greenwich Observatory,** built by Wren in 1675. It has a fine display of time-keeping ephemera, and a brass rule on the ground marks the dividing line between the Eastern and Western Hemispheres. Here it is possible to have a foot in both worlds. In the early days a

Former figureheads below deck in the *Cutty Sark*, Greenwich.

newly-employed caretaker is reported to have helped a scientist point a massive telescope skywards, spot a falling star, and then congratulate the scientist on his "good shot".

Over the brow of the hill and behind the Observatory, another green area spreads out like a tablecloth. **Blackheath** village has the atmosphere of a quaint country town.

To the east of Greenwich Park is **Vanbrugh Castle**, a castellated private house said to have been the first "folly" constructed in England. It is an imitation of the Bastille, where Van Brugh was imprisoned for two years on charges of being a British spy. The park is also the traditional start for the London Marathon, which attracts more than 20,000 athletes each spring.

A towpath extends downriver from Greenwich through an atmospheric old waterfront. En route are old attractive pubs: the **Trafalgar Tavern** and **Yacht Tavern**.

Travelling to Greenwich, it is possible to buy an all-in ticket which covers the return boat trip from London, admission to the Maritime Museum, the Maritime Trust and the Cutty Sark, plus a guide to central Greenwich.

Highgate: This pleasant hill-top suburb, built round a pretty central square could well claim to be the dead centre of London. Highgate (the gate was removed in 1769 because it was too low) contains London's grandest cemetery, where 300 famous people are buried. Consecrated in 1839, **Highgate Cemetery** was the fashionable resting place for Victorian Londoners before it became neglected and overgrown. It is now being restored by private funds (the Friends of Highgate Cemetery).

Besides its catacombs and impressive memorials, the main attraction remains the rather grim bust of Karl Marx, who was buried here in 1883. Nearby are the graves of Christina Rossetti, Michael Faraday and George Eliot. The cemetery was the setting for part of the original book *Dracula* and remains pretty eerie.

The views from **Highgate Hill**, the main road back to town, are as spectacular as those from the cemetery. They are said to have persuaded poor Dick Whittington to turn back again and give the city another chance, after which he became Lord Mayor three times. However, this is an image of Whittington perpetuated by pantomime: the real Whittington was far from poor, and was only Mayor, not Lord Mayor. Whittington's stone stands by the roadside at the foot of Highgate Hill.

West Hill was the scene of a near calamity in 1837 when the horses drawing the carriage of the recently-crowned Queen Victoria bolted. The landlord of the Fox and Crown public house stopped the runaways and was rewarded with permission to display the royal coat of arms on his premises.

Essayist Francis Bacon died here of pneumonia after ill-advisedly stuffing a chicken with snow in an attempt to

Many a village graveyard is now surrounded by suburbs.

BLUE PLAQUES

One of many pointers to London's varied past are the blue plaques slapped on sundry sites to commemorate famous people, famous events and famous buildings. There may be times when Mrs Margaret Thatcher goes to bed after a particularly bad day in the office with one consolation in mind: 20 years after her death someone will slap a blue plaque on a building to remind visitors and Londoners of Britain's first woman prime minister. It may not be a tribute that would have satisfied Ozymandias, but in the immortality stakes every little counts.

London is strewn with such commemorative plaques. Around 400 of them have appeared, like some sort of historic mould, on the sites of the dwelling places of the famous and the long dead. The first plaque was erected by the Royal Society of Arts in memory of the poet Byron in 1866. In 1901 the London County Council took over the service, which is today administered by English Heritage.

Bona fide plaques are ceramic with white lettering on a circular blue background. They are bald statements of fact, giving few snippets of biography beyond name, date and profession.

The awarding of a plaque is almost haphazard in that there is no overall register of famous people who have lived in London. Many plaques are put up because descendants or adherents of the deceased put forward the suggestion to English Heritage. Thus plaques function as a barometer of public taste, as notions change about what constitutes fame. Until now the range has been unsurprisingly dominated by politicians and artists, particularly those from the Victorian era.

However, there is a plaque at the site of the building of the *Great Eastern*, the largest steamship of the 19th century. Mahatma Gandhi has one as a result of his quick stopover in the city. Louis Kossuth, the not so famous Hungarian patriot, earned one for his visit, and Mozart has one because he composed his first symphony in a house in Ebury Street.

Isaac Newton is remembered by a plaque on

his house in Jermyn Street, although he had made his major discoveries about gravity before residing in the city. There are two plaques to the memory of the poet Samuel Taylor Coleridge, despite the fact that his private life was not one of unblemished rectitude.

A plaque-spotting tour would certainly not lack variety. Matthew Arnold lived at 1–3 Robert Street, WC2; John Logie Baird first demonstrated television at 22 Frith Street, W1; Captain William Bligh of *Bounty* fame lived at 100 Lambeth Road, SE1; Charlie Chaplin lived at 287 Kennington Road; Sir Winston Churchill lived at 34 Eccleston Square, SW1; Charles Dickens lived at 48 Doughty Street, WC1; Benjamin Franklin lived at 36 Craven Street, WC2; Sigmund Freud lived at 20 Maresfield Gardens, NW3; Henry James lived at 34 De Vere Gardens, W8; T.E. Lawrence (of Arabia) lived at 14 Barton Street, SW1; Karl Marx lived at 28 Dean Street, W1; Florence Nightingale lived and died on the site of 10 South Street, W1; George Bernard Shaw lived at 29 Fitzroy Square, W1; Mark Twain lived at 23 Tedworth Square, SW3; and Oscar Wilde lived at 24 Tite Street, SW3.

Perhaps in the future entertainers and sporting personalities will play a more prominent role, with a plaque adorning Elizabeth Taylor's London apartment and another for tennis stars Pat Cash and Stefan Edberg, who both live in the city.

Most candidates for plaques are submitted to lengthy scrutiny before their sojourn on earth is immortalised on a London wall. They must have been dead for at least 20 years; they must be regarded as eminent by luminaries in their profession; they should have made an important contribution to human welfare; the well-informed passer-by should readily recognise their name; and they should, by the kind of infuriatingly nebulous "general agreement" that has traditionally characterised British decision-making, *deserve* recognition.

And, of course, the honoured do not have to be British. In 1971 the Greater London Council agreed that plaques could be erected in memory of foreigners, provided that their stay in London was somehow significant. It's all a bit of a lottery, but at least anyone can play, albeit posthumously.

discover refrigeration. The chicken's ghost is still said to haunt the hill.

Hampstead: Highgate's even more upmarket neighbour, Hampstead, has long been regarded as one of the most desirable addresses in the city. Today's famous people live in the same houses as the famous of previous centuries. Between Highgate and Hampstead **Bishop's Avenue** has earned the sobriquet of Millionaire's Row.

Open spaces predominate. The Heath, Parliament Hill Fields and Primrose Hill all provide splendid views. Hampstead also has one of the deepest tunnels on the Underground system: 200 ft (60 metres). In 1880 this smart village was still 4 miles (7 km) away from the edge of London; now it is swamped by the urban life. **Whitestone Pond**, at the top of the hill on the main road, is the highest point in London located at 440 ft (134 metres) above sea level.

Hampstead is full of chic shops, restaurants and pubs. Its population is relatively young and rich. On the northern edge of the Heath, the **Jack Straw's Castle** pub is named after one of the ringleaders of the Peasant Revolt. The **Spaniards Inn** figures in another story of insurrection. In the 18th century, angry Gordon rioters rampaged up Hampstead Hill and looted Lord Mansfield's stately house, Kenwood. The landlord of the Spaniards plied the rioters with free drink until the military arrived to restore order.

The **Old Bull and Bush**, still a very popular pub, was immortalised in a music hall song which is sung on stage today. An ancient tollgate narrows the road outside the Spaniards Inn, and the Hampstead rich are constantly driving their Porsches into it.

Kenwood House is now a major art gallery with works by Rembrandt, Vermeer, Reynolds, Gainsborough and Turner. Poetry readings and chamber music recitals are held in the Orangery.

Much of the poet John Keats' greatest work, including *Ode to a Nightingale*,

was composed during the two years he lived at Wentworth Place in Hampstead. The building, known as **Keats' House**, is open to the general public and houses memorabilia such as his letters and even a lock of his hair. Keats fell in love with the daughter of his neighbour. His mentor, Leigh Hunt, also lived nearby – when he wasn't in gaol for describing the Prince Regent as a "fat Adonis of fifty". The surrounding streets of old Hampstead, especially Flask Walk and Well Walk, have to be walked to be seen.

Islington: Ironically, while it is dubbed "the Red Republic of Islington" because of its left-wing administration, **Islington** symbolises more than any other district the new-style gentrification of London's inner city.

House prices in the area have escalated in a dizzying fashion as whole areas of the borough have been restored to their original Georgian and Victorian graciousnesss.

At the southern end of Islington, on **Rosebery Avenue**, stands **Sadler's Wells**, a 1,500-seat theatre built in 1683 by Thomas Sadler. The well is under the floor backstage. Islington Spa, which stood opposite, was known as New Tunbridge Wells because its medicinal waters were claimed to be of similar properties to those of the very fashionable spa town of Tunbridge Wells in Kent. The qualities of the local water led to the development of the huge Whitbread Brewery in Chiswell Street and the Gordon's Dry Gin distillery.

The **Regent's Canal** passes discreetly under Islington, in a 960-yard tunnel. The towpath disappears and tow-horses had to be led overland while the bargemen propelled their boats by pushing off the roof of the tunnel. Today boat-hirers need a good torch, a reliable motor and a strong constitution for long periods of darkness while travelling through the dank tunnel.

Standing on the crossroads at the heart of Islington's shopping district is the **Angel**. The one-time pub building is

A terrace in Islington, very popular with young professionals.

a familiar destination sign on London's red buses.

Restorers have also been at work on the old **Royal Agricultural Hall**, on Liverpool Road. Established originally in 1798 as home for the Smithfield Club's annual agricultural and livestock shows, the Hall is known locally as the "Aggie". An impressive edifice, the main hall contains 1,000 tons of cast iron and boasts a 130-ft (40-metre) roof span. Within, the hall space of nearly 5 acres (2 hectares) was the venue for the 1873 World's Fair. Aggie is now the London Business Design Centre, used for conferences and exhibitions.

One of Islington's prettiest assets – though something of a tourist trap – is **Camden Passage**. The elegant buildings and arcades have been turned into a treasure trove of antique shops, ranging from simple stalls to grand shops. Prices tend to reflect the popularity of the place and it is difficult to find any stunning bargains.

Dotted around Islington are several fringe theatres which are worth investigating (magazines such as *Time Out* carry details). The borough has a history of entertainment, as it was regarded a safe haven from the muggings and plague in the City. The gentry also liked to travel "out of town". In the 17th century there were five theatres, and the first-ever actress (as opposed to men dressed as women) appeared on stage here. Today there are seven regular venues, of which the better known are the **Almeida** (with a good lunchtime food bar) in Almeida Street, the **King's Head** in Upper Street and the **Old Red Lion** in St. John Street.

Notting Hill: Notting Hill is a melting pot in which several races and social classes of all grades rub shoulders. Grand and very expensive Georgian townhouses contrast with their run-down counterparts which are divided into dozens of seedy bed-sitters.

The **Notting Hill Carnival**, which brings the spirit of Caribbean street festivals to London, was started in 1966 in an attempt to unite the local communities – an attempt which has been largely successful. Months of work go into the elaborate costumes worn by the dancers in the procession. The event features Trinidadian steelbands and attracts 750,000 onlookers.

The Carnival, however, is a major policing operation, with 10,000 officers on duty. In 1976 revellers resented the heavy police presence and confrontations occurred. Although full-scale violence has not been repeated, pickpocketing and mugging do persist, and the 1987 Carnival ended in tragedy when a street vendor was stabbed to death.

In **Ladbroke Grove**, the air thumps with the reggae beat most of the year-round. Ladbroke Grove's restaurants and shops are the centre of local Afro-Caribbean life. By contrast, **Westbourne Grove** and **Queensway**, which runs down into it, have a strong continental flavour, with immigrants from Germany, Italy, Greece, and Arabic

The Notting Hill Carnival, Europe's largest street festival.

countries.

Westbourne Grove was originally planned as a shopping street to rival Kensington High Street and at one time Whiteley's department store was the largest in the world. But development in nearby centres gradually drew away customers, and Westbourne Grove returned to being a sleepy, elegant backwater. In 1989 Whiteley's was restored to its former glory and is a multi-shop complex, with multi-screen cinema.

Until the 1940s, **Portobello Road** was just one of London's many street markets. However, it has gradually gained a world-renowned reputation as a source of antiques. The first market traders in the 19th century included gypsies who came to sell horses for the Hippodrome race track which was nearby. The traders were licensed from 1929, and increased when the Caledonian Market closed down in 1948. Today, traders pretend to be local characters, but are much sharper than they may seem. The busiest market times are on Saturday and Sunday.

All Saints Road is a market of a different sort, being one of the principle London streets for drug trafficking. In recent years police have clamped down but trade is still done on the street, which can be dangerous late at night.

Brixton: Once an elegant and classy 19th-century suburb, Brixton won worldwide notoriety during the riots in 1981 which set the local West Indian community against the police. Tension built up over the launching of "Swamp 81", a police operation designed to reduce the amount of street crime in the area. Violence erupted when a hostile crowd gathered as police questioned a minicab driver.

The arson and looting which ensued was on a scale unseen in the UK. It was a symptom of the discontent which was bred in a run-down and deprived district, stricken by severe unemployment. Riots in other parts of the country soon followed.

Brixton, known as a black ghetto,

Thirty percent of visitors to London find their way to Portobello Road market.

actually has a population which is 60 percent white. The balance includes a high proportion of Cypriots, Vietnamese and Chinese. The first West Indians arrived in 1948. Though its side-streets are not the place for non-locals after dark, the centre of Brixton is safe. It has a good late-night venue for rock music, the **Brixton Academy**, and one of London's trendiest discos, the **Fridge**. The **Ritzy** is one of the city's most interesting independent cinemas.

Besides the branches of the major chain stores, there are several markets, including a number of fascinating covered Victorian arcades which sell a wide variety of ethnic Caribbean, African, Asian and European food. Here are salted pig's tails, snappers, jackfish, green bananas, ackee and callaloo.

The crescent of **Electric Avenue** – one of London's first streets to be lit by electricity in 1888 – is the heart of these markets. Electric Avenue is also featured in Jamaican singer Eddie Grant's lyrics: "We're going to rock down to /

Electric Avenue".

On the street corner heading south up Brixton Hill is the imposing **Lambeth Town Hall**, headquarters of one of London's most radical local borough councils.

Further up the hill, **Brixton Prison** is the main centre for prisoners who are on remand waiting trial. The authorities were embarrassed a few years ago when it was discovered that one of the inmates used to escape every evening for a few hours to the local pub, returning to his cell at closing time.

The **Brixton Windmill** was built in 1816 and still stands, although vandalism has destroyed its mechanism. The fringes of Brixton, notably towards Stockwell, are being gentrified by young professionals keen to own their own homes. In **Coldharbour Lane**, testifying to the survival of traditional Londoners is a "pie and mash" shop offering such delicacies as jellied eels, meat pies, mashed potato, and "liquour" (a rich, parsley-flavoured sauce).

Railton Road market, Brixton.

MARKETS

"Billy buys almost everything", the sign reads. Billy's selection of "almost everything" is piled high within a six-foot square cubby hole in one corner of Camden Lock Market, located on Regent's Canal in Camden. Billy himself is tiny and stands on two milk crates so that he can see over shoppers' heads to watch his junk. Around him an enormous variety of vendors whose accents come from all parts of the globe, let alone London, sell earrings made out of innards of clocks, hand painted shoes, and even life membership to the Finsbury Park Insect Club.

Fly-pickers (illegal traders selling from suitcases) appear and disappear like shadows on the pavements outside, according to whether or not a policeman is in sight. Camden Lock (best on a Saturday or Sunday) catalogues the charivari of English domestic life from the war years onwards, as well as amassing state-of-the-art crafts of the 1990s, but it is not cheap. And, like so many other areas of London, parts of it have attracted the attention of the redevelopers.

On the other hand, stall-holders in Petticoat Lane and Brick Lane in the East End would claim their prices are rock bottom, although goods here (clothes, bric-a-brac, electronic goods, etc.) could be "dodgy" meaning either acquired below the counter (illegally) or liable to go wrong at the flick of a switch; there is a popular saying that by the time a tourist has walked the length of the Petticoat Lane market he could be sold his own handkerchief by the last stall.

Brick Lane market starts very early in the morning. While the Camden markets reflect the hidden riches of the city, Brick Lane reflects the hidden poverty. In the sidestreets of this market Eastenders spread their wares on the wet, grey pavement, within a few hundred yards of the Stock Market. Here the latest CD player retails at less than £100, unchipped despite "falling off the back of a lorry". There are tremendous bargains for the brave, and tremendous rip-offs for the unwary or unlucky.

The West End's Covent Garden and neighbouring Jubilee Market are well known and described elsewhere in this book, but in fact it is the City which has hosted London's major markets. Billingsgate, the home of fresh fish and foul language, has since been moved from the City to Docklands; Smithfield meat market still functions although there are plans afoot to move it; Spitalfields organic produce market has expanded to include crafts; Leadenhall (so called because of its original lead roofing, at a time when other markets were thatched) has been revived, and now provides market shopping for City workers; ironically, most of the produce sold here which was trucked in from surrounding countryside ends up being eaten in the suburbs near where it was grown.

Antique markets are widespread throughout London. Chelsea's enclosed markets Chenil Galleries and Antiquarius, networks of tiny passages and crammed stalls on King's Road, are staffed by experts but are rather stuffy.

There is a much better chance of picking up a bargain at the open-air Portobello Road market (selling antiques on Saturdays) in Notting Hill, where dealers do their shopping. Stall-holders here may seem almost unaware of what they have on their stalls and more concerned to perpetuate their images as street "characters", but don't be fooled. Not only do they know intimately what they have; they also know what all their neighbours have.

Camden Passage market in Islington is also strong on (quite pricey) antiques and

Berwick Street market.

particularly features bric-a-brac on Wednesdays and Saturdays.

For designer fashion sold from market-type stalls, Kensington High Street offers two good venues in Kensington Market and Hyper Hyper, which looks deceptively like a large store from the outside. The former retails a mixture between punk chic and post-Carnaby Street tat; the latter (almost facing Kensington Market) offers the work of young clothing designers at competitive prices.

Outside the central areas of London in the local boroughs – the areas of home life rather than work and play – the local market remains a feature of community life. These venues are not arty, crafty or creaking with antiques like the central markets, but are largely composed of fruit and vegetable vendors selling less variety than supermarkets but at lower prices.

These markets make an interesting microcosm of London life, with the vendors being old Londoners (both old in terms of age and in tradition) and the shoppers being a mixture of both old and new residents. The Berwick Street market in Soho, even though it is in the centre of the city, is a good example.

Brixton is more a market for atmosphere than for shopping, although amongst a lot of unremarkable merchandise there is a good assortment of tropical fruit and other West Indian foods and spices that aren't available in other markets.

Popularly associated with the markets of the East End, Pearly Kings and Queens are more frequently seen in London these days since the TV programme *Eastenders*, Britain's most popular series, focused on the city's traditions. The Pearlies, so named because of the pearl-like buttons they wear on their costumes, supposedly came from market-vendor stock.

The first Pearly was Henry Croft, an orphan and a crossing-sweeper, who started to collect buttons from his stretch of road and wove them into a suit in 1880. He supposedly then sold the suit in order to raise money for a children's home, thus beginning the fund-raising role of the Pearlies which still persists.

Today Pearlies are ceremonial figures. Their positions are inherited, not elected and a Pearly generally opens fetes, does advertising work for charity, and appears regularly at his or her local markets. Visitors can see Pearlies in large concentrations at the Pearly Harvest Festival (October) and the Lord Mayor's Festival (November).

aluable *ovelties in* *'ortobello* *Road.*

WIGS AND PENS

On the northwest corner of Ludgate Circus, at the foot of Fleet Street, there is a plaque dedicated to the great crime writer Edgar Wallace, who had his first newspaper job in the building that stands on this site.

The greening plaque has an almost ideal vantage. Behind it is the street that was once the capital of the British and world newspaper industry and whose name is still synonymous with that industry, though much of it is now scattered down-river.

Facing the plaque, at the top of Ludgate Hill, is the magnificent dome of **St Paul's Cathedral**, which peers sternly back down at Fleet Street. The satirical magazine *Private Eye* made this view famous in its regular "Street of Shame" feature which set out to expose the foibles and puncture the pretensions of Britain's newspaper industry. Wallace's plaque may be central, but he was just one of the many writers, lawyers and intellects this area has nurtured for generation upon generation.

Wren's greatest work: St Paul's, which was the somewhat controversial choice of the Prince and Princess of Wales for their wedding (Westminster Abbey would have been more traditional), is undoubtedly Sir Christopher Wren's greatest work. A tablet above Wren's plain marble tomb reads: *Lector, si monumentum requiris, circumspice*, "Reader, if you wish to see his memorial, it is all about you."

Historians believe that the first church on the St Paul's site was built in the 7th century, although it only really came into its own as Old St Paul's in the 14th century, and by the 16th century it was the tallest cathedral in England. However, much of the building was destroyed in the Great Fire of 1666. Construction on the new St Paul's Cathedral began in 1675, when Wren was 43 years old.

However, the architect was an old man of 78 when his son Christopher finally laid the highest stone of the lantern on the central cupola in 1710. In total, the cathedral cost £747,954 to build, and most of the money was raised through taxing coal arriving in the port of London. The building is massive and the Portland stone dome alone weighs over 50,000 tons.

Generations of school children have giggled secret messages in St Paul's **Whispering Gallery**, an incredible feature of over 100 ft (30 metres) of perfect acoustic (as the most musical of Royal Weddings bore witness).

Associated with the church were the great "Metaphysical" poet John Donne, who was Dean, and the victor of Trafalgar, Admiral Nelson, whose body lies

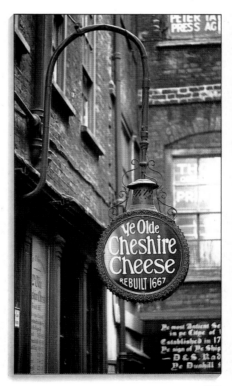

in the crypt. The magnificent, much copied Holman Hunt painting *The Light of the World*, hangs in the south aisle. There are fine statues by Flaxman and Bacon of the painter Sir Joshua Reynolds and of the great wit and dictionary maker Samuel Johnson.

The area is full of Johnsoniana. He lived for a time at St John's Gate, Clerkenwell. The back-courts of Fleet Street were Johnson's stamping grounds and drinkers in **Ye Olde Cheshire Cheese** pub in Wine Office Court will still raise a glass or two to honour his memory.

The area around St Paul's and in particular the ancient market site known as **Paternoster Square** have been developed. The only contemporary echo of the shepherding and marketing that used to be done here is Elizabeth Frink's sculpture of a flock of sheep, a sight that has sobered up many a drinker on a foggy night. The mediocrity of most of the buildings hemming in St Paul's has long been criticised and recently Prince

Charles joined in the chorus of disapproval. New plans are afoot to reconcile God and Mammon by replacing the box-like offices with new buildings and giving the cathedral room to breathe.

Friars and theatres: Down the hill from St Paul's and closer to the river is the quaintly named **Puddle Dock**, which today looks unquaintly like a motorway. There was once, apparently, a Mr Puddle. In 1616, the year Shakespeare died, a movement to open a theatre here was thwarted by the monks at the nearby monastery of Black Friars (who gave this area its modern name). It wasn't until 1956 that the **Mermaid Theatre** was founded, a bare mile across the river from the site of Shakespeare's Globe. The weirdly shaped **Black Friar** pub, with a tubby statue of its namesake above the door and a resident ghost upstairs stands on the corner by Blackfriars Bridge.

Street of shame: The **El Vino** wine bar, at No. 47 Fleet Street, became notorious for maintaining, even in the face of

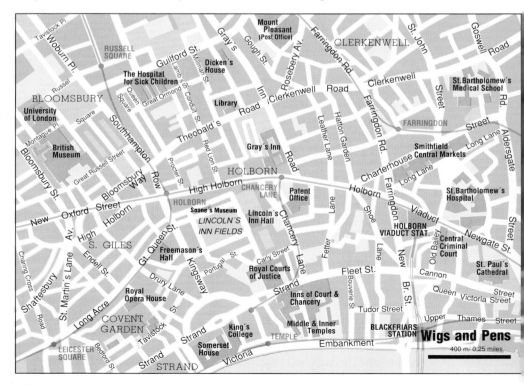

court action by feminists, its stuffy policy of not serving unaccompanied ladies at the bar. It will still not admit women in trousers and requires men to wear a jacket and tie. Not so long ago, it was packed daily with lawyers and with hard-drinking and hard-gossiping national newspaper journalists. The lawyers are still there, but the ranks of journalists have been thinned out by the flight of newspapers from what used to be the Street of Ink and Adventure (or, to the more cynical, the Street of Shame), once the centre of Britain's national newspaper publishing.

The Times was the first to quit the area. After leaving Blackfriars, it went first to Gray's Inn Road to join the *Sunday Times*, but took with it the print unions' Luddite practices. Thomson International, tiring of lost production, sold the paper to Rupert Murdoch, who decisively defeated the unions by moving all his national newspapers downriver to a new site at Wapping. That meant that *The Sun* and the *News of the*

Forsaking the desk for the green baize: a snooker club at Blackfriars.

World, Britain's biggest-selling daily and Sunday tabloids, were uprooted from their offices just off Fleet Street. The beginning of the end was in sight for Fleet Street as a newspaper centre.

Soon the *Daily Telegraph* left its magnificent Elcock and Sutcliffe building near the foot of Fleet Street for Docklands. *The Observer* uprooted itself to a striking new building in Battersea. The *Daily Express*, Lord Beaverbrook's pride, also moved south of the river, abandoning its famous art deco black-and-silver fronted offices on Fleet Street. And its long-time rival, Lord Northcliffe's *Daily Mail*, migrated to offices above a department store in Kensington High Street.

It was a breathtakingly fast death for a centuries-old tradition of print in the area. Now Fleet Street is just another street of shops and offices.

Up **Shoe Lane** from Ludgate Circus, passing the impressive International Press Centre on the way, is the *Daily Mirror* **building** at Holborn Circus. It's

a patriotically striped multi-storey block on the corner, contrasting sharply with the elaborate Gothic fantasy of the Prudential Assurance building opposite which sits on the site of Charles Dickens's first married home.

The liberal *Guardian* and communist *Morning Star* operate from Farringdon Road, a low-lying thoroughfare built on the line of the Fleet River which flows through a culvert underneath. Reduced these days to a dark and muddy stream, the Fleet continues on running under the solid Victorian ironwork of Holborn Viaduct opened in 1896.

Degrees of socialism: The area north of the viaduct has other associations with socialism and freedom. The Italian nationalist Mazzini, once made his home in the small Italian enclave at Clerkenwell. Here there is an ornate Italian church, packed for early Mass on Sundays, after which the congregation spills on to the street to gossip and shop. The church sits just opposite the end of **Hatton Garden**, London's famed diamond centre, where the bulk of the working population is Jewish.

A few hundred yards further east is **Clerkenwell Green**, with **St James's** church, the ancient **Clerk's Well** and the **Marx Memorial Library** at no. 37 (where the exiled Lenin published his revolutionary newspaper *Iskra*, "The Spark").

Market at work: Through the stone arch of St John's Gate is the unlikely confection of iron and plaster that is **Smithfield Meat Market**, which should be visited (by non-vegetarians) early on a winter's morning. Here the porters and "bummarees" thunder about with their barrowloads of carcases, the refrigerated lorries roar and rumble, and the knife-grinders shower sparks out of the backs of their vans. Through all the commotion, it's still possible to hear "backchat", Smithfield's equivalent of Billingsgate profanity, designed to fool unwanted listeners. The Smithfield day ends as most people's day begins. The area has long

Golden boys: the younger marks the end of the Great Fire and (right) the older discuss the state of British justice.

been a haunt for late-night and early-morning revellers who like to rub shoulders in the pubs and cafés with market workers, while pursuing the high cholesterol "breakfasts" which are the porters' dinners.

Smithfield is the last of the great markets still on its original site. It originally traded in live animals which were herded in from the country, but the gore of slaughter proved too much for the Victorians, who made some changes: Stinking Lane became Newgate Street, Blow Bladder Lane became King Edward Street, and the Smithfield meat was slaughtered outside the capital.

There are plans afoot to turn Smithfield into a shopping "piazza" like Covent Garden, home of the old fruit market. In readiness, the area has already gone "up-market". However, little change manages to penetrate the quiet of the Georgian **Charterhouse Square**, a favourite location for "period" film-makers with its gas lamps and cobbles.

On the opposite side of the market, in **West Smithfield**, are memorials to the Scottish hero William Wallace, victim of a spot of judicial butchery here in 1305, and to the 270 "Marian martyrs", Protestants burned at the stake for religious heresy by Queen Mary before her own unhappy end. The church of **St Bartholomew's** hides in a corner of the square, perhaps a trifled shocked or shamed by what has passed before, for this was also the site of the Bartholomew Fair, immortalised in Ben Jonson's noisy play. Behind is the great block of **St Bartholomew's Hospital**, founded in 1122 and the oldest in London. Opposite it, high on the wall at the corner of **Giltspur Street** and **Cock Lane**, is a naked golden figure of a boy, symbolizing (in the most obvious way imaginable) the eventual extinguishing of the Great Fire at this point.

Legal London: Wedged between Little Britain and St Martin's-le-Grand, two of the more exotic local street names, is the main London Post Office. Out on

Inside the exclusive Wig and Pen Club (**left**) and the Old Bailey.

Newgate Street, the extension of Holborn eastwards to St Paul's tube station, is the **Central Criminal Court**, universally known by its street front address in **Old Bailey**.

The court was built on the site of the infamous Newgate Gaol and was originally an open air construction to lessen the risk of judges and jurors catching "gaol fever". It has been the scene of many famous trials notably that of Peter Sutcliffe, "the Yorkshire Ripper" who eventually met his nemesis a scant mile or two from where the original Ripper plied his grisly course.

History, in the shape of the Luftwaffe in the 1940s and more lately the IRA in the 1970s, has taken occasional revenge on the building. But in recent years it has been substantially renovated and cleaned and the stonework now gleams almost as brightly as does the golden figure of blind Justice on the pinnacle.

The whole area is associated with the legal system and it's hard to say which are the most impressive of its buildings, the churches or the courts. British law, particularly in cases involving insurance or incidents at sea, is still textbook stuff for much of the rest of the world.

Fleet Street boasts two remarkable churches. **St Bride**, another building struck by bombs in the war, reveals the macabre site of a crypt jam-packed with coffins. Three hundred years ago Pepys had to bribe a sexton to find room for his brother's corpse.

At the head of **The Strand** is the church well-known from the "Oranges and Lemons" rhyme, **St Clement Dane**. No-one knows what the connection with the Danes actually was but there is a present day association with the Royal Air Force.

Places of record: Nearby the **Royal Courts of Justice**, which deal with all civil cases (as the Old Bailey does with criminal cases), is **Chancery Lane**, running between Fleet Street and Holborn. Once home of the feared Chancery Courts, which was the foggy bureaucracy of Dickens's *Bleak House*, Chancery Lane now houses part of the **Public Record Office**. The modern explosion in documentation, which Dickens only saw in its infancy, means that most of the office's material is rehoused at Kew.

On the Strand is the building which once functioned as the "hatch 'em, match 'em, and dispatch 'em department", **Somerset House** where "every little boy and every little gal / That's born into the world alive" was registered, at birth, at marriage and at death. Births, marriages and deaths have moved across to the other side of Aldwych to St Catherine's House, and Somerset House now contains the impressive **Courtauld Institute Art Collection**.

Just up the road from the handsome limestone front of the Public Record Office is that cartoonists' staple, the **Patent Office** on Theobald's Road.

Professional inns: All around this area are the famous **Inns of Court**, home of London's legal profession. (The old

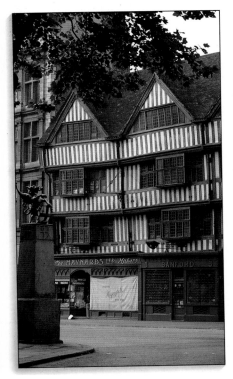

Left, Staple Inn dates from 1586. Right, the stern face of Dickens's House, now the Dickens Museum.

Inns of Chancery, from which the lane takes its name, are no more.) The "Inns" were once, much as they sound, places of rest and comfort for trainee lawyers.

From the 19th century onward, law was taught at **King's College**, next to Somerset House in the Strand, and at **University College** in Gower Street. Before that time the only way to obtain legal training was to serve an apprenticeship like the one young Dickens suffered in **Gray's Inn**.

As with most of the others, this Inn is 14th-century in origin, its grounds lying just to the west of Gray's Inn Road. The magnificent garden was laid out by Francis Bacon, the Elizabethan essayist. Among the host of other famous people to serve here were the poets Sir Philip Sydney and Hilaire Belloc and the social thinker and Fabian, Sidney Webb. With an irony that must have tickled Dickens's sense of the ridiculousness of the law, Gray's Inn Hall saw the first production of Shakespeare's *Comedy of Errors*.

Plays and planners: A similar distinction is enjoyed by the **Middle Temple**, near the **Inner Temple** on the Embankment. Here in 1601 was the first performance of *Twelfth Night*. Founded by the Knights Templar, the Temple is architecturally magnificent, with cloisters and gardens. A horn still summons members to dinner and would-be lawyers are still required to dine here a certain number of times during the year.

Staid though it might all seem today, these Inns used to be far from respectable. A 17th-century Act of Parliament restrained the young lawyers; "they were not to wear beards of more than three weeks' growth upon pain of a fine of forty shillings".

Besides Shakespeare, entertainment included dice and dancing, and archery, football and westling. All were practised in the now-quiet quadrangles.

A short distance away is **Lincoln's Inn**, alma mater of Cromwell, and the great 19th-century prime ministers and rivals for Queen Victoria's favour,

Left, The BBC beams radio programmes worldwide from Bush House. **Right**, Bloomsbury is the heart of publishing.

William Gladstone and Benjamin Disraeli. Ben Jonson designed the gate house. **Lincoln's Inn Fields** were created for students' recreation but the best sport of all was watching the early city planners try to outmanoeuvre each other. There was a Royal Commission to decide the area's 17th-century fate and Inigo Jones was a member.

Today, visitors can puzzle out the significance of Barry Flanagan's large sheet steel sculpture "Camdonian" in the northeast corner, or pass on to the **Sir John Soane Museum**. The museum is a self-endowed monument to London's most important architect and collector who died in 1837, the year of Victoria's accession. He left his house and collection much as they had been during his lifetime.

Soane was also responsible for the Dulwich Picture Gallery in South London which was Britain's first public art gallery. He built his private home on three sites along the north edge of the Lincoln's Inn Fields.

Dickens's world: Dickens's ghost haunts these streets. His most famous settings are here: **Bleeding Heart Yard**, scene of much of the domestic action in *Little Dorrit*, is only a quiet step or two away from the bustle of Hatton Garden and **Leather Lane**, a crowded street market presided over by the diminutive Dickensian figure of Little Jimmy, who is its unofficial policeman and traffic warden. The market sells a wide variety of household goods and foodstuffs.

The **Dickens House Museum** is at 47 Doughty Street; the offices of *The Spectator*, an influential right-wing weekly magazine with a distinguished history, are a few doors away.

Dickens was brought to London at an early age, and started work in a bootblacking factory off the Strand. He later became a reporter in the House of Commons, and began to write books which reflected areas and themes of London which he knew well.

An ethical riot: A bare half mile down

One of several specialist bookshops in Great Russell Street.

Doughty Street and to the right along Theobald's Road is **Red Lion Square**. Here, in **Conway Hall**, the South Place Ethical Society deliberates and holds its famous Sunday-night subscription chamber concerts; they've been going for nearly a century, with undimmed enthusiasm.

In 1974, in keeping with the ideal of free speech, they rented their main hall to the extreme right-wing National Front. A left-wing group called Liberation hired a back room. Ensuing were marches and counter marches, a demonstration and eventual violence in which a young demonstrator was killed. Red Lion Square marked the apogee of political unrest in 1970s Britain.

Today the square is disturbingly quiet. A statue of the veteran campaigner Fenner Brockway, chairman of Liberation, stands in characteristic pose by the roadside, lecturing the cars and buses.

At the end of **Kingsway** at night, is one of London's most striking architectural sights, the floodlit front of the British Broadcasting Corporation's **Bush House**, headquarters of its overseas service. It's remarkable frontage and the optimistic motto, "Nation shall speak unto nation", is echoed by the soaring arch with its twin figures. The world service broadcasts in most major languages in most corners of the world.

Back up Kingsway (named for George V and a miracle of urban engineering in its day) is the **Kingsway Hall**, once a favourite venue of "live" Third Programme classical music broadcasts on the BBC. Listeners grew used to hearing Beethoven or Mozart mingled with the subterranean rumble of the underground, which runs directly beneath.

Old fossils: An even more remarkable feat of organisation and classification than the great legal record offices is the **British Museum and Library** on Great Russell Street in Bloomsbury. Behind the famous Athenian frontage are the famous Elgin Marbles and the

The London Transport Museum, Covent Garden.

162

linguist's codebook, the Rosetta Stone. There is also Sir Anthony Panizzi's circular Reading Room in the British Library, which will soon to move to a new site near Euston station.

Here Karl Marx did much of his research for *Das Kapital* and visitors are shown his favourite seat. Outside again in the main museum, the current attractions are the mummified figure of murdered primeval man "Pete Marsh", preserved by a peat bog for centuries until he was turned up by a farmer's plough, and archaeopteryx, the controversial bird-fossil that still divides the experts over its origins.

Literary London: Bloomsbury is blue plaque territory *par excellence*. Virginia Woolf, Roger Fry and Queen Victoria's biographer Lytton Strachey all lived at various addresses around these streets.

At the beginning of the 20th century, they were christened "The Bloomsbury Group" and although their inclinations spread across painting, philosophy and writing their common thread was to challenge the accepted conventions of the day. They probably had more influence as a body than as individuals, and they were bookish men and women in a bookish world.

The area's industry is publishing. The art publishers Thames and Hudson have their offices, with the steps decorated in magnificent Vanessa Bell tiles, at the bottom of Gower Street. Faber and Faber, publishers of *Lord of the Flies* and one-time employers of T. S. Eliot, have moved from **Russell Square** to **Queen Square** behind Southampton Row, where they share the quiet backstreets with a curious knot of hospitals: the National Hospital for Nervous Diseases, the Homoeopathic Hospital, and, best known, the Royal Hospital for Sick Children. The Royal is usually known by its address "Great Ormond St.", although the kids call it by its initials: GOSH. The bookshops here are full of skeletons and diagrams that will help you postpone lunch.

Across Russell Square is the grey turret of the University of London **Senate House** built in 1936. The First World War tank that sat outside as a charity gimmick is long gone, sold for scrap, but in these straitened, fund-raising times, some version of it may be back to play a part during university rag-week.

Moving down Gower Street, past **Dillon's** university booksellers, the mood becomes a little less sombre. **Shaftesbury Avenue** is the beginning of theatre land and modern **Covent Garden**, with its mime artists and buskers, and its shops and restaurants.

The market area is bracketed by two London opera houses: the more traditional **Royal Opera House** in Bow Street and the **Coliseum** in St Martin's Lane, where the programmes are all in English and sometimes in questionable taste. In the centre, the **London Transport Museum** displays the more mundane aspects of modern culture. Beside it are the new premises of the **Theatre Museum**.

Shopping in Covent Garden.

THE CITY

Preceding pages: a 20th-century sculpture in front of Tower Bridge. Left, the National Westminster Tower looms over the City. Right, today's Beefeater is more of a guide than a guardian.

"I am still unable to decide whether the City is a person, or a place, or a thing... You read in the morning paper that the City is "deeply depressed"...at noon it is "buoyant", and by four o'clock it is "wildly excited".

– Stephen Leacock,
My Discovery of England

The City, London's ancient financial quarter, is a world apart from the rest of the capital. It runs its own affairs and is quite apart from the rest of London's local government organisation. It has its own police force and a very distinct set of hierarchies. Here, even the Queen treads carefully: on her coronation drive in 1953, she was obliged – by tradition rather than force – to stop at Temple Bar and declare, before continuing into the City, that she came in peace. The name "Square Mile" is given to this financial district that was until relatively recently regarded as "the clearing-house of the world", but it signifies far more than a limited geographical area.

For most of its 2,000-year history, the City *was* London. Today the area is humming with late 20th-century technology, but is still heavy with archaic traditions which has helped a potentially faceless world retain a certain degree of character.

Here, in microcosm, the visitor will find the class system of England – complacency, uniforms, snobbishness; the very poor rubbing shoulders with the astonishingly rich. It's easy in such surroundings to recall the remark of American comedienne Bette Midler: "When it's three o'clock in New York, it's still 1938 in London."

Like any closed world the City does not open up easily to the outsider. Peering out of a tourist bus at acres of glass and concrete is far too superficial; time and leg work in the network of alleys and backstreets which thread through the office blocks, will reveal much, much more.

Landmarks of history: The City's past isn't readily accessible through its buildings. It has been devastated twice. In 1666 the **Great Fire** devoured four-fifths of the City, and in the winter of 1940–41 Goering's Luftwaffe pounded it night after night during the Blitz, leaving a third in smoking ruins. However, the 2,000 years of history are still accessible through a section of Roman Wall in Moorgate, through a Tudor oriel window in Cloth Fair, through the street names and through the people.

The Romans established the City in AD 45, but there are few remains. The **Roman Wall** which was 2 miles (3 km) long, 20 ft high and 9 ft wide (6 by 3 metres) and had six magnificent gates (Ludgate, Newgate, Aldersgate, Cripplegate, Bishopsgate and Aldgate) is now found only in fragments. Good sections can still be seen at London Wall, Noble Street, Cooper's Row and the Museum of London.

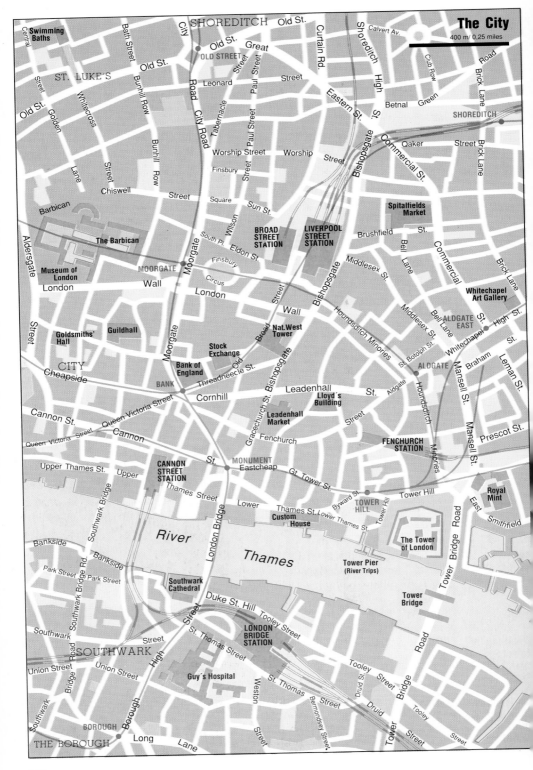

The City

400 m / 0,25 miles

SHOREDITCH

Swimming Baths

ST. LUKE'S

OLD STREET

SHOREDITCH

Spitalfields Market

The Barbican

Museum of London

BROAD STREET STATION

LIVERPOOL STREET STATION

Whitechapel Art Gallery

MOORGATE

Goldsmiths' Hall

Guildhall

Nat. West Tower

ALDGATE EAST

CITY

Stock Exchange

Bank of England

Leadenhall Lloyd's Building

ALDGATE

Cheapside

BANK

Cornhill

Leadenhall Market

Fenchurch

FENCHURCH STATION

CANNON STREET STATION

MONUMENT
Eastcheap

TOWER HILL

Royal Mint

Custom House

TOWER HILL

River Thames

The Tower of London

Tower Pier (River Trips)

Southwark Cathedral

Tower Bridge

LONDON BRIDGE STATION

SOUTHWARK

Guy's Hospital

THE BOROUGH

Long Lane

Constant building is always unearthing new finds. In 1869 the **Bucklersbury Mosaic** was discovered in Cannon Street and in 1954 the **Temple of Mithras** was found under the Bucklersbury building. The reconstructed temple can now be seen on the Bucklersbury site and the mosaic and sculptures found at the original site are in the **Museum of London**.

The Museum is an essential stop. The galleries run in chronological order from prehistoric London to the present day and feature lovingly reconstructed rooms – from an Elizabethan parlour to a 1930s barber shop. A highlight of the visit is the audio-visual recreation of the Great Fire.

The museum gives a good taste of the City's trading past, a flavour of which remains today in the main shopping throughfare, **Cheapside**. In medieval times Cheapside (from the old English word *ceap* – to barter) was the City's mercantile heart. The names of the side-streets, Bread Street, Milk Street and Wood Street, give an idea of the merchandise. Just beyond Cheapside was the poulterers area, now known simply as **Poultry**. **Cannon Street** (a corruption of candlewick), which runs parallel, was the candlemakers area. **Garlick Hill** could be smelt from Cheapside.

City guilds: Craftsmen with the same trade tended to congregate in small areas, and clubbed together to form medieval guilds. Like trade unions, the guilds operated to ward off foreign competition and established an apprenticeship system. They set standards for their goods and ran mutual aid schemes which helped members in difficulty. The more prosperous guilds built halls to meet and dine in and wore lavish uniforms or "liveries", in due course becoming **livery companies**.

For years there was considerable inter-guild rivalry and in 1515 the Lord Mayor interceded and named a top 12 based on wealth: Mercers (dealers in fine cloth), Grocers, Drapers, Fishmongers, Goldsmiths, Skinners, Merchant

Taylors, Haberdashers, Slaters, Ironmongers, Vintners and Clothworkers. Competition between the Skinners and Merchant Taylors who both claimed the number six slot was particularly vicious. The Lord Mayor, with Solomon-like decisiveness, decreed they should alternate positions six and seven every year. His action originated the expression "at sixes and sevens" meaning "uncertain".

Down the centuries the livery companies shed their Mafia image and became part of the establishment promoting charities and founding some of England's better educational institutes, including Haberdashers' College and Goldsmiths' College.

Livery halls: Today some of the most impressive entry ways in the City belong to livery halls. Behind their gleaming paintwork and elaborate carvings members dine as lavishly as ever. Most spectacularly pompous is **Goldsmiths** in Foster Lane where the integrity of gold and silver issued the previous year

omp and
eremony
eep alive
e City's
aditions.

is checked in an annual ceremony. The use of the word "hallmark" as a seal of value originated here. Unfortunately visitors are not usually allowed inside the livery halls, except in special circumstances.

While the 96 livery companies today have little connection with their original crafts they still exert influence in their home territory.

The City is governed by the City Corporation, chaired by the **Lord Mayor**. The office of Lord Mayor dates back to 1189 and in the past 800 years a number of colourful and sometimes bizarre ceremonies have become attached to the job. The new Mayor is elected each year on Michaelmas Day, 29 September, when the reigning Lord Mayor and his aldermen parade through the streets carrying small posies of flowers to ward off the stench which filled the City when the ceremony originally began.

In November the mayor is sworn in at the **Guildhall**, taking up his symbols of office in a ceremony known as the Silent Change, so called because no words are spoken. The next day is the Lord Mayor's show, a colourful parade through the streets which starts at the Guildhall and passes through the City, culminating at **Mansion House**, the Lord Mayor's official residence.

Market forces: The few remaining City markets are on the move – logically enough, as it is a long time since the Square Mile was just a trading Centre for foodstuffs. **Smithfield**'s future is in doubt. **Spitalfields** has reopened as an organic produce market and crafts centre. **Billingsgate** has already moved to Docklands, its former building taken over by banking groups.

Leadenhall. once the wholesale market for poultry and game, will remain. It has been prettified and its magnificent airy Victorian structure is now home to a collection of sandwich bars, stylish restaurants, food and book shops. The market, however, remains an excellent place to browse and barter.

The new Lord Mayor celebrates his office while Metal Exchange dealers earn their keep.

Trading has certainly not diminished in the City. Today's traders are not dealing in beef or boxes of carnations, but commodities measured in thousands of tons. The commodity markets, the **London Commercial Sale Rooms** and **Plantation House** in Fenchurch Street, fix prices and place orders for commodities as diverse as coffee and rubber. Impersonal deals are struck by phone and on screen except for "futures" (promises to take deliveries in the future) where dealing is done in person on the trading floor.

For a real sense of the cut and thrust of buying and selling visit the ring of the **London Metal Exchange** in Fenchurch Street or the dealing floor of **Liffe** (London International Financial Futures Exchange) in the **Royal Exchange** at **Cornhill**. Each metal is traded for five minutes only and the record number of bargains struck in a day is 45,000.

Liffe's visitors' gallery is open daily between 11.30 a.m. and 1.45 p.m., but

get there early. Inside are animated young men in traditional garish blazers shouting and waving for their professional lives. A trip to the Metal Exchange must be arranged through Brian Reidy Associates (telephone: 071-626 1828).

Outside the Royal Exchange is the heart of the City – the triangular intersection known as **Bank**. The sight can be intimidating. Civic architecture abounds with the **Mansion House** on the western corner and the implacable facade of the **Bank of England** to the North. Bear in mind that all the City's great institutions grew from the fulfilment of the most basic needs and have only subsequently acquired their superior air.

Bank roots: Banking first came to the City in the 17th century when Italian refugees set up lending benches (*banca* in Italian) in **Lombard Street**. Today the businesses seem far from temporary, and range from merchant banks in quaint 18th-century houses to major

Commodity exchange dealers wear bright jackets for easy identification on the trading floor.

clearing banks like the National Westminster in its 600-ft (180-metre) tower in Old Broad Street.

The Bank of England dominates the Bank square as it does the British financial scene. Popularly known as the Old Lady of Threadneedle Street, a name which probably was drawn from a late 18th-century cartoon depicting an old lady (the bank) trying to prevent the then Prime Minister, Pitt the Younger, from securing her gold. The name stuck because it rather aptly describes the conservative, maternalistic role the Bank plays in stabilising the country's economy.

The Bank of England was set up in 1694 to finance a war against the Dutch. In return for the £1.2 million loan, it was granted a charter and became a bank of issue (with the right to print notes and take deposits). Today it prints and destroys five million notes daily and stores the nation's gold reserves.

Big Bang: The **Stock Exchange**, just along Threadneedle Street, was formed in a similar fashion, by merchants who were trying to raise money for a Far Eastern trip in 1553.

It has changed enormously since late 1986. Before that time it was an exclusive club with cosy, restrictive practices which benefitted members and excluded competition. Members were divided into jobbers and brokers. Brokers traded in the market for their clients while jobbers acted as whole-salers. A minimum commission was charged for any transaction.

In October 1986, threatened with legal action from the Government, the Stock Exchange agreed reluctantly to radically alter its practices. The Big Bang abolished the fixed commission system, merged jobber and broker functions, and transferred dealing to SEAQ, a computerised quotation system. Institutions were allowed to become members, not just individuals, which meant foreign securities houses could buy in.

The market is now a much fairer place, but for the visitor a duller one.

The Stock Exchange, a quieter place now that dealing has been computerised.

The trading floor once crowded with frantic, pin-striped figures, now echoes like a vast swimming bath; empty apart from a handful of options traders. A game of cricket is even rumoured to have been played on this, the holy turf of the financial world.

A trip to the visitors gallery (Monday–Friday, 9.45 a.m. to 5.15 p.m.) is still worthwhile. A film describes the exchange's history and on the battery of screens you can see the 7,000 listed securities changing hands. Sixty thousand bargains are struck here daily – business amounting to £4.5 billion.

High rise, high risk: A short walk from the exchange along Cornhill is another great City institution which began in a coffee house. **Lloyd's of London**, the biggest insurance group in the world, is now housed in a building designed by Richard Rogers. Rogers' use of blue, yellow and chrome service pipes look out of place sitting amidst the beige of the establishment.

Lloyd's practices, which have re-mained largely unchanged for 300 years, belie this modern exterior. Taking the spectacular, transparent glass lift to the fourth floor and walking through the audio-visual recreation of Lloyd's history to the visitors' gallery, you can appreciate the building's cathedral-like plan. All floors are linked by a central window higher than the holy windows of Chartres Cathedral.

Lloyd's is not a single company, but composed of 31,000 paying members. The conservative looking men on the trading floors are in the high-risk business. Policies range from the insurance of Marlene Dietrich's legs to the rust-buckets in the Greek merchant fleet.

There are two job functions here. The brokers sell the risks. Originally they were only marine related, but now cover everything from personal possessions to a satellite launch. Buying the risks are the underwriters who sit at their boxes, and draw on years of experience to assess the deals.

Set in the magnificent marble floor is

a wooden rostrum housing the **Lutine Bell**, which rings once for bad news and twice for good. The huge **Casualty Book** contains a record of every ship lost at sea.

City spire: The best view of Lloyd's is from the top of the **Monument**, in Monument Yard. After the destruction of the Great Fire, Sir Christopher Wren was asked to redesign large parts of the City, including numerous churches. The Monument, a Roman Doric column erected according to Wren's designs to commemorate the fire, stands 202 ft (61 metres) high. The height is exactly the same as the distance between the monument's base and the King's baker's house in Pudding Lane where the fire began.

The Great Fire lasted five days and spread through 460 streets, destroying 89 churches and more than 13,000 houses in all.

At the base of the column is a relief depicting the King and his citizens fighting the blaze. Inside, 311 steps wind giddily up to a small platform, from which the view is spectacular. Ron Koster of the Netherlands holds the record for ascending and descending the column in a speedy two minutes and forty seconds.

The City skyline is constantly changing and the maps on the viewing platform are always out-of-date. A notable omission are the red granite towers to the northeast, which were also born out of destruction.

The **Barbican Centre**, comprising an arts centre and housing and business space, was devised by the Corporation after World War II to attract residents and boost a falling City population. It took over 20 years to build and has been attacked since its opening for its inaccessibility and the maze-like interior. The community ideal was never realised as the flats were sold at exorbitant prices and were acquired by City firms. However, anyone who braves the ubiquitous orange carpet will find a cultural cornucopia including an art gallery, a

Left, the Barbican Centre. Right, legend has it that, when the ravens leave the Tower of London, doom will befall the country.

cinema, the Royal Shakespeare Company and the London Symphony Orchestra within the centre. During the day there are foyer performances and live music on the terrace of the Waterside café which overlooks the fountains.

Wren's vision: Appropriately enough the Monument gallery affords a chance to appreciate the remarkable vision Wren imposed on the City through his spires. There are 56 Wren spires, and you risk severe Wren-fatigue if you attempt to see them all. Selected visits reveal the work of the artist at the height of his powers.

St Mary-Le-Bow is the home of the famous Bow bells, which give their own kind of baptism – that of being a true Londoner, or cockney – to anyone born within earshot.

The original bells were destroyed in the war, but new ones were recast from the fragments. The church interior after restoration is rather vulgar, but the Norman crypt is worth a look. **St Stephen Walbrook**, dating from 1096, has a dome believed to be a dry run for St Paul's and a controversial Henry Moore, "cheeseboard" altar.

Ravens and jewels: East of the Monument is a building which is regarded with considerably greater affection than the Barbican. At first sight the **Tower of London**, the City's oldest building, looks like a cardboard model, but closer inspection reveals an awesome solidity. The Tower merits a book in itself and there are many on sale in the gift shop. This is London's biggest tourist attraction, hosting several thousand daily. There is plenty to savour. The Tower was built by William the Conqueror to guard eastern approaches to the city, but has been extended by monarchs since, so that it is now a complex of 22 towers. Inside the original building, the central White Tower, is a massive Norman chapel which is the oldest piece of church architecture in England.

The **Crown Jewels** are not a disappointment, with the Star of Africa (a

The Tower of London.

diamond in the Imperial State Crown) measuring the size of a cricket ball. The **Armoury** is a reminder of the number of ingenious ways humankind has found to kill each other. Hordes of ghosts reputedly stalk the walls seeking their heads, which were lost on the execution block on **Tower Hill**. Another legend has it that when the ravens which live in the Tower leave, the Tower and the country will fall. The authorities, with a healthy mistrust of fate, have clipped their wings.

Port and ale: After the exertions of the Monument and surrounding area, traditional refreshment is within easy walking distance. The **Ship** pub off Eastcheap and the **Samuel Pepys** on the river have real character and real ale. Lunchtime in the City can be chaotic: the 350,000 commuters who swell the resident 7,000 population and turn the streets into a seething, pinstripe river, are out shopping or fighting for taxis.

The City lunch used to be something of an institution. Many spent two hours lingering over port and stilton in unpretentious chop houses, but in the post-Big Bang era the work-obsessed now tend to have sandwiches delivered to their desks.

For a taste of real City fare visit **Sweetings** in Queen Victoria Street. The City's oldest fish restaurant, Sweetings is an institution, and behaves like one. You cannot book and must fight for a drink in the bar. The menu ranges from excellent fresh fish to stodgy nursery puddings which cater to the public school clientele.

Around the corner in Cannon Street is the less genteel world of **Corney and Barrow**, an exclusive wine bar. Here you can sip the latest "in" tipple-pink champagne, and listen to the under-30s crowd swap details of their six figure salaries. Downstairs the expense-account priced restaurant offers *nouvelle cuisine* to the newly moneyed.

Nouveau traders: The Big Bang revolutionised more than the Stock Exchange trading floor. For centuries the

City reflected British society, where *who* you knew was more important than *what* you knew. With the technological revolution, old school ties no longer inevitably buy into a cosy broking sinecure. Brains and quick wits are what count and the accents heard at Corney and Barrow are as likely to be flat cockney vowels as the refined tones of Oxford or Cambridge.

City decay: The new affluence has not touched everyone and the East End today is still a contrast between the rich and the poor as it was in the past. Frederick Engels visiting **Whitechapel** in 1844 wrote: "close to the splendid houses of the rich such a lurking place of the bitterest poverty may be found". In Engels' time the East End poor were Jewish rag traders, but today Bengalis work in **Bell Street** hunched over sewing machines night and day for little more than £1 an hour. In nearby **Brune Street,** the homeless who cannot find a place in the Catholic refuge sleep in a car park.

In **Brick Lane** are some of London's finest and cheapest Indian restaurants and a Sunday street market with a very distinctive East End character.

The area, however, has a gruesome past. It has been the scene of race riots against the Bengalis by the extreme right-wing National Front. In an earlier era, from 30 August to 9 November 1888, Jack the Ripper terrorised the streets, murdering five prostitutes, identified by his gruesome trademark – a double slash of the throat. His victims were destitute women who pawned their petticoats in **Middlesex Street**, better known as **Petticoat Lane**, and sold their bodies.

Brick Lane and neighbouring streets have yet to defeat the problems of racism and it can still be foolhardy to walk there alone at night. A half mile away under the red beacon of the massive National Westminster Tower, you can enter the more comfortable world of orderly finance and international billion-dollar deals.

City panorama, as seen from Lloyd's of London.

DOCKLANDS AND THE RIVER

The river Thames is a ribbon of liquid history, both for the city of London and for Great Britain. Grain Spit, Deadman's Point and Mucking flats witnessed the arrival of all those people who have contributed to the composition of the English – the Celts, Romans, Anglos, Saxons, Jutes, Danes, and Vikings. Shoeburyness, Sheerness and Sheppey watched the Elizabethan explorers sail out centuries later to stick the Union Jack in various far-off corners of the world.

Between 1860 and 1900 the British reaped the harvest of the empire. London's trade trebled and its docklands became the warehouse of the world. The massive dock system had 55 miles of wharf and quay within minutes of the city centre.

The importance of the river declined through the first half of the 20th century. However, its significance increased for a different reason in World War II: the Thames acted as a flight path for German bombers. Today helicopters are allowed to fly lower over the river than over the rest of the metropolis, and flights heading for Heathrow airport follow its route.

Boat trips covering the river upstream as far as Hampton Court and downstream to Greenwich run from Kew, Putney, Westminster, Tower and Greenwich piers. A fast river bus service started in 1988.

Docklands: Over the years the advent of larger and larger vessels and containerisation killed off the once mighty docklands. The Pool of London, the stretch of water between London Bridge and Tower Bridge, used to be a massive parking lot for boats. Today, practically no cargo moves over the wharves. The dockland cranes are silent; warehouses have crumbled and sagged, and lock gates have rotted on their hinges. The warehouse of the world became the backyard to the City that no-one liked to look at, although eager film crews travelled from Hollywood to shoot scenes from various disaster films amidst the dereliction.

In 1981 Billingsgate Market, the home of fresh fish and foul language, moved from the Pool of London in the city's financial centre to a new site. Billingsgate's move was one of the first in a massive redevelopment of the 25 sq. miles (65 sq. km) of docklands.

The government earmarked £350 million for the regeneration of the area, and set up the London Docklands Development Corporation (LDDC) to oversee it. In the first six years of the LDDC's operation another £3.5 billion of private money was pumped into the area, attracted by such incentives as a property taxes amnesty for businesses which relocated to Docklands. Newham and Tower Hamlets, two of London's poorest boroughs, will be awash with cash once the amnesty is over.

Property boom: Land values within

Docklands have changed enormously. A prime site that was valued at £70,000 per acre in 1981 increased to £3 million by 1987, and then slumped massively. Property prices read like telephone numbers. In a 26-flat development next to Tower Bridge, two-bedroom flats were priced at between £300,000 and £800,000, with the top penthouse valued at £2.5 million. Space is so valuable that units erected in the mid-1980s were replaced with taller buildings within a couple of years.

The development corporation believes that the new water city will be London's major tourist attraction of the 1990s, but the beginning of the decade saw a big slow-down in the development of the area, partly because of the property market's stagnation and partly because of the lack of adequate transport facilities. Docklands remains a massive construction site in which thousands of people live and work.

Docklands is worth visiting, even if just viewed through the window of the high-tech **Docklands Light Railway**, which runs at the command of a computer rather than a driver over much of the developed **Isle of Dogs**. The once marshy area was used by Henry VIII for hunting, and supposedly his hunting dogs gave the area its name. Certainly it has the most dramatic view of any train ride within London.

The LDDC divides the area into four sections: Wapping, the Isle of Dogs, the Royal Docks on the north bank and the Surrey Docks on the south.

Piazzas with pizzazz: Notable in **Wapping** is **St Katharine's Dock**, the last to fall into dereliction in the 1950s and the first to be refurbished as a tourist attraction. Captain Scott and his ship the *Discovery* set sail from here on their disastrous voyage to the North Pole.

The **Prospect of Whitby**, along Wapping High Street past atmospheric refurbished warehouses, dates from 1520 and is probably London's oldest pub still in use.

Regent's Canal slips almost unno-

The Thames Barrier at Woolwich.

ticed into the Thames at Limehouse. Built in 1812, it makes a complete loop around North London. Canal barge trips are available from Regent's Park.

The controversial **Canary Wharf** complex boasts London's tallest tower at 800ft (244m). It was originally planned to have 75 restaurants, but a year after opening its owners were bankrupt and much of its space, both office and retail, was still unlet. The tower dominates the view from Christopher Wren's beautiful Royal Naval College at Greenwich, which is just over the river. The little-used Greenwich foot tunnel, opened in 1902, has begun to carry a growing tide of new visitors. The Docklands **Visitor Centre** at 3 Lime Harbour arranges tours and has displays relevant to both tourists and potential tenants.

Dock flights: So far development within the **Royal Docks** has been largely residential. However it is also the site of the **London City Airport**, with scheduled flights to UK and north-ern European destinations. The airport, aimed particularly at businessmen, is served by small aircraft only, with strict noise limits.

The massive **Thames Barrier**, which protects 45 sq. miles (117 sq. km) of the City from flooding, spans the river by the Royal Victoria Dock. In 1953, 300 people died in disastrous floods. With southeast England subsiding at a rate of 12 inches (30 cm) every 100 years the situation will not improve. The barrier was finished in 1982, at a cost of £435 million. It has a visitor centre on the south side.

Over the river in **Surrey Docks,** the massive new and aesthetically pleasing shopping centre **Hay's Galleria** (off Tooley Street near the London Dungeons) forms part of London Bridge City. The fascinating working sculpture in the centre is called "The Navigators". It is the work of Cornwall-based sculptor David Kemp and took a year to build.

The river: Commenting on the Thames, Julius Caesar said it "could

The Docklands Light Railway glides above the new water city.

only be forded at one place and that with difficulty". Time has marched on, and the stretch of tidal water from Tower Bridge to Teddington lock now has 27 bridges and 11 tunnels, although not all are in public use.

Tower Bridge dating from 1894, has become a symbol of London. During the days when London was a flourishing port, it lifted open several times a day. Nowadays openings are rare. The view from the high walkways is magnificent on a clear day. Initially these walkways were intended to allow pedestrians to cross whilst the bridge was up, but they were closed for a long time because of the number of suicides and the night-time population sleeping rough. The bridge now houses an exhibition and museum.

Ordinary-looking, though more exotic in historical terms is **London Bridge**, the fifth to be built on this site. The first, built in AD 43, was for 1,700 years the only place where the river was spanned. The second bridge, built in 1176, was heavy with shops and houses, and the tax paid by the occupants kept the bridge open. It also acted as an effective dam for the river, which became so slow moving that it regularly froze over in the winter. Frost Fairs were held on its surface. Unfortunately the slow movement of the river could not cope with the increasing drainage demands made on it, and in the summer it smelt strongly of sewage.

Banking solution: In 1870 the engineer Sir Joseph Bazalgette solved two massive problems – the increasing congestion of the city and the overwhelming stink of the river – with the new **Victoria Embankment**.

This roadway, which runs from Blackfriars to Westminster, was built over the mudflats of the river. The Embankment contains sewage pipes and Underground lines and carries a substantial road and gardens. Its size is indicated by the present position of the Strand, which used to run along the water's edge. Lost to sight, however,

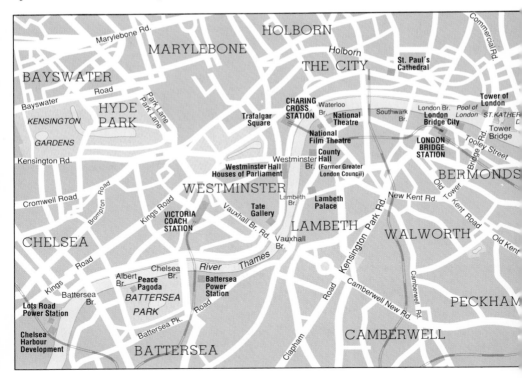

are the old watergates to riverside buildings such as Somerset House.

Moored on the Embankment next to **Waterloo Bridge** (built largely by women during World War II) are various boats converted into restaurants and bars, including a Thames sailing barge. These latter used to be very common on the river. They have the largest sail area of any boat crewed only by a skipper and his boy. Many are preserved by large companies and compete in annual races on the river.

The **South Bank Arts Centre** dominates the view from the deck of the Wilfred. The **National Theatre** was built at a cost of £17 million, and contains three theatres. Also within the complex is the **Hayward Gallery**, home to many modern art exhibitions, the **National Film Theatre**, the **Museum of the Moving Image** and the **Royal Festival Hall.** Under the arches of these austere, arty buildings is a cardboard city of houses for the down-and-outs, grouped around the heating ventilators. Many critics consider the South Bank buildings ugly and there is a plan afoot to place a single roof over the lot of them.

The next road bridge upstream is **Westminster Bridge**, with the oppressive building of County Hall on the south side and the Houses of Parliament on the north. **Westminster Pier** is the central point for the river's boat trips. Above it, on the corner of the bridge, is a statue of Queen Boadicea, one of London's earliest celebrities. The statue has been much criticised, especially because the chariot has no reins. One archaeologist described it as an "armoured milkfloat" when it was first unveiled. **County Hall** was the headquarters of the Greater London Council until it was disbanded. The imposing building contains 7 miles (11 km) of corridors. It is to become a hotel.

Terraces: Between the Houses of Parliament and the water's edge is a hidden terrace where Members of Parliament take tea and no doubt discuss the truths

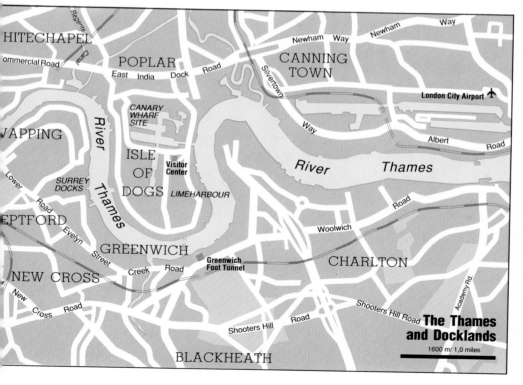

The Thames and Docklands

1600 m / 1,0 miles

behind government. Previous buildings were not so well protected from the river. In 1236 the Thames rose, flooding the building. The water level in the corridors was so high that you could row down them.

On the southern end of **Lambeth Bridge** two pillars are topped with the shapes of pineapples in memory of famous gardener John Tradescant, who first introduced the fruit to this country. The church of **St Mary**, by the bridge end, is now a gardening museum. Next to the church are the gates to **Lambeth Palace**, largely invisible from the road, which is the London seat of the Archbishop of Canterbury, who is the head of the Church of England. Parts of the Palace date from 1490.

Prison site: Further upstream on the north bank is the **Millbank Tower**, once heralded as the highest building in London, but now much overshadowed. Next to it is the **Tate Gallery**, built on the site of the massive Millbank penitentiary. Early in the 19th century, pris-oners sentenced for deportation to Australia embarked from here.

Some distance upriver, on the south end of the **Victoria Railway Bridge** (once the widest railway bridge in the world) is **Battersea Power Station**, a major London landmark. The building, no longer used to generate power, was in the process of being converted into a massive indoor theme park when the developer ran out of money.

The suspension bridges, **Chelsea Bridge** and **Albert Bridge**, are both lit at night, as is the **Peace Pagoda** on the river wall of Battersea Park. The pagoda was built by Japanese buddhist monks to commemorate 1985's Year of Peace.

On the north end of **Battersea Bridge** is the largest collection of houseboats moored on the river. Rates for these moorings are high and the boats themselves sell for upwards of £75,000. Upriver from the boats is Lots Road Power Station, which provides independent electricity supply for the city's Underground network. Alongside is the **Detail from Chelsea Bridge.**

new development of **Chelsea Harbour**. The development surrounds a marina, and now commands very high property prices. It also boasts the world's largest car park.

Boat races: Industry lines the banks to **Putney**, which is the start of the **University Boat Race**, an annual competition between the universities of Oxford and Cambridge. The race between the two opposing rowing eights was started in 1829 and still attracts media attention. It is rowed upstream, with the tide.

In early days the race was umpired from a rowing boat manned by Thames watermen, who managed to keep pace with the university gentlemen. The watermen have their own single scull race between London Bridge and Chelsea, raced on much rougher water against the tide. Sadly this **Doggett's Coat and Badge Race** has waned in recent years as the number of true watermen has dwindled.

Riverside walks: The waterside becomes increasingly green further upriver. Bomb damage from World War II was limited here, and riverside malls at Hammersmith and Chiswick remain unspoilt, with some of the most elegant housing in London. **Strand on the Green** boasts a fine pair of waterside pubs, the **Bull's Head** and the **City Barge**, both over 350 years old and ideal for a summer riverside drink.

The trees of **Kew Gardens** line the southern bank beyond Kew bridge to Richmond, matched by the gardens of **Syon House** on the north. The bridge in this elegant outer London community dates from 1774, and is the oldest still in use on the river. The 18th-century **Marble Hill Park** and House, beyond Richmond, are open to the public, although most riverboat passengers who get this far will finally disembark at **Hampton Court Palace**.

Walking tour: The riverboat is not the only way to enjoy the Thames. It is possible to walk the length of the river from Tower Bridge to Hampton Court. Towpaths begin at Putney.

County Hall, former headquarters of London's local government.

DAY TRIPS

London's need for breathing space has long been recognised. Thankfully, planning authorities have jealously guarded the "Green Belt" which surrounds the capital from hands of developers. It is still possible to escape fairly quickly from the city's streets into the countryside. Planning restrictions have forced property values in the Green Belt ridiculously high and farmers in Kent can no longer afford to insure their barns because they are worth so much.

Tube country: Some excellent countryside is even reachable by Underground. The last remnant of a once vast Royal hunting preserve, **Epping Forest** still has hundreds of rare deer. **Epping** itself is an interesting country town straggling along the old London to Newmarket main road. It is on the Central Line and the trains run overground for the last dozen or so miles.

Further out is delightful **Chipping Ongar**. One of the prettiest small towns in rural Essex, it is worth visiting for the nearby Saxon church at **Greensted**.

The Central Line also reaches into the countryside to the northwest where **Chesham** and **Amersham** are good starting points for a country ramble in the **Chiltern Hills**. Most of London's countryside is beyond reach of the Underground but regular London Transport Green Line buses and British Rail trains provide a good service.

Going south: Down in Kent, the picturesque small town of **Westerham** is full of historical interest. It was here that General Wolfe stayed before embarking on his conquest of Quebec. Sir Winston Churchill's country home at **Chartwell** is just down the road and open to visitors.

Sadly, the hurricanes of October 1987 and January 1990 destroyed many of the superb trees for which London and the surrounding countryside were so well known. Among the victims were the fine old specimens which gave **Sevenoaks** (like Westerham, best reached by train) its name, but this lovely town still has plenty to offer.

Knole is one of the great stately homes of England, built by Thomas Bouchier, the Archbishop of Canterbury, between 1456 and 1486, and later lived in by Thomas Cranmer from whom it was appropriated by Henry VIII. The house contains a wealth of fine furniture and one of the largest extant collections of period tapestries, rugs and bed hangings.

Closer to London and even grander than Knole is **Hampton Court**, (reached by train from Waterloo); another vast house which Henry VIII took over from a disfavoured courtier, Cardinal Wolsey. Most of the palace is the creation of architect Sir Christopher Wren, working in the 17th century on behalf of King William III (William of Orange) and his Queen Mary (the daughter of James II, the Jacobean king whom he deposed).

Intended to rival Versailles, Hampton Court is not quite as grand but does feature imposing state rooms, fine mature gardens on the banks of the Thames and an extensive maze. The palace has not been used by a reigning monarch since George II's death in 1760. However, it still remains a symbol of regal splendour, despite a fire in 1989 that destroyed part of the roof.

Castles: Particularly fascinating for those interested in England's once turbulent history are some fine castles within easy reach of London. **Leeds Castle**, near Maidstone in Kent (served by British Rail) has been described as "the most perfect castle in the world". Still occupied and set like a jewel in a placid moat, Leeds was transformed by Henry VIII from a Norman fortress into a magnificent royal palace.

Another monument to suffer recently from fire is **Windsor Castle** (accessible by coach excursions and rail), still a favourite residence of the Royal Family. William the Conqueror commenced fortification here in 1066, immediately after defeating King Harold at the Battle of Hastings. The present stone castle was begun 100 years later by Henry II.

It was here that Edward III founded the prestigious Order of the Garter in 1348, giving special status to the castle in which he had been born. Queen Victoria also had a special love for Windsor and she is buried, along with her beloved Albert, at the **Frogmore Mausoleum**, about a mile away.

Though overshadowed by its vast castle, **Windsor** is a vibrant town in its own right. It boasts a waxworks and a restored Victorian railway station as well as pleasant riverside walks. Take the bridge across the Thames to **Eton**, famed for its public school that nourishes the nation's future leaders – hence the old saying that Britain's wars were won on the playing-fields of Eton.

Spreading to the south and west of Windsor, the **Great Park** offers unspoilt woodland and parkland.

A gaunt ruin, **Rochester's** huge cas-

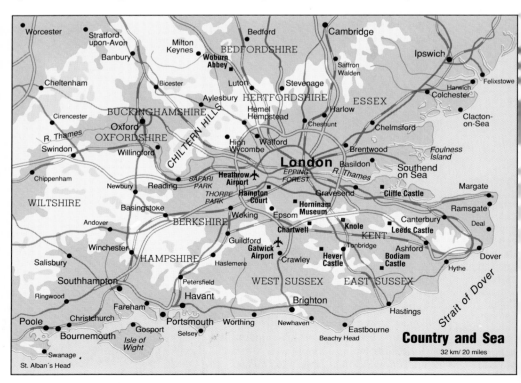

tle stands brooding over this **Medway** town, 30 miles (48 km) east of London from London Bridge station. Home to Charles Dickens for many years, his novels were set here and the town still has a Dickensian atmosphere. Here there is a fine **Dickens museum.** In the winter when Medway is covered with snow, the quaint old High Street can look like the archetypal Dickens Christmas card.

Near Rochester, but far less accessible out on the Kent marshes, **Cliffe Castle** is worth a visit though you can only admire it from outside.

The castle at the Sussex seaside resort of **Hastings** is less satisfying, being a total ruin. Better to visit **Bodiam,** a bit further inland, which reflects a castle's original role as a fortress rather than a stately home, or quaint **Hever Castle** near **Edenbridge** in Kent. Hever was the family home of Anne Boleyn who lost her head, figuratively and literally, to Henry VIII.

Worlds of adventure: Children enjoy the attractions of **Thorpe Park**, a lively theme park situated just where the M25 orbital motorway crosses the Wessex-bound M3. There are dozens of different rides (all included in the admission price), but there can be long waits for the more popular ones.

Located on the fringe of the Surrey countryside near Kingston, **Chessington World of Adventure** is a fun fair and zoo combined, with features like a runaway goldrush mine train and the Safari Skyrail monorail.

Run by the London Zoological Society, **Whipsnade Wild Animal Park** covers 500 acres (200 hectares) of chalk downs at the eastern end of the Chiltern Hills near Dunstable. Steam trains run through the "plains of Asia" and there are dolphin and bird of prey shows.

A similar wildlife park with additional funfair is the **Wild Animal Kingdom** at **Woburn Abbey**, just off the M1, 45 miles north of London.

In pre-war times, Londoners who could not afford a proper holiday would

take their families hop picking in **Kent**, a county often described as "the garden of England". Nowadays trips to the countryside are centred around more leisurely pursuits such as watching cricket on the village green and sampling ale and rough "scrumpy" cider in the local pub.

By the seaside: An old fashioned seaside is still a favoured weekend pastime for Londoners. The seafronts of London's favourite resorts (all best reached by rail) are now somewhat seedy and run down, though efforts are being made to smarten them up. **Brighton's** long-time derelict **West Pier**, for instance, is currently subject to redevelopment plans. Apart from the beach, Brighton offers interesting shopping. The web of old-fashioned pedestrianised streets known as **The Lanes** are a mass of antique shops, booksellers and souvenir stores. The main shopping area has branches of all the big national chain stores.

The exotic Indian-style **Royal Pavil-ion** was built between 1787 and 1822. It was originally intended as a summer home for the Prince Regent who, more than anyone else, made Brighton a fashionable resort. The interior has more of a Chinese feel with its luxurious furnishings.

An important conference hall capable of seating up to 5,000 delegates, the **Brighton Centre** also hosts concerts by major international stars and big sporting events. The **Theatre Royal**, established in 1806, is one of Britain's most lovely provincial theatres.

Brighton's other attractions include an aquarium and dolphinarium, a fine racecourse high on the South Downs and one of Europe's largest marinas, with moorings for 1,800 yachts.

Eastbourne, to the east of Brighton, is a more gentle resort, much favoured by retired people. It has good concert facilities, an interesting lifeboat museum, and a heritage museum. The **Redoubt Fortress**, an impressive citadel, was built to defend against invasion during the Napoleonic wars; as were the numerous **Martello Towers** seen along the Sussex and Kent coasts.

Northwards, up the coast, **Broadstairs**, is the quietest of the three main Isle of Thanet resorts. The other two are Margate and Ramsgate. The resort is proud of its Dickensian connections and **Bleak House** can still be seen perched on its clifftop.

On the Essex coast, **Southend On Sea** is a mere shadow of what it was years ago. Hundreds of charabancs (motor buses) full of day-trippers used to flock to the resort to see the famous Southend Lights. Each autumn the town's seafront was lit up in a spectacular display.

In Town: If you do not want to stray to the coast or the open countryside, London's outer suburbs have much to offer. At **Hendon**, in North London, is the impressive **RAF Museum** which houses warplanes of every vintage. A special attraction is the evocative Battle of Britain display, complete with appro-

priate noises of bomb blasts and warning sirens. The **Horniman Museum** in **Forest Hill** has a marvellous collection of natural history exhibits put together last century by a tea magnate.

Further afield but within a two-hour train ride are cities such as Cambridge (served by Liverpool Street station), Oxford (Paddington), Winchester (Waterloo) and Canterbury (Charing Cross), all of which make interesting all-day outings.

Henry James called **Oxford** "the finest thing in England" and John Keats was even more smitten, declaring it "the finest city in the world". Coach-loads of tourists seem to agree as they troop respectfully round the University's three dozen colleges, some of which have been centres of learning for seven centuries. There's something about the light in Oxford, reflecting off the ancient stones, that gives it a unique allure.

The town's setting is equally magical. Oxford is not a large place and you don't need to climb far up one of its dreaming spires in order to spy the green countryside which encircles it. The **Cotswolds** beckon, their showpiece villages appearing to grow out of the earth, so perfect is their relationship with the landscape.

Winchester is now very much a refined country town, but it was once the capital of England (in Saxon times) from which King Alfred unified the Anglo-Saxon nation for the first time in the face of Danish invasions. The town is compact and boasts enticing alleyways and shopping streets. For those interested in archaeology, Winchester is the site of a most ambitious dig.

Canterbury, like Winchester, has an importance in English history which far exceeds its size. The cathedral was where Thomas Beckett was martyred and is one of the finest religious buildings in Europe. It is surrounded by interesting buildings from every period of English history, including some with Roman mosaics. The city's ancient walls are virtually intact to this day.

197

INSIGHT GUIDES
Travel Tips

FOR THOSE
WITH MORE THAN
A PASSING INTEREST
IN TIME...

Before you put your name down for a Patek Philippe watch *fig. 1*, there are a few basic things you might like to know, without knowing exactly whom to ask. In addressing such issues as accuracy, reliability and value for money, we would like to demonstrate why the watch we will make for you will be quite unlike any other watch currently produced.

"Punctuality", Louis XVIII was fond of saying, "is the politeness of kings."

We believe that in the matter of punctuality, we can rise to the occasion by making you a mechanical timepiece that will keep its rendezvous with the Gregorian calendar at the end of every century, omitting the leap-years in 2100, 2200 and 2300 and recording them in 2000 and 2400 *fig. 2*. Nevertheless, such a watch does need the occasional adjustment. Every 3333 years and 122 days you should remember to set it forward one day to the true time of the celestial clock. We suspect, however, that you are simply content to observe the politeness of kings. Be assured, therefore, that when you order your watch, we will be exploring for you the physical—if not the metaphysical— limits of precision.

Does everything have to depend on how much?

Consider, if you will, the motives of collectors who set record prices at auction to acquire a Patek Philippe. They may be paying for rarity, for looks or for micromechanical ingenuity. But we believe that behind each $500,000-plus

bid is the conviction that a Patek Philippe, even if 50 years old or older, can be expected to work perfectly for future generations.

In case your ambitions to own a Patek Philippe are somewhat discouraged by the scale of the sacrifice involved, may we hasten to point out that the watch we will make for you today will certainly be a technical improvement on the Pateks bought at auction? In keeping with our tradition of inventing new mechanical solutions for greater reliability and better time-keeping, we will bring to your watch innovations *fig. 3* inconceivable to our watchmakers who created the supreme wristwatches of 50 years ago *fig. 4*. At the same time, we will of course do our utmost to avoid placing undue strain on your financial resources.

Can it really be mine?

May we turn your thoughts to the day you take delivery of your watch? Sealed within its case is your watchmaker's tribute to the mysterious process of time. He has decorated each wheel with a chamfer carved into its hub and polished into a shining circle. Delicate ribbing flows over the plates and bridges of gold and rare alloys. Millimetric surfaces are bevelled and burnished to exactitudes measured in microns. Rubies are transformed into jewels that triumph over friction. And after many months—or even years—of work, your watchmaker stamps a small badge into the mainbridge of your watch. The Geneva Seal—the highest possible attestation of fine watchmaking *fig. 5*.

Looks that speak of inner grace *fig. 6*.

When you order your watch, you will no doubt like its outward appearance to reflect the harmony and elegance of the movement within. You may therefore find it helpful to know that we are uniquely able to cater for any special decorative needs you might like to express. For example, our engravers will delight in conjuring a subtle play of light and shadow on the gold case-back of one of our rare pocket-watches *fig. 7*. If you bring us your favourite picture, our enamellers will reproduce it in a brilliant miniature of hair-breadth detail *fig. 8*. The perfect execution of a double hob-nail pattern on the bezel of a wristwatch is the pride of our casemakers and the satisfaction of our designers, while our chainsmiths will weave for you a rich brocade in gold *figs. 9 & 10*. May we also recommend the artistry of our goldsmiths and the experience of our lapidaries in the selection and setting of the finest gemstones? *figs. 11 & 12*.

How to enjoy your watch before you own it.

As you will appreciate, the very nature of our watches imposes a limit on the number we can make available. (The four Calibre 89 time-pieces we are now making will take up to nine years to complete). We cannot therefore promise instant gratification, but while you look forward to the day on which you take delivery of your Patek Philippe *fig. 13*, you will have the pleasure of reflecting that time is a universal and everlasting commodity, freely available to be enjoyed by all.

Should you require information on any particular Patek Philippe watch, or even on watchmaking in general, we would be delighted to reply to your letter of enquiry. And if you send

fig. 1: The classic face of Patek Philippe.

fig. 4: Complicated wristwatches circa 1930 (left) and 1990. The golden age of watchmaking will always be with us.

fig. 6: Your pleasure in owning a Patek Philippe is the purpose of those who made it for you.

fig. 9: Harmony of design is executed in a work of simplicity and perfection in a lady's Calatrava wristwatch.

fig. 2: One of the 33 complications of the Calibre 89 astronomical clock-watch is a satellite wheel that completes one revolution every 400 years.

fig. 5: The Geneva Seal is awarded only to watches which achieve the standards of horological purity laid down in the laws of Geneva. These rules define the supreme quality of watchmaking.

fig. 7: Arabesques come to life on a gold case-back.

fig. 10: The chainsmith's hands impart strength and delicacy to a tracery of gold.

fig. 3: Recognized as the most advanced mechanical regulating device to date, Patek Philippe's Gyromax balance wheel demonstrates the equivalence of simplicity and precision.

fig. 8: An artist working six hours a day takes about four months to complete a miniature in enamel on the case of a pocket-watch.

fig. 11: Circles in gold: symbols of perfection in the making.

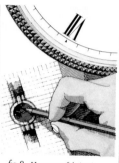

fig. 12: The test of a master lapidary is his ability to express the splendour of precious gemstones.

✣
PATEK PHILIPPE
GENEVE
fig. 13: The discreet sign of those who value their time.

So, you're getting away from it all.

Just make sure you can get back.

AT&T Access Numbers
Dial the number of the country you're in to reach AT&T.

*AUSTRIA†††	022-903-011	*GREECE	00-800-1311	NORWAY	800-190-11
*BELGIUM	0800-100-10	*HUNGARY	00◇-800-01111	POLAND¹◆³	0◇010-480-0111
BULGARIA	00-1800-0010	*ICELAND	999-001	PORTUGAL¹	05017-1-288
CANADA	1-800-575-2222	IRELAND	1-800-550-000	ROMANIA	01-800-4288
CROATIA¹◆	99-38-0011	ISRAEL	177-100-2727	*RUSSIA¹ (MOSCOW)	155-5042
*CYPRUS	080-90010	*ITALY	172-1011	SLOVAKIA	00-420-00101
CZECH REPUBLIC	00-420-00101	KENYA¹	0800-10	SOUTH AFRICA	0-800-99-0123
*DENMARK	8001-0010	*LIECHTENSTEIN	155-00-11	SPAIN•	900-99-00-11
*EGYPT¹ (CAIRO)	510-0200	LITHUANIA◆	8◇196	*SWEDEN	020-795-611
*FINLAND	9800-100-10	LUXEMBOURG	0-800-0111	*SWITZERLAND	155-00-11
FRANCE	19◇-0011	F.Y.R. MACEDONIA	99-800-4288	*TURKEY	00-800-12277
*GAMBIA	00111	*MALTA	0800-890-110	UK	0500-89-0011
GERMANY	0130-0010	*NETHERLANDS	06-022-9111	UKRAINE¹	8◇100-11

Countries in bold face permit country-to-country calling in addition to calls to the U.S. **World Connect℠** prices consist of **USADirect**® rates plus an additional charge based on the country you are calling. Collect calling available to the U.S. only. *Public phones require deposit of coin or phone card. ◇ Await second dial tone. ¹May not be available from every phone. †††Public phones require local coin payment through the call duration. ◆ Not available from public phones.• Calling available to most European countries. ¹Dial "02" first, outside Cairo. ³Dial 010-480-0111 from major Warsaw hotels. ©1994 AT&T.

Here's a travel tip that will make it easy to call back to the States. Dial the access number for the country you're in to get English-speaking AT&T operators or voice prompts. Minimize hotel telephone surcharges too.

If all the countries you're visiting aren't listed above, call **1 800 241-5555** for a free wallet card with all AT&T access numbers. Easy international calling from AT&T. **TrueWorld Connections.**

AT&T

TRAVEL TIPS

Getting Acquainted

202 The Place
202 Government
202 Climate
202 Time
202 Business Hours
202 Public Holidays

Planning the Trip

202 Visas & Passports
203 Money Matters
203 Health
203 Customs
203 Getting There

Practical Tips

204 Loss
204 Left Luggage
204 Tipping
205 Media
205 Postal Services
205 Telephones
206 Tourist Information
206 Embassies

Getting Around

206 Driving
207 Public Transport
208 Underground Tube Map

Where to Stay

209 Hotels
214 Youth Hostels
214 A Place of Your Own

Eating Out

215 Restaurant Listings
221 Drinking Notes

Attractions

222 Tours
224 Other Visits
225 Museums
227 Art Galleries
228 Historical Houses
229 Concerts
230 Ballet
230 Opera
230 Theatre
231 Cinema
231 Diary of Events
232 Architecture
233 Other Attractions
235 Nightlife
237 Cabaret
237 Casinos
237 Round-the-Clock
238 Shopping
239 Clothing
241 Antiques
242 Art
243 Sports

Further Reading

244 Other Insight Guides

Art/ Photo Credits

Index

Getting Acquainted

The Place

London, situated on the tidal River Thames 40 miles (64 km) from its estuary, covers 610 sq. miles (1,580 sq. km) and has a population of just under 7 million. The population has been declining in recent years as manufacturing firms have closed or moved out, but it is still a leading financial, insurance and corporate centre.

Thanks to its location, you can probably find more nationalities in London at any given time than in any other city, even New York. Many are visitors, since tourism is a major business. But many are members of immigrant groups from Britain's former colonies, especially from the Indian subcontinent and the West Indies.

Specific groups often congregate in particular areas of town: blacks in Brixton, for example, Australians in Earls Court, Irish in Kentish Town, Jews in Golders Green. London has often been described as a series of villages – which, in fact, it once was until they eventually merged into one another – and each "village" possesses its own distinctive characteristics.

Government

When people refer to London, they mean the county of Greater London. When they speak of the City of London, they generally mean the financial district, the historic square mile east of St Paul's Cathedral which is governed by the Corporation of London, headed by the Lord Mayor, and which even has its own police force. The rest of the metropolis is run by 12 inner boroughs and 20 outer boroughs, each of which is responsible for local services.

Lodon is one of the few major capitals which has no overall elected administration. The Greater London Council used to fulfil this role until Margaret Thatcher's government, deeming it to be too left-wing, abol-ished it in the 1980s and sold its splendid Thames-side headquarters to Japanese investors. Many feel that Greater London's planning and services would be better coordinated if the body was restored.

Climate

The English are justly famous for their preoccupation with the weather, a fascination which is largely due to its unpredictable nature. The climate in London is mild, with the warming effects of the city itself keeping off the worst of the cold in winter.

Snow and temperatures below freezing are unusual, with January temperatures averaging 43°F/6°C. Temperatures in the summer months, average 64°F/18°C, but they can soar, causing the city to become airlessly hot (air-conditioning is rare).

However, temperatures can fluctuate considerably from day to day and surprise showers catch people unawares all year round. Therefore visitors should come prepared with wet weather clothes whatever the season. Generally speaking, short sleeves and a jacket are fine for summer, but a warm coat and woollens are recommended for the winter.

The London "smogs" beloved of old Hollywood movies are long gone, thanks to the passing of Clean Air legislation in the 1950s and 1960s which stopped chimneys belching out smoke.

For recorded weather information, tel: 01898-141214.

Time

British time is governed by Greenwich Mean Time (GMT). Zones west of the Greenwich Meridian (located in south-east London) are ahead in time and those to the east are behind. British Summer Time (BST) begins in March when the nation puts its clocks forward one hour and ends in October when clocks go back to GMT.

Most of Continental Europe is one hour ahead of Britain.

Some time differences:
Athens (+2), Brasilia (–3), Buenos Aires (–3), Canberra (+10), Hong Kong (+8), Jerusalem (+2), Moscow (+3), Los Angeles (–8), New Delhi (+2), New York (–5), Pretoria (+2), Rio de Janeiro (–2), Singapore (+8), Sydney (+10), Tokyo (+9), Washington DC (–5), Wellington (+12)

Business Hours

Shop and office hours in London are usually 9 or 9.30am–5.30pm Monday–Saturday. Shops in the centre of town rarely close for lunch and may stay open later, particularly around Covent Garden and Piccadilly Circus. Increasing numbers of shops are open on Sunday, particularly supermarkets and large warehouse stores away from the centre. Late-night shopping until as late as 8pm is on Thursday in Oxford and Regent streets and on Wednesday in Knightsbridge and Kensington.

Public Holidays

New Year's Day, Good Friday, Easter Monday, May Day (first Monday in May), Spring Bank Holiday (last Monday in May), August Bank Holiday (last Monday in August), Christmas Day, Boxing Day.

Planning The Trip

Visas and Passports

You need a valid passport (or any form of official identification if a citizen of the European Union) to enter the UK. Visas are not needed if you are an American, EU national (or come from most other European or South American countries), or are a Commonwealth citizen. Health certificates are not required unless you have arrived from Asia, Africa or South America.

If you wish to stay for a protracted period or apply to work in Britain, contact the Home Office, 50 Queen Anne's Gate, SW1, tel: 0171-273 3000.

A Wise Man Never Thinks How Far He's Come. He Thinks How Far He Can Still Travel.

REMY **XO BECAUSE LIFE IS WHAT YOU MAKE IT**

American Express offers Travelers Cheques built for two.

Cheques *for Two*℠ from American Express are the Travelers Cheques that allow either of you to use them because both of you have signed them. And only one of you needs to be present to purchase them.

Cheques *for Two* are accepted anywhere regular American Express Travelers Cheques are, which is just about everywhere. So stop by your bank, AAA* or any American Express Travel Service Office and ask for Cheques *for Two*.

Money Matters

Most banks are open between 9.30am–4.30pm Monday–Friday, with Saturday morning banking being slowly introduced. The major English banks tend to offer similar exchange rates; it's only worth shopping around if you have large amounts of money to change. Banks charge no commission on travellers cheques presented in sterling. If a London bank is affiliated to your own bank back home, it will make no charge for cheques in other currencies either. However, there will be a charge for changing cash into another currency.

Some High Street travel agents, like Thomas Cook, operate **bureaux de change** at comparable rates. These have the advantage of being open during shop hours, Monday–Saturday. There are also a great many privately run bureaux de change all over London. However, you should be wary of changing money at them – rates can be very low and commissions high. If you do have to use one, try to ensure it's carrying a London Tourist Board code of conduct sticker. For those who are truly desperate for cash, there are various 24-hour bureaux de change located in central London. **Chequepoint** is a reputable chain with branches at Piccadilly Circus, Leicester Square, Marble Arch, Bayswater Underground and Victoria mainline station.

International credit cards are widely accepted in shops, hotels and restaurants in London. However, there are some notable exceptions, and many a visitor has been embarrassed at the check-out of Marks & Spencer. Eurocheques are gaining in popularity; look out for the EC sticker in shop and restaurant windows. Most hotels will accept them.

Health

If you fall ill and are an EC national, you are entitled to free medical treatment for illnesses arising while in the UK. Many other countries also have reciprocal arrangements for free treatment. However, most visitors will be liable for medical and dental treatment and should ensure they have adequate health insurance.

In the case of a serious accident or emergency, dial 999. In the case of minor accidents, your hotel will know the location of the nearest hospital with a casualty department. If you sprain your wrist in the street, hail a cab. Amazingly, cab drivers seem to know just about everything.

Chemists: Boots is a large chain of pharmacies with numerous branches throughout London that will make up prescriptions. The branch at 75 Queensway, W2 is open until 10pm daily whilst Bliss Chemist at Marble Arch is open until midnight daily.

Customs

There are no restrictions on the amount of British or foreign currency you can bring into the country.

Following the introduction of the European Union's Single Market in 1993 there are no longer any official restrictions on the movement of goods within the community, provided those goods were purchased within the EU. However, British Customs have set the following "guide levels" on the following: cigarettes 800 pieces; cigarillos 400 pieces; cigars 200 pieces; tobacco 1kg; spirits 10 litres; fortified wines etc 20 litres; wine 90 litres and beer 110 litres. EU nationals no longer need to exit through a red or green channel.

Travellers from further afield are subject to the following allowances: 1 litre of spirits, or 2 litres of fortified or sparkling wine, or 2 litres of table wine (an additional 2 litres of still wine if no spirits are purchased); plus 200 cigarettes or 100 cigarillos, or 30 cigars, or 250g of tobacco; plus 60cc perfume, 250cc toilet water.

The following are **prohibited entry** into the United Kingdom: plants and perishable foods such as meats and meat products, eggs, fruit; some drugs (check with your doctor if you need to bring strong medication with you on your trip); firearms and ammunition brought without special arrangement; animals, and obscene film/written material.

Getting There

By Air

London is served by two major international airports: Heathrow to the west (mainly scheduled flights) and Gatwick to the south (charter flights), with the smaller airports of Stansted and Luton to the northeast. There is also the tiny London City Airport in Docklands, a few miles from the City, used by small aircraft connecting London with European capitals.

Arriving at **Heathrow airport** can be a demanding experience (the walk to the central building from an international gate can seem like miles). It's important to plan how you'll get into central London in advance. It may be a further trek through a maze of passages, but the **Underground** (usually known as the **Tube**) is the simplest way. It takes around 45 minutes, costs around £3, and no change of train is needed. The Piccadilly line, which runs from Heathrow to Kensington, Knightsbridge, Park Lane (Hyde Park Corner) Piccadilly, Covent Garden and Bloomsbury (Russell Square) operates as early as 5am (6am on Sunday) until 11.40pm daily.

London Regional Transport (LRT) runs an **Airbus** service with red double decker buses picking up from all Heathrow terminals; the A1 goes to Victoria, via Earls Court and Knightsbridge, while the A2 goes to Euston via Marble Arch and Baker Street. Buses leave at half-hour intervals from 6.30am–10.15pm daily, take about an hour and stop at major hotels on the way. A single fare costs £5 and can be purchased from the driver who will accept sterling and American dollars. For 24-hour Airbus travel information, tel: 0171-222 1234.

Heathrow is also well-served for **taxis**. A ride into town in a familiar London "black cab" will cost upwards of £30. Don't get into a private or unlicensed "minicab" unless you're prepared to spend a lot more.

If you want to hire a car, the following are the Heathrow offices of major **car rental** companies:
Avis tel: 0181-897 9321; Budget Rentacar tel: 0181-759 2216; Europcar tel: 0181-897 0811; Hertz tel: 0181-679 1799; Swan National Eurodollar tel: 0181-897 3232.

Gatwick airport isn't on the Underground network, but it has sophisticated train and coach services into London running to and from Victoria. The **Gatwick Express** leaves every 15 minutes from 5.30am–9pm, otherwise every hour round the clock. It takes just half an hour and costs £8.60 one way.

Flightline 777 coaches leave from both the North and South terminals and take about 70 minutes to reach Victoria. A single fare is £7.50. Green Line also operates Jetlink and Speedlink services between Heathrow and Gatwick. Tel: 0181-668 7261.

National Express run a coach service connecting Heathrow, Gatwick, Stansted and Luton airports with each other and the first three airports with Victoria. Enquiries and credit card bookings, tel: 0171-730 0202.

Car rental from Gatwick: Avis, tel: 01293-29721; Budget Rentacar., tel: 01293-540141; Europcar, tel: 01293-31062; Hertz, tel: 01293-30555; Swan National Eurodollar, tel: 01293-513031.

Luton Airport is served with a regular train service to St Pancras Station, taking 45 minutes, and the Luton and District bus service to London taking 70 minutes (tel: 01582-404074).

From **Stansted Airport** a direct rail link goes straight in to Liverpool Street Station every half-hour, with a journey time of 41 minutes.

London City Airport is badly served by transport despite its close proximity to the City (6 miles/10 km). There is a courtesy bus to the Docklands Light Railway, which then links with the Underground network. A courtesy bus also links with the River Bus at Canary Wharf, with departures every half hour from 7am until 8pm. The River Bus runs upstream to Charing Cross, Waterloo and Chelsea, and downstream to Greenwich. Ticket price is £3 to Charing Cross, tel: 0171-987 0311 for information. Reduced frequency at weekends.

It's worth stopping off at the **Tourist Information Centres** (TICs) at Heathrow or Gatwick if you have time. The London Tourist Board produces a pack, free to visitors, which is full of interesting and useful information. At Heathrow the TIC is at the entrance to the Underground for terminals 1, 2 and 3.

Numbers for flight information:
Heathrow:
Terminal 1: tel: 0181-745 7702
Terminal 2: tel: 0181-745 7115
Terminal 3: tel: 0181-745 7412

Terminal 4: tel: 0181-745 4540.
Gatwick Airport, tel: 01293-535353
Luton Airport, tel: 01582-405100
Stansted Airport, tel: 01279-680500
London City Airport, tel: 0171-474 5555

By Channel Tunnel

The Channel Tunnel opened in late 1994, providing Eurostar passenger services by rail from Paris Nord (3 hours, tel: Paris 1-45 82 50 50) and Brussels Midi (3 hours 15 minutes, tel: Brussels 22 48 856) to London's Waterloo Station. UK bookings, tel: 011233 617575. Vehicles are carried by train through the tunnel from Folkestone in Kent to Nord-Pas de Calais in France. Bookings not essential; just drive up. Enquiries in France: (33) 21 00 60 00) and in UK, (44) 1303-271100.

By Ferry

Would the Channel Tunnel kill off the ferries? Such a demise, in fact, was never likely since the sea services operating between 12 British ports and more than 20 Continental ones were able to compete on price and, before the long delayed tunnel opened, lavishly refurbished their vessels. Also, for many people, arriving by boat has a sense of occasion that can never be matched by an underground train.

Ferry crossings from the Continent are operated by the following companies:

Sealink Stena. (UK tel: 01233 647047) sails to Dover from Calais (33-21 46 80 00), to Newhaven from Dieppe (33-50 63 90 00), and to Southampton from Cherbourg (33-33 20 43 38).

Brittany Ferries (UK tel: 01705-827701) sails to Portsmouth from St Malo (33-99 82 80 80) and Caen (33-33 22 38 98), to Poole in Dorset from Cherbourg (33-33 22 38 98), and to Portsmouth or Plymouth, depending on season, from Santander in Spain (34-42 214 5000).

P&O European Ferries (UK tel: 0181-575 8555) sails to Dover from Calais (33-21 46 04 40), and to Portsmouth from Cherbourg (33-33 88 65 70) and Le Havre (33-35 19 78 50).

Sally Line (UK tel: 01843-595522)

sails to Ramsgate in Kent from Dunkirk (33-28 21 43 44) and Ostend (32- 59 55 99 66).

Hoverspeed (UK tel: 01304-240241) runs a hovercraft service to Dover from Calais (33-21 46 14 14).

Seacat (UK tel: 01304-240241) has a fast service to Folkestone from Boulogne (33- 21 30 27 26).

Practical Tips

Loss

If you can't find a policeman, dial 192 and ask for the number of the nearest police station. Don't call the emergency number 999 unless there has been a serious crime or accident. If your passport has been lost, let your Embassy know as well.

For possessions lost on public transport, contact London Transport Lost Property, 200 Baker Street, NW1 5RZ (tel: 0171-486 2496) between 9.30am and 2pm Monday–Friday, or fill in an enquiry form, available from any London Underground station or bus garage. Allow 2 full working days to elapse after the loss before making a visit. If you left something in a taxi, the Taxi Lost Property office is at 15 Penton Street, N1 9PU, tel: 0171-833 0996.

Left Luggage

Most of the main British Rail (BR) stations have left luggage departments where you can leave your suitcases on a short term basis, although all are very sensitive to potential terrorist bombs. These left luggage offices close at 10.30pm with the exception of Euston (open 24 hours) and Paddington (open until midnight).

Tipping

Most hotels and many restaurants automatically add 10–15 percent service charge to your bill. It's your right to deduct it if you're not happy with the service. Sometimes when service has been added, the final to-

Swatch. The others just watch.

seahorse/fall winter 94-95

Don't be overcharged for overseas calls.

Save up to 70% on calls back to the U.S. with WorldPhone.®*

While traveling abroad, the last thing you need to worry about is being overcharged for international phone calls. Plan ahead and look into WorldPhone – the easy and affordable way for you to call the U.S. and country to country from a growing list of international locations.

Just dial 1-800-955-0925 to receive your free, handy, wallet-size WorldPhone Access Guide – your guide to saving as much as 70% on phone calls home.

When calling internationally, your WorldPhone Access Guide will allow you to:

- Avoid hotel surcharges and currency confusion
- Choose from four convenient billing options
- Talk with operators who speak your language
- Call from more than 90 countries
- Just dial and save – regardless of your long distance carrier back home

WorldPhone is easy. And there's nothing to join. So avoid overcharges when you're traveling overseas. Call for your free WorldPhone Access Guide today – before you travel.

Call 1-800-955-0925.

THE TOP 25 WORLDPHONE COUNTRY CODES.

COUNTRY	WORLDPHONE TOLL-FREE ACCESS #
Australia (CC)♦	
To call using OPTUS■	008-5511-11
To call using TELSTRA■	1-800-881-100
Belgium (CC)♦	0800-10012
China (CC)	108-12
(Available from most major cities)	
For a Mandarin-speaking Operator	108-17
Dominican Republic	1-800-751-6624
El Salvador♦	195
France (CC)♦	19▼-00-19
Germany (CC)	0130-0012
(Limited availability in eastern Germany.)	
Greece (CC)♦	00-800-1211
Guatemala♦	189
Haiti (CC)+	001-800-444-1234
Hong Kong (CC)	800-1121
India (CC)	000-127
(Available from most major cities)	
Israel (CC)	177-150-2727
Italy (CC)♦	172-1022
Japan♦	
To call to the U.S. using KDD■	0039-121
To call to the U.S. using IDC■	0066-55-121

COUNTRY	WORLDPHONE TOLL-FREE ACCESS #
Japan (cont'd.)	
To call anywhere other than the U.S.	0055
Korea (CC)	
To call using KT■	009-14
To call using DACOM■	0039-12
Phone Booths+	Red button 03, then press*
Military Bases	550-2255
Mexico ▲	95-800-674-7000
Netherlands (CC)♦	06-022-91-22
Panama	108
Military Bases	2810-108
Philippines (CC)♦	
To call using PLDT■	105-14
To call PHILCOM■	1026-12
For a Tagalog-speaking Operator	108-15
Saudi Arabia (CC)+	1-800-11
Singapore	8000-112-112
Spain (CC)	900-99-0014
Switzerland (CC)♦	155-0222
United Kingdom (CC)	
To call using BT ■	0800-89-0222
To call using MERCURY■	0500-89-0222

(CC) Country-to-country calling available. May not be available to/from all international locations. Certain restrictions apply.

+ Limited availability.

▼ Wait for second dial tone.

▲ Rate depends on call origin in Mexico.

■ International communications carrier.

♦ Public phones may require deposit of coin or phone card for dial tone.

WORLDPHONE℠ From MCI

Let it take you around the world.

tal on a credit card slip will still be left blank, the implication being that a further tip is expected. In London, you don't tip in pubs, cinemas, theatres or elevators. You do tip hairdressers, sightseeing guides, railway porters and cab drivers. They get around 10 percent.

Media

Newspapers

There's no lack of choice. Politically speaking, the *Daily Telegraph* and *The Times* are on the right, *The Independent* is in the middle, and *The Guardian* is on the left. On Sunday *The Observer* is more liberal than the *Sunday Times*, *Independent on Sunday* and *Sunday Telegraph*. The *Financial Times* is renowned for the clearest, most unslanted headlines in its general news pages (plus, of course, its exhaustive financial coverage).

The tabloids are the smaller ones. *The Sun* and *The Star* are on the right (and obsessed with royalty, soap operas and sex), ditto the Sunday *News of the World*. The *Daily Sport* likes sex and flying saucers. The *Daily Mirror* and *Sunday Mirror* are left-ish, as is the Sunday *People*. The *Daily Mail* and *Mail on Sunday* are slightly more upmarket equivalents of the right-wing *Daily Express* and *Sunday Express*. *Today* is Rupert Murdoch's presence in the middle market.

Editions of the London-only *Evening Standard* come out Monday-Friday from late morning and are good for cinema and theatre listings.

Listings magazine: Supreme in this field is the long-established weekly *Time Out*.

Foreign newspapers and magazines: These can be found at many street news-stands, at mainline stations, and at the following outlets:

John Menzies: 104 Long Acre, WC2, tel: 0171-240 7645.

Capital Newsagents: 48 Old Compton Street, W1, tel: 0171-437 2479.

A Moroni & Son: 68 Old Compton Street, W1, tel: 0171-437 2847.

Selfridges: Oxford Street, W1, tel: 0171-629 1234.

Eman's: 123 Queensway, W2, tel: 0171-727 6122.

Gray's Inn News: 50 Theobald's Road, WC1, tel: 0171-405 5241.

Radio

Many new commercial stations have sprung up in London in recent years. Among the most popular are:

Capital Radio – 95.8FM, 24-hour pop.

Capital Gold – 1548AM, 24-hour golden oldies.

LBC Newstalk – 97.3FM, news, discussions, phone-ins.

JFM – 102.2FM, started life as Jazz FM but has broadened its interest to include soul and blues.

Kiss FM – 100FM, 24-hour dance.

The BBC still offers stiff competition with the following advertising-free stations:

Radio 1 – 98.8 FM, mainstream pop.

Radio 2 – 89.2FM, easy-listening music, light chat shows.

Radio 3 – 91.3FM, classical music, serious drama.

Radio 4 – 93.5FM, heavyweight discussions, news, current affairs and plays.

Radio 5 – 909MW, rolling news, sport.

GLR (Greater London Radio) – 94.9FM, London-oriented music and chat.

BBC World Service - broadcasts international news worldwide.

Television

Britain has a reputation for broadcasting some of the finest television in the world. There are four national channels, BBC1, BBC2, ITV and Channel 4 (C4). Both the BBC (British Broadcasting Corporation) and ITV (Independent Television) have regional stations throughout the country which broadcast local news and varying programme schedules in between links with the national networks based in London. The BBC is financed by compulsory annual television licences (anyone with a TV set must buy one) and therefore does not rely on advertising for funding. The independent channels, ITV and C4, are funded entirely by commercials.

BBC1 and ITV broadcast programmes aimed at mainstream audiences; BBC2 and C4 cater for arts, cultural and minority interests. However, with the advent of a host of satellite and independent franchising, things are forecast to change in the future as stations become more commercially motivated and biased towards gaining high audience ratings, with pro-

grammes such as soap operas, game shows and situation comedies.

The pricier hotels rooms will often offer a choice of cable stations such as CNN.

Postal Services

Post offices are open 9am–5pm Monday–Friday, 9am–noon Saturday. Stamps are available from post offices and selected shops, usually newsagents, and from machines outside most post offices. Within the UK sending a letter first class costs 25 pence and second class, which is slower, costs 19 pence. These are increased by weight.

A letter weighing less than 10 grammes to a destination outside Europe costs 41p.

London's main post office is at Trafalgar Square, situated on the east side behind the church of St Martin in the Fields. It stays open until 8pm Monday–Saturday. Beware, queues tend to be long over the lunch period.

Telephones

It is usually cheaper to use a public telephone than the one in your hotel room as some hotels make high profits out of this service.

There are two separate telephone companies, British Telecom (BT) and Mercury, plus various mobile phone companies. Public telephones are operated by BT and make no charge for service calls such as directory enquiries. An increasing number of kiosks will accept only plastic phone cards (which resemble credit cards and mean that you don't have to carry pockets full of heavy change); these cards are widely available from post offices and newsagents in varying amounts between £1 and £20. Credit card phones can be found at major transport terminals.

Central London numbers have the prefix 0171 and outer areas 0181. You need use these codes only when calling from one area to the other.

Useful numbers

Emergency – police, fire, ambulance: **999**

Operator (for difficulties in getting through): **100**

Directory Enquiries: **192**
Directory Enquiries (for international
    telephone numbers): **153**
London Regional Transport
    24-hr information: **0171-222 1234**
Speaking Clock: **123**
Talking Pages : **0171-600 9000**

International Calls

You can telephone abroad directly
from any phone. Dial **00** followed by
the international code for the country
you want, and then the number. Some
country codes: Australia (61); France
(33); Germany (49); Italy (39); Japan
(81); Netherlands (31); Spain (34);
US and Canada (1).

    If using a US credit phone card, dial
the relevant company's access
number as follows – Sprint, tel: 0800-
890877; MCI, tel: 0800-890222;
AT&T, tel: 0800-890011. (For Mercury
phones, replace 0800 with 0500.)
    The International Operator is on
155. Operator-assisted calls are more
expensive. To send telegrams (now
called telemessages), dial 190.

Information by Phone

The following provide useful information to visitors in London:
London Tourist Board, tel: 0171-730
3488. For accommodation, tel: 0171-
824 8844. For information about England in general, tel: 0171-824 8000.
British Travel Centre, 12 Regent
Street, W1. Tel: 0171-730 3400.
Leisureline for recorded information
of events; English, tel: 0171-246
8041, French, tel: 0171-246 8043,
German, tel: 0171-246 8045.
Arts Council of Great Britain for exhibition information. Tel: 0171-629
9495.
National Trust for information on
stately homes. Tel: 0171-222 9251.
British Rail information: Paddington
tel: 0171-262 6767; Kings Cross tel:
0171-278 2477; Euston tel: 0171-
387 7070; Victoria and Waterloo tel:
0171-928 5100.

Tourist Information

To contact the London Tourist Board
for information before your visit, write
to them at: 26 Grosvenor Gardens,
Victoria, London SW1W 0DU, tel:
0171-730 3488. In London, their

main centre is the Victoria Station
office. These tourist information centres (TICs) can book hotels in London
and tours for people who come to
their office. The Victoria Station office
also makes theatre bookings and hotel reservations within England, and
sells tourist tickets.
Heathrow TIC: In the Underground
station foyer for terminals 1–3. Daily
8am–6pm.
Selfridges TIC: Selfridges, Oxford
Street, W1. Open during store hours.
Liverpool Street Stn TIC: In the Underground station, EC2. Open
8.15am–7pm daily and until 4.45pm
on Sunday.
Victoria Station TIC: Victoria Station
forecourt, SW1. Open daily 8am–7pm
Easter–1 November, and 9am–7pm
throughout the rest of the year. (9am–
5pm on Sunday in winter).

Embassies

Austria: 18 Belgrave Mews West,
SW1.
Tel: 0171-235 3731.
Brazil: 32 Green Street, W1. Tel:
0171-499 0877.
Denmark: 55 Sloane Street, SW1.
Tel: 0171-333 0200
Egypt: 26 South Audley Street, W1.
Tel: 0171-499 2401.
Finland: 66 Chesham Place, SW1.
Tel: 0171-235 9531.
France: 58 Knightsbridge, SW1.
Tel: 0171-235 8080.
Germany: 23 Belgrave Square, SW1.
Tel: 0171-235 5033.
Greece: 1A Holland Park, W11. Tel:
0171-229 3850.
Hong Kong: 6 Grafton Street, W1.
Tel: 0171-499 9821.
Iceland: 1 Eaton Terrace, SW1. Tel:
0171-730 5131.
Indonesia: 38 Grosvenor Square,
SW1.
Tel: 0171-499 7661.
Ireland: 17 Grosvenor Place SW1.
Tel: 0171-235 2171.
Israel: 2 Palace Green, Kensington
Palace Gardens, W8. Tel: 0171-957
9500.
Italy: 14 Three Kings Yard, W1. Tel:
0171-629 8200.
Japan: 101 Piccadilly, W1. Tel: 0171-
465 6500.
Kuwait: 45 Queen's Gate, SW7. Tel:
0171-589 4533.
Mexico: 42 Hertford Street, W1.

Tel: 0171-499 8586.
Netherlands: 38 Hyde Park Gate,
SW7.
Tel: 0171-584 5040
Norway: 25 Belgrave Square, SW1.
Tel: 0171-235 7151
Poland: 47 Portland Place, W1. Tel:
0171-580 4324.
Portugal: 11 Belgrave Square, SW1.
Tel: 0171-235 5331.
Russian Federation: 5 Kensington
Palace Gardens, W8. Tel: 0171-229
8027.
Saudi Arabia: 30 Charles Street, W1.
Tel: 0171-917 3000.
Spain: 24 Belgrave Square, SW1.
Tel: 0171-235 5555.
Sweden: 11 Montagu Place, W1. Tel:
0171-724 2101.
Switzerland: 16 Montagu Place, W1.
Tel: 0171-723 0701.
United States 24 Grosvenor Square,
W1.
Tel: 0171-499 9000.

Getting Around

Driving

If you're only staying a short while in
the Greater London area, and are un-
familiar with the geography of the capital, don't hire a car. Central London
is now more than ever a nightmare to
drive in, with its web of one-way
streets, bad signposting, and impa-
tient drivers who will cut you up at the
first hesitation (taxi drivers in particular seem to regard hesitation as virtually a capital offence).
    Parking is a major problem in con-
gested central London. Meters are
slightly cheaper than NCP car parks,
but only allow parking for a maximum
of two or four hours. If parking at a
meter, keep your wits about you. Do
not leave your car parked a moment
longer than your time allows and do
not return and insert more money
once your time has run out. These are
considered offences for which you
can face a fine in the region of £30
and there are plenty of thorough and

THOMAS COOK MASTERCARD TRAVELLERS CHEQUES...

...HOLIDAY ESSENTIALS

Travel money from the travel experts

THOMAS COOK MASTERCARD TRAVELLERS CHEQUES ARE
WIDELY AVAILABLE THROUGHOUT THE WORLD.

INSIGHT GUIDES

North America
160 Alaska
173 American Southwest
184I Atlanta
227 Boston
275 California
180 California, Northern
161 California, Southern
237 Canada
184C Chicago
184 Crossing America
243 Florida
240 Hawaii
275A Los Angeles
243A Miami
237B Montreal
184G National Parks of America: East
184H National Parks of America: West
269 Native America
100 New England
184E New Orleans
184F New York City
133 New York State
147 Pacific Northwest
184B Philadelphia
172 Rockies
275B San Francisco
184D Seattle
Southern States of America
186 Texas
237A Vancouver
184C Washington DC

Latin America and The Caribbean
150 Amazon Wildlife
260 Argentina
188 Bahamas
292 Barbados
251 Belize
217 Bermuda
127 Brazil
260A Buenos Aires
162 Caribbean
151 Chile
281 Costa Rica
282 Cuba
118 Ecuador
213 Jamaica
285 Mexico
285A Mexico City
249 Peru
156 Puerto Rico
127A Rio de Janeiro
116 South America
139 Trinidad & Tobago
198 Venezuela

Europe
155 Alsace
158A Amsterdam
167A Athens
263 Austria
107 Baltic States

219B Barcelona
1187 Bay of Naples
109 Belgium
135A Berlin
178 Brittany
109A Brussels
144A Budapest
213 Burgundy
122 Catalonia
141 Channel Islands
135E Cologne
119 Continental Europe
189 Corsica
291 Côte d'Azur
165 Crete
226 Cyprus
114 Czech/Slovak Reps
238 Denmark
135B Dresden
142B Dublin
135F Düsseldorf
149 Eastern Europe
148A Edinburgh
123 Finland
209B Florence
154 France
135C Frankfurt
135 Germany
148B Glasgow
279 Gran Canaria
124 Great Britain
167 Greece
166 Greek Islands
135G Hamburg
144 Hungary
256 Iceland
142 Ireland
209 Italy
202A Lisbon
258 Loire Valley
124A London
201 Madeira
219A Madrid
157 Mallorca & Ibiza
117 Malta
101A Moscow
135D Munich
158 Netherlands
111 Normandy
120 Norway
124B Oxford
154A Paris
115 Poland
202 Portugal
114A Prague
153 Provence
177 Rhine
209A Rome
101 Russia
130 Sardinia
148 Scotland
261 Sicily
264 South Tyrol
219 Spain
220 Spain, Southern
101B St. Petersburg
170 Sweden
232 Switzerland

112 Tenerife
210 Tuscany
174 Umbria
209C Venice
263A Vienna
267 Wales
183 Waterways of Europe

Middle East and Africa
268A Cairo
204 East African Wildlife
268 Egypt
208 Gambia & Senegal
252 Israel
236A Istanbul
252A Jerusalem-Tel Aviv
214 Jordan
270 Kenya
235 Morocco
259 Namibia
265 Nile, The
257 South Africa
113 Tunisia
236 Turkey
171 Turkish Coast
215 Yemen

Asia/Pacific
287 Asia, East
207 Asia, South
262 Asia, South East
194 Asian Wildlife, Southeast
272 Australia
206 Bali Baru
246A Bangkok
234A Beijing
247B Calcutta
234 China
247A Delhi, Jaipur, Agra
169 Great Barrier Reef
196 Hong Kong
247 India
212 India, South
128 Indian Wildlife
143 Indonesia
278 Japan
266 Java
203A Kathmandu
300 Korea
145 Malaysia
218 Marine Life in the South China Sea
272B Melbourne
211 Myanmar
203 Nepal
293 New Zealand
205 Pakistan
222 Philippines
250 Rajasthan
159 Singapore
105 Sri Lanka
272 Sydney
175 Taiwan
246 Thailand
278A Tokyo
255 Vietnam
193 Western Himalaya

merciless traffic wardens in this city ready to give you a ticket. Meter parking is free after 6.30pm each evening, after 1.30pm in most areas on Saturday afternoons and all day Sunday. However, always check the details given on the meter.

Don't ever leave your car on a double yellow line. If you escape a ticket, it is probably only because you have been clamped instead. Clamping, whereby your vehicle is rendered completely immobile until you pay to have it released some hours later, is now an epidemic in London. If your car disappears consult a policeman as it will most likely have been towed away to a car pound. To retrieve it will cost you £95 plus the £30 parking fine. Don't take the risk!

When driving in England you should drive on the left-hand side of the road and observe the speed limits: 30 mph (50 kph) in urban areas (unless otherwise indicated), 60 mph (100 kph) on normal roads away from built-up areas and 70 mph (112 kph) on motorways and dual carriageways (divided highways). It is strictly illegal to drink and drive and penalties are severe. The law also states that drivers and passengers (front-seat and back-seat) must wear seat belts. Failure to do so can result in a fine. For further information on driving in Britain consult a copy of the *Highway Code*, widely available in bookshops.

Car Rental

To rent a car in Britain you must be over 21 years old and must have held a valid full driving licence for more than a year. The cost of hiring a car will usually include insurance and unlimited free mileage. It does not, however, include insurance cover for accidental damage to interior trim, wheels and tyres or insurance for other drivers without prior approval. It can be worth shopping around as some companies offer special weekend and holiday rates.

Car rental companies: The following selection are all members of the London Tourist Board:

Europcar Interrent, tel: 0171-834 8484 (SW1)

Alamo Car Rentals, tel: 0171-408 1255 (W1)

Eurodollar, tel: 0171-730 8773 (SW1)

Hertz Rentacar, tel: 0171-679 1799

Avis, tel: 0171-848 8733

Weekly hire rates start at around £170.

24-hour petrol stations in London:
– Underground car park, Park Lane, W1
– 170 and 195 Marylebone Road, NW1
– 383 Edgware Road, W2
– Chelsea Cloisters Garage, Sloane Avenue, SW3.

Car Breakdown

The following motoring organisations operate 24-hour breakdown assistance. All telephone calls to these numbers are free:

AA, tel: 0800-887766

RAC, tel: 0800-828282

National Breakdown, tel: 0800-400600

Public Transport

The Tube

The **Underground** (colloquially known as the **Tube**, *see map overleaf*) is the quickest way to get across London and every kind of Londoner uses it from school children to grand old ladies who failed to catch a cab. In the rush hours between 8am–9.30pm and 5–6.30pm every station is packed with workers keen to get home; they cram into carriages like sardines in a tin. The Underground starts at 5.30am and runs until the last trains start their final journeys at around midnight.

Make sure you have a valid ticket and keep hold of it after you have passed it through the electronic barrier – you will need it to exit at your destination. Note that on-train inspectors charge anyone without a valid ticket £10, payable on the spot. There is no flat-fare system throughout London, though a £1 fare operates within the central zone.

It is illegal to smoke within the Underground system or on the buses.

The downside of being the world's oldest underground railway – the first trains puffed through smoke-filled tunnels between Paddington and Farringdon in 1863 – is that the system

has become noticeably creaky. Lack of investment during the 1980s has meant that trains and station escalators increasingly break down and it is only because of the docility of English commuters that there aren't more public protests about the inadequacy of the service. More money is now being spent, however – the first signs are in refurbished stations – and better things are promised for the future.

The **Docklands Light Railway** (tel: 0171-918 4000) opened in 1987, and is one of the best (and cheapest) ways to see the old but revived docks area. This fully automated service runs from Bank station (where it links with the Underground network) all the way up to Stratford, east London. The second branch line starts from Island Gardens, on the Isle of Dogs, close to the Greenwich foot tunnel.

The railway is part of London Regional Transport and operates like the Tube, with similar fares. Expect some weekend disruption of service (buses are provided), as the line is being upgraded to cope with the increased number of passengers. Some of the views along the routes are superb.

Buses

London buses follow the same working pattern as the Underground although their routes are intended to supplement the Tube lines. The Night Buses take over the most popular routes running hourly throughout the night. Trafalgar Square is their starting point; a full bus route map and Night Buses leaflet are available at travel information centres. Night buses are a lifesaver for nightclubbers and lovers of romantic after-theatre suppers who can't afford a taxi home, but on weekends thousands of people congregate in Trafalgar Square and your bus journey home could be spent wedged between very loud and very drunk people.

Sightseeing tours

One of the best ways for first-time visitors to orient themselves is to take a special one-hour or two-hour ride on a double-decker tour bus. Some are open-topped so that, weather permitting, you can enjoy fresh air and unin-

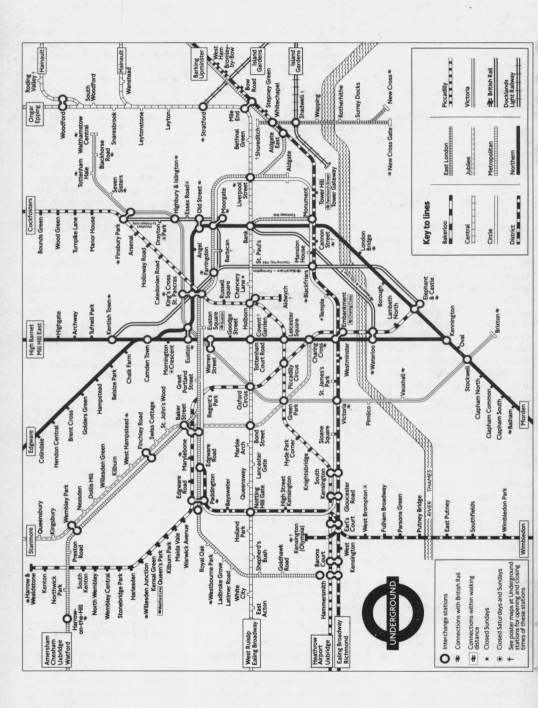

terrupted camera angles. Others allow to jump off at various stops and catch a later bus without buying an additional ticket.

You can begin the tours at many points around London, such as Marble Arch or Trafalgar Square.

For further details and telephone numbers, see the *Tours* entry in the "Attractions" section.

Taxis

Taxis in London are licensed and display the regulated charges on the meter. If you should have a complaint, make a note of the driver's license number and contact the Carriage Office, tel: 0171-230 1631. Remember if you telephone for a taxi you will be charged for the time and miles it takes to pick you up as well. Minicabs are unlicensed, and can only be hired by telephoning for one; they're not allowed to compete with the black cabs for business on the streets.

London black cab drivers are well trained, having had to complete a rigorous study of London's streets, called "The Knowledge", before they can take to the road. Minicabs, however, as a rule are cheaper but are unlikely to know precise destinations. They are also more likely to charge what they think fit.

Travel Passes

The Travelcard is a day pass that allows you unlimited travel on the Tube, buses, Docklands Light Railway and British Rail's Network SouthEast for a fixed fee of £3.80 (all zones) or £2.80 (zones 1 & 2). The Travelcard can be used after 9.30am on weekdays and all day Saturday, Sunday and public holidays. Available from all Underground and Network SouthEast stations and some newsagents.

Travel Passes are valid for a week (£31.20 all zones) or a month (£119.90 all zones) and can be used at any time. To buy a Pass you will need to supply a passport-sized photograph.

Day Trips: Rail

These are the principal British Rail stations in London, with the areas they serve.

Charing Cross Station, Victoria, Waterloo. Tel: 0171-928 5100. Services to South London and the South of England.
Euston Station, St Pancras, Marylebone. Tel: 0171-378 7070. Services to North West London and beyond to Liverpool, Glasgow.
Kings Cross Station. Tel: 0171-278 2477. Services to North London and beyond to York, Edinburgh and Aberdeen.
Liverpool Street Station, Fenchurch St. Tel: 0171-928 5100. Services to East, North East London and East Anglia.
Paddington Station. Tel: 0171-262 6767. Services to West London and beyond to Oxford, Bristol, and the west.
Victoria Station. 0171-928 5100. Services to south London and southeast England, including Gatwick airport, Brighton and Dover.
Waterloo Station. 0171-928 5100. Services to southwest London, Southampton, and southern England as far as Exeter.

Day Trips: Coach

Coach travel in England is considerably cheaper than travelling by train. **National Express** runs a comprehensive service throughout the country leaving from Victoria Coach Station, Buckingham Palace Road, SW1. Tel: 0171-730 0202.

For day trips out of town to places such as Oxford, the Cotswolds, Stratford-upon-Avon, Canterbury, Windsor and Hampton Court, try **Green Line Coaches** (tel: 0181-668 7261) which also leave from Victoria. For guided tours to such destinations, try **London Coaches** (operated by London Regional Transport, tel: 0181-877 1722), **Golden Tours** (tel: 0181-743 3300), **Frames Rickards** (tel: 0171-837 3111) or **Cityrama** (tel: 0171-627 8512). These operators also provide guided tours of London.

Where to Stay

The feeling is that London hotels are getting better. Some couldn't get better, like the Berkeley and the Connaught, many are getting better, and some are just being "improved." It's always sad to see tatty but charming London landmarks dressed up with mock velvet and theme bars by the giant hotel chains.

Generally, though, facilities are becoming more international in standard, and this is good news for business travellers at least. Business visitors are now the dream customer of most luxury class hotels. Conference rooms, secretaries and fax machines are everywhere. Business visitors are wanted. They may not stay long, but they use hotel facilities to the fullest. Partly propelled by business incentives, the hotel restaurant is once again being taken seriously by London gourmets. They're attracting serious chefs, serious eaters, and serious Michelin stars – the restaurants within the Dorchester, the Connaught, the Capital, and the Britannia, particularly so.

Prices in London for decent, comfortable hotel accommodation are high. Whatever your income, up to £300 for one night's bed and breakfast for two is a lot to pay. If a clean room and a hot breakfast in a central location is all you ask, you can get it for a tenth of the price. For a truly English experience, a more moderately priced hotel can often be better. It's certainly smaller, yes, but it comes with a friendly smallness.

There are hotels everywhere in London, but some areas have more than others. SW1 is traditionally the hotel district. The area around Victoria is, of course, an established one, and there are some delightfully old-fashioned hotels here, in most price brackets, chiefly the medium range. There are streets full of terraced bed and breakfast accommodation close to Victoria Station. There are also streets full of terraced (or rather town-housed, for this is Kensington) hotels in the second big hotel area of SW5 and SW7. This zone, around Kensington High Street, Earl's Court and the Gloucester Road is another major centre for medium range hotels of dependable comfort and, at least, some style.

The West End is the third area and the best-known zone. You'll pay more for budget or moderate accommodation here than you will in SW1 or SW5 because of the location. W1 hotels at the bottom end of the price range can be *very* humble. WC1 is a clever choice: it's central and has reasonable prices, and there is still some dignity, even romance, in Bloomsbury (don't expect to find either of these qualities in Oxford Street).

The following listings are arranged into price brackets. The categories are based on one night's accommodation for one person, exclusive of breakfast. Generally you can get whatsoever your heart desires in expensive hotels. In budget accommodation, you're not paying for a view, and if you get one it's a bonus.

Book ahead. London fills up in the summer months (May and September are particularly crowded because of conference traffic), but if you arrive without a reservation, head straight for a Tourist Information Centre. The London Tourist Board operates an efficient bed-booking service. Nevertheless, 18 million visitors a year do not fit easily into 150,000-odd registered beds, especially when so many visitors want to arrive at the same time.

Service is usually included in the bill. No extra tip is necessary, but if you wish to repay particularly good service, 10 percent split between the deserving is the custom. Equally, you can insist that service be deducted if you feel you've been treated less than impressively.

Ensure when booking that the price quoted is inclusive, and isn't going to be bumped up by a mysterious "travellers' charge" or other extras on the final bill. If you reserve in advance, you may be asked for a deposit. Bear in mind that reservations made, whether in writing or by telephone, can be regarded as binding contracts,

and you could be prosecuted for failing to honour that contract by not turning up on the day. In many hotels you'll find it's standard practice to vacate rooms by midday on the day of departure.

Finally, make the most of your hotel. Many offer a wide range of services to their guests – free information, theatre ticket booking, etc., all of which are much harder to obtain on the street.

Price categories (based on single occupancy without breakfast): £ = under £40; ££ = £41–69; £££ = £70–109; ££££ = over £110

Top Class

Berkeley Hotel, Wilton Place, SW1X 7RL. Tel: 0171-235 6000. Many rate the Berkeley as the best in London. It's low key, seldom advertised, with a country house atmosphere. Not a business hotel. Swimming pool. A lot of English customers. ££££

Claridges, Brook Street, W1A 4ZX. Tel: 0171-629 8860. Has long had a reputation for dignity and graciousness. ££££

The Dorchester, Park Lane, W1A 2HJ. Tel: 0171-629 8888. One of the most expensive in London. Lovely views over Hyde Park. ££££

Hyatt Carlton Tower, 2 Cadogan Place, SW1X 9PY. Tel: 0171-235 5411. Luxury hotel away from the bright lights of Park Lane with a health centre. Knightsbridge location. Good English breakfasts. ££££

Four Seasons (Inn on the Park), Hamilton Place, Park Lane, W1A 1AZ. Tel: 0171-499 0888. Another temple of modern opulence. Friendly staff. ££££

Hotel Intercontinental, 1 Hamilton Place, Hyde Park Corner, W1V 0QY. Tel: 0171-409 3131. One of the Intercontinental hotel group, and the most opulent of the Park Lane "millionaire's row." Modern, and well equipped. Superb views over the park. ££££

Luxury

Athenaeum Hotel, 116 Piccadilly, W1V 0BJ. Tel: 0171-499 3464. Small hotel (112 rooms) in the heart of smart London, close by shops and with views over Green Park. A very

English hotel, full of character of the "gentlemen's club" kind. Excellent service. ££££

The Britannia Intercontinental, Grosvenor Square, W1A 3AN. Tel: 0171-629 9400. Modern and comfortable, with one of the best hotel restaurants in London in The Best of Both Worlds. ££££

The Churchill, 30 Portman Square, W1A 4ZX. Tel: 0171-486 5800 . Large hotel in the heart of the West End, very much geared towards the business visitor. Stylish split level bedrooms. ££££

The Connaught, Carlos Place, W1Y 6AL. Tel: 0171-499 7070. One of the best hotels in London, and very popular with British visitors. Discreet but immaculate service, superb decor (if a little gentlemen's club-ish) and a restaurant with a Michelin star. Only 110 rooms. ££££

Conrad Hotel, Chelsea Harbour, Lots Road, SW10 0XG. Tel: 0171-823 3000. Luxury hotel opened in 1990 within the exclusive Chelsea Harbour complex on the banks of the Thames. ££££

Duke's Hotel, 35 St James's Place, SW1A 1NY. Tel: 0171-491 4840. Small (64 rooms) traditional hotel in smart St James's. The courtyard is still lit by gas-lamps, and every bedroom is named after a duke. ££££

Grosvenor House Hotel, Park Lane, W1A 3AA. Tel: 0171-499 6363. Least showy of the Park Lane set, owned by the Forte chain. Large banqueting room a popular choice for smart London parties. Also has apartments for rent. ££££

Hyde Park Hotel, Knightsbridge, SW1Y 7LA. Tel: 0171-235 2000. A hotel of character, located right on Knightsbridge, close to Harrods and Hyde Park. Sumptuous in a Victorian marble-and-chandeliers style. ££££

Langham Hilton, Portland Place, London W1V 3AA. Tel: 0171-636 1000. Elegant hotel renovated to a high standard. Two bars and a good restaurant. The attractive fountain room is a good place for taking afternoon tea. 385 rooms. ££££

Le Meridien, 19-21 Piccadilly, W1V 0BH. Tel: 0171-734 8000. Traditional, smart hotel. Has its own leisure club and pool. Food is excellent. ££££

London Hilton on Park Lane, 22 Park

Lane, W1A 2HH. Tel: 0171-493 8000. Not the best of the chain. Double rooms are classed as "executive," "deluxe" or plain "superior." ££££

Mayfair Intercontinental, 28 Stratton Street, W1A 2AN. Tel: 0171-629 7777. Smart, modern hotel with popular Polynesian restaurant and its own small cinema. Top price rooms include a jacuzzi bath. ££££

Montcalm Hotel, Great Cumberland Place, W1A 2LF. Tel: 0171-402 4288. It's part of an elegant Georgian crescent. Rather plush. ££££

The Ritz, Piccadilly, W1V 9DG. Tel: 0171-493 8181
One of the most famous hotel names in the world. Not quite what it was, despite refurbishment. Jackets and ties must be worn. Tea at the Ritz available. Casino. Tel: 0171-491 4678. ££££

The Savoy, Strand, WC2R OEL. Tel: 0171-836 4343
Another of London's legends, with a solid reputation for comfort (rooms are excellent) and personal service (if a little overformal in atmosphere). Couldn't be more central, but set back from the main road. Very convenient for theatreland and Covent Garden. ££££

Sheraton Park Tower, 101 Knightsbridge, SW1X 7RN. Tel: 0171-235 8050. The modern circular tower of this popular hotel is five minutes walk from Harrods, and close to Hyde Park. Attracts a lot of business visitors. Casino next door. Friendly service. ££££

Stafford Hotel, 16 St James's Place, SW1A 1NJ. Tel: 0171-493 0111. Owned by the Cunard group, and beautifully located in its own gaslit courtyard just minutes away from Piccadilly. Good choice for those who like small hotels (74 rooms), old-fashioned service. ££££

Moderate

Blakes Hotel, 33 Roland Gardens, SW7 3PF. Tel: 0171-370 6701. Very trendy and up-to-the-minute hotel popular with theatrical and media folk. Cosmopolitan, tolerant, laid-back in style. 52 rooms. £££–££££

Brown's Hotel, Albemarle Street, W1A 4SW. Tel: 0171-493 6020. A distinguished, very British, Victorian-

style hotel, owned by the Forte Group. Smart Mayfair location. 120 rooms. £££–££££

Cadogan Thistle Hotel, Sloane Street, SW1X 9SG. Tel: 0171-235 7141. Another 19th-century style hotel, this time owned by the Thistle chain. Interesting position between Knightsbridge and Chelsea. Lily Langtry lived in what's now the bar! £££–££££

Capital Hotel, 22-24 Basil Street, SW3 1AT. Tel: 0171-589 5171. Luxurious little hotel (56 rooms) in the heart of Knightsbridge. Restrained in style, with tasteful decor, and rooms in the Laura Ashley style. Friendly service. Restaurant has Michelin star. £££–££££

Forte Crest St James's, Jermyn Street, SW1Y 6JF. Tel: 0171-930 2111. Smart but bustling location. Large and modern hotel. £££–££££

The Gloucester, 4 Harrington Gardens, SW7 4LH. Tel: 0171-373 6030. Large modern City Development Limited owned hotel just off Gloucester Road and its useful Tube station, but otherwise a rather soulless locale. The hotel itself is a bit office-like. Handy for the big museums. £££–££££

Goring Hotel, 15 Beeston Place, Grosvenor Gardens, SW1W OJW. Tel: 0171-834 8211. Family-owned (the present manager, George Goring, is last in a long line of Goring managers) delightfully traditional hotel not far from Buckingham Palace. Relaxed atmosphere. Homemade food, including the bread. £££–££££

Londoner Hotel, Welbeck Street, W1H 8HS. Tel: 0171-935 4442. Very central but quiet hotel, modern behind its Edwardian facade. 144 rooms. £££–££££

Park Lane Hotel, Piccadilly, W1Y 8BX. Tel: 0171-499 6321. Established grand hotel in a grand position, but equally gaudy. The 17th floor has spectacular views over Buckingham Palace gardens. £££–££££

Royal Court Hotel, Sloane Square, SW1W 8EG. Tel: 0171-730 9191. A stone's throw from the King's Road, and within walking distance from Harrods. A variety of eating and drinking places: the No. 12 Sloane Square restaurant, the Courts Café Wine Bar, and a "traditional English tavern". 102 rooms. £££–££££

Royal Garden Hotel, 2-24 Kensington High Street, W8 4PT. Tel: 0171-937 8000. Modern but stylish hotel overlooking Kensington Gardens, its Palace and High Street shopping. Very friendly with good facilities and food. 398 rooms. £££–££££

Royal Horseguards Thistle Hotel, Whitehall Court, SW1A 2EJ. Tel: 0171-839 3400. Unusual location, overlooking the Thames and the Royal Festival Hall. 376 rooms. £££–££££

Royal Westminster Thistle Hotel, Buckingham Palace Road, SW1W OQT. Tel: 0171-834 1821. Close to Buckingham Palace and St James's Park. Half the size of its sister above, with 134 rooms. £££–££££

St George's Hotel, Langham Place, W1N 8QS. Tel: 0171-580 0111. Forte hotel close to the BBC and Oxford Street. Impressive views from its public rooms. Only 85 rooms. £££–££££

Waldorf Hotel, Aldwych, WC2B 4DD. Tel: 0171-836 2400. This renowned Edwardian hotel is now owned by the Forte Group. Modernised with a superb location, close to Covent Garden and theatreland. £££–££££

Inexpensive

Academy Hotel, 17-21 Gower Street, WC1 6HC. Tel: 0171-631 4115. A small and welcoming Bloomsbury hotel. Licensed bar; evening meal available. 35 rooms, 5 with private bath. £££

Adelphi Hotel, 127-129 Cromwell Road, SW7 4DT. Tel: 0171-373 7177. On a busy street, but a short ride from Harrods, and the West End. Museums are within walking distance. 76 rooms. £££

Barkston Hotel, Barkston Gardens, SW5 OEW. Tel: 0171-373 7851. Set in a quiet tree-lined street, but close to the bustle of Earls Court. Meals available. 80 rooms, all with private bath. £££

Basil Street Hotel, Basil Street, Knightsbridge, SW3 1AH. Tel: 0171-581 3311. Hotel with a tremendous reputation, and certainly lots of old-fashioned charm. For those who like a country house atmosphere. Rooms and service can vary with rates. Close to Harrods. 94 rooms, 82 with private bath. £££

Bayswater Inn, 8-16 Princes Square, W2 4NT. Tel: 0171-727 8621. Situated in a quiet residential square, close by Portobello Road Market, and handy for the Underground. 127 rooms, all with private bath. £££

Charing Cross Hotel, Charing Cross, Strand, WC2N 5HX. Tel: 0171-839 7282. Located right next door to the station and Underground. Comfortable and reliable, in a busy, central location close to Covent Garden. £££

Coburg Hotel, 129 Bayswater Road, W2 4RJ. Tel: 0171-229 3654. Traditional hotel in a convenient but not quite charming neighbourhood. Recently refurbished to 4-star standard. 132 rooms, all with bathroom. £££

Commodore Hotel, 50-52 Lancaster Gate, W2 3NA. Tel: 0171-402 5291. Situated in a quiet Victorian square close to Hyde Park, only one stop from Oxford Street on the Tube. 90 rooms, including 8 family. ££

Durrants Hotel, George Street, W1H 6BJ. Tel: 0171-935 8131. A sedate, traditional hotel close to Marylebone High Street, a distinguished neighbourhood just behind Oxford Street. Reports vary on quality. £££

Eccleston Hotel, 82-83 Eccleston Square, SW1V 1PS. Tel: 0171-834 8042 . Close to Victoria station, with its own conference and banqueting facilities. 114 rooms. £££

Forte Crest Bloomsbury, Coram Street, WC1N 1HT. Tel: 0171-837 1200. Modern but pleasant hotel in a cental quiet area. Close to the British Museum. 284 rooms, all with private bath. £££

Hazlitts, 6 Frith Street, W1V 5TZ. Tel: 0171-434 1771. One of London's oldest houses, dating from 1718, unusually located in the heart of Soho. 23 rooms, all with bath and all furnished with antiques – even the baths. £££

Kennedy Hotel, Cardington Street, NW1 2LP. Tel: 0171-387 4400. Modern air-conditioned hotel located next to Euston station. 320 rooms with private bath. £££

Knightsbridge Green Hotel, 159 Knightsbridge, SW1X 7PD. Tel: 0171-584 6274. Astonishingly good value for its area, a family-run hotel. Unusual in that it consists mostly of suites, double and family-sized rooms. 23 rooms. £££

London Embassy Hotel, 150 Bayswa-ter Road, W2 4RT. Tel: 0171-229 1212. Overlooking Kensington Gardens, on the busy road leading to the West End. 195 rooms. £££

Mount Royal Hotel, Bryanston Street, W1A 4UR. Tel: 0171-629 8040. A truly central hotel, overlooking Oxford Street. Very large, with 700 rooms. £££

Norfolk Towers Hotel, 34 Norfolk Place, W2 1QW. Tel: 0171-262 3123. Elegant hotel with its own cocktail bar and restaurant, convenient for the West End attractions. 86 rooms. £££

One Cranley Place Hotel, 1 Cranley Place, SW5 0LA. Tel: 0171-589 7944. Small Chelsea hotel decorated prettily in the Laura Ashley style. 10 rooms, 6 with bath. £££

Regent Crest Hotel, Carburton Street, W1P 8EE. Tel: 0171-388 2300. Comfortable Crest hotel close to Regents' park and the zoo. 320 rooms. Special weekend break prices, up to 75 percent off normal prices. £££

Rubens Hotel, 39-41 Buckingham Palace Road, SW1. Tel: 0171-834 6600. Traditional style hotel with a newly fitted Regency Floor of 45 rooms. Smart location opposite the Royal Mews, and close to Victoria station. 188 rooms. £££

Hotel Russell, Russell Square, WC1B 5BE. Tel: 0171-837 6470. Spacious Forte hotel in the heart of Bloomsbury. Close to the British Museum and the Underground. 328 rooms, all with bath. Meals. £££

Sherlock Holmes Hotel, 108 Baker Street, W1M 1LB. Tel: 0171-486 6161. Handy for Oxford and Regent street shopping. 126 rooms. £££

Strand Palace Hotel, The Strand, WC2R 0JJ. Tel: 0171-836 8080. Massive, long-established London hotel. Terrific location, refurbished in 1992. 781 rooms. £££

Tophams, 26 Ebury Street, SW1W 1SD. Tel: 0171-730 8147. Old-style hotel with faded charm. Very popular and certainly one of the best value places to stay in London. Homely atmosphere. ££

Tower Thistle Hotel, St. Katherine's Way, E1 9LD. Tel: 0171-481 2575. A big modern hotel situated on the fringes of docklands. It's more central than it sounds, and the locale is breathtaking, with Tower Bridge and the river. Handy for the City. A brisk five-minute walk to the nearest Tube station. 826 rooms, all with private bath. Meals. £££–££££

The White House, Albany Street, Regents Park, NW1 3UP. Tel: 0171-387 1200. Nicely situated close to the park, and a few minutes from Oxford Street. Three Tube stations nearby, and Euston BR. Meals. 576 rooms. £££

Least Expensive

(Prices usually include breakfast)

Abcone Hotel, 10 Ashburn Gardens, SW7 4DG. Tel: 0171-370 3383. Not far from Kensington High Street in a pleasant, rather old-fashioned hotel district. 35 rooms, 26 with bath. ££

Airway Hotel, 29 St George's Drive, SW1V 4DG. Tel: 0171-834 0205. Pleasant hotel close to Buckingham Place, Westminster Abbey, and Harrods. Friendly service. 32 rooms, 19 with bath. ££

Andrews House Hotel, 12 Westbourne Street, Hyde Park, W2 2TZ. Tel: 0171-723 5365. Family-run, in a busy area close to Lancaster Gate, Paddington and Marble Arch. 17 rooms, 10 with bath. £

Beverley House Hotel, 142 Sussex Gardens, W2 2TZ. Tel: 0171-723 3380. Well-equipped hotel between Oxford Street and Hyde Park. 23 rooms. £

Chester House, 134 Ebury Street, SW1W 9QQ. Tel: 0171-730 3632. Bed and breakfast accommodation in a good location close to Sloane Square. 12 rooms including 2 family-sized. 4 with private bath. £££

Clearlake Hotel, 19 Prince of Wales Terrace, W8 9PQ. Tel: 0171-937 3274. Comfortable bed and breakfast in a quiet location with views of Hyde Park. 17 rooms. Good value. ££

Crescent Hotel, 49-50 Cartwright Gardens, WC1H 9EL. Tel: 0171-387 1515. Pleasantly situated in a quiet Bloomsbury crescent, with private gardens and tennis courts. 6 double, 3 single rooms en suite. ££

Curzon House Hotel, 58 Courtfield Gardens, SW5 0NF. Tel: 0171-373 6745. Economical but comfortable small hotel which is close to Gloucester Road Underground station. 2 single, 2 twin, 2 doubles, 2 triples, 9 four-bedded, 2 five-bedded dormitories costing £11–£12 a person. £

Eden House Hotel, 111 Old Church Street, SW3 6DX. Tel: 0171-352 3403. Family-run bed and breakfast hotel situated in an elegant Chelsea townhouse. 14 rooms (5 family), 8 with bath. ££

Elizabeth Hotel, 37 Eccleston Square, SW1. Tel: 0171-828 6812. Friendly hotel set in an elegant period square, only two minutes' walk from Victoria station. 40 rooms, 22 with bath. ££

Enterprise Hotel, 15-25 Hogarth Road, SW5 0QJ. Tel: 0171-373 4502. Good location close to Kensington High Steet and the Underground in a popular hotel area. 95 rooms, 63 with bath. ££

Garden Court Hotel, 30-31 Kensington Gardens Square, W2 4BG. Tel: 0171-229 2553. Friendly bed and breakfast hotel set in a traditional English garden square. 37 rooms, 12 with bath. £

Georgian House Hotel, 35 St George's Drive, SW1V 4DG. Tel: 0171-834 1438. Bed and breakfast hotel close to Victoria station. Friendly family atmosphere. 34 rooms, 21 en suite. £

Hanover Hotel, 30-32 St George's Drive, SW1V 4BN. Tel: 0171-834 0134. Friendly, privately-owned hotel in Victoria. Good English breakfast (no meals). 32 rooms. ££

Kenwood House Hotel, 114 Gloucester Place, W1H 3DB. Tel: 0171-935 3473. Friendly family-run hotel with bed and breakfast accommodation in a central location. 16 rooms, 5 family rooms. £

Hotel Lexham, 32-38 Lexham Gardens, W8 5JU. Tel: 0171-373 6471. Owner-managed hotel overlooking a garden square handy for the South Kensington museums. 66 rooms, 48 with bath. ££

London House Hotel, 81 Kensington Gardens Square, W2 4DJ. Tel: 0171-727 0696. Cheap, friendly and comfortable hotel in a pleasant location, close to public transport. 73 rooms, 26 with bath. £

Lonsdale Hotel, 9-10 Bedford Place, WC1B 5JA. Tel: 0171-636 1812. Old-established bed and breakfast hotel with real character in the heart of Bloomsbury. 34 rooms, 3 with private bath. ££

Montagu House Hotel, 3 Montagu Place, W1H 1RG. Tel: 0171-935 4632. Well-equipped bed and breakfast hotel. All rooms have TV, phones and tea-making facilities. 18 rooms (3 with baths). ££

Oliver Plaza Hotel, 33 Trebovir Road, SW5 0LR. Tel: 0171-373 7183. Bed and breakfast hotel with good service and comfortable rooms. All 35 have private baths. Good value. ££

The Regency Hotel, 19 Nottingham Place, W1M 3FF. Tel: 0171-486 5347. An elegantly converted mansion in the heart of the West End close to Regent, Oxford and Harley streets. Comfortable and well-furnished. 20 rooms. ££

Royal Adelphi Hotel, 21 Villiers Street, WC2N 6ND. Tel: 0171-930 8764. Behind Charing Cross station, and close to the Embankment Tube station and the river, in a busy little street. A short walking distance from Covent Garden and theatreland. 55 rooms, 17 with bath. ££

Stanley House Hotel, 19-21 Belgrave Road, SW1V 1RB. Tel: 0171-834 5042. Modern family-style bed and breakfast hotel. Spacious rooms. 31 rooms, 13 with bath. £

Hotel Strand Continental, 143 Strand, WC2R 1JA. Tel: 0171-836 4880. Despite the fancy name, one of the cheapest hotels in London, and one of the most central! Superb location. 22 rooms, none with private bath. No credit cards. £

Wilbraham Hotel, 1 Wilbraham Place, Sloane Street, SW1X 9AE. Tel: 0171-730 8296. Smart location between Knightsbridge and the King's Road, in a quiet street. The hotel is converted from three Victorian terraced houses. Old-fashioned and charming. 52 rooms, 43 with bath. Exceptional value. No credit cards. ££

North London

Buckland Hotel, 6 Buckland Crescent, Swiss Cottage, NW3 5DX. Tel: 0171-722 5574. Victorian bed and breakfast hotel in a smart, bustling area. 15 rooms, 12 with private baths. ££

The Clive Hotel, Primrose Hill Road, Hampstead, NW3 3NA. Tel: 0171-586 2233. Near pretty Primrose Hill. Relaxed atmosphere. Restaurant and bar. 96 rooms. £££

Dillons Hotel, 21 Belsize Park, Hampstead, NW3 4DU. Tel: 0171-794 3360. Small family-style guesthouse in affluent Hampstead. Charming area close to transport. 13 rooms, 10 with private bathrooms. No credit cards. £

Hendon Hall Hotel, Ashley Lane, Hendon, NW4 1HF. Tel: 0181-203 3341. A converted 18th-century Georgian mansion with its own grounds in the middle of suburban north London. Fully modernised. Meals available. 52 rooms. £££

Forte Post House Hotel, 215 Haverstock Hill, NW3 4RB. Tel: 0171-794 8121. Forte hotel close to Hampstead Heath. 140 rooms. ££

Swiss Cottage Hotel, 4 Adamson Road, NW3 3HP. Tel: 0171-722 2281. Furnished in a superb Victorian house-style. 65 rooms, 24 with shower, the rest with bath. £££

South London

Bardon Lodge Hotel, 15 Stratheden Road, Blackheath, SE3 7TH. Tel: 0181-853 4051. Elegant Victorian house close to Greenwich and its magnificent park. 37 rooms. £££

Selsdon Park Hotel, Addington Road, South Croydon, CR2 8YA. Tel: 0181-657 8811. Between London and Gatwick, and the country's biggest owner-managed hotel. Set in over 200 acres of parkland, with 175 bedrooms. Swimming pool. ££££

Southwest London

Kingston Lodge Hotel, Kingston Hill, Kingston upon Thames, KT2 7NP. Tel: 0181-541 4481. Country house hotel in a pretty location to the west of London. 64 rooms. £££

The Petersham Hotel, Richmond Hill, Richmond upon Thames, TW10 6UZ. Tel: 0181-940 7471. Great views over parkland and the river. Richmond BR or Tube for easy transport into London (40 minutes). 54 rooms. ££££

Richmond Hill Hotel, 146-150 Richmond Hill, Richmond on Thames TW10 6RW. Tel: 0181-940 2247. Traditional English hotel with a friendly atmosphere, and panoramic views over parkland. Close to Richmond village, Kew Gardens and Richmond station. 124 rooms. Meals available. £££

West London

Foubert's Hotel, 162-166 High Road, Chiswick, W4 1PR. Tel: 0181-995 6743. Small family-run hotel with its own restaurant and wine cellar-bar. Live music on weekends. 21 rooms, 10 with private baths. ££

Near Heathrow Airport

The Ariel, Bath Road, Hayes, Middlesex, UB3 5AJ. Tel: 0181-759 2552. 177 rooms, all with private bath. ££–£££

Berkeley Arms Hotel, Bath Road, Cranford, Middlesex, TW5 9QE. Tel: 0181-897 2121. About 10 minutes from the airport, smaller and less international in style than other airport hotels. Lovely English garden. 56 rooms. ££

Edwardian International, Bath Road, Hayes, Middlesex, UB3 9AW. Tel: 0181-759 6311. 450 rooms. Swimming pool. £££

The Excelsior, Bath Road, West Drayton, Middlesex, UB7 0DU. Tel: 0181-759 6611. Near airport entrance. 839 rooms. ££

Heathrow Ambassador, London Road, Colnbrook, Slough, SL3 8QB. Tel: 01753 684001. 112 rooms. ££

Heathrow Park, Bath Road, Longford, Middlesex, UB7 0EQ. Tel: 0181-759 2400. 306 rooms. £££

Hotel Ibis, 112-114 Bath Road, Hayes, Middlesex, UB3 5AL. Tel: 0181-759 4888. 354 rooms. Courtesy coach service to Heathrow. ££

Osterley Hotel, Great West Road, Isleworth, Middlesex, TW7 5NA. Tel: 0181-568 9981. Small hotel with its own pub. 63 rooms, 56 with bath. Meals. Special weekend discounts. ££

Sheraton Heathrow, Colnbrook Bypass, West Drayton, Middlesex, UB7 0HJ. Tel: 0181-759 2424 440 rooms. £££

Sheraton Skyline, Bath Road, Hayes, Middlesex, UB3 5BP. Tel: 0181-759 2535. Rather showy, with indoor tropical garden, pool. 354 rooms. £££

Near Gatwick Airport

Gatwick Hilton International, Gatwick Airport, West Sussex RH6 0LL. Tel: 01293 518080. Just a covered walkway away from airport terminals. 550 rooms. ££–£££

Gatwick Skylodge, London Road, County Oak, Crawley, West Sussex RH11 0FF. Tel: 01293-514341. Small comfortable hotel with a courtesy bus to the airport. 51 rooms. Weekend discounts. ££

Holiday Inn Gatwick, Langley Drive, Tushmore Roundabout, Crawley, West Sussex, RH11 7SX. Tel: 01293 529991. In a pleasant area with a courtesy bus to the airport. 223 rooms. £££

Youth Hostels

The English describe Youth Hostel accommodation as spartan. Visitors might regard it as extremely basic. You get a single bed in a dormitory with basic washing and cooking facilities. Most hostels also have restaurants. The price is cheap: around £15 for bed and breakfast in any of the five hostels. You must be a member to stay in a hostel. Write to the YHA, Trevelyan House, St Albans, Herts AL1 2DY. Or fill in a form at one of the hostels located at:

36 Carter Lane, EC4 5AD (City Hostel). Tel: 0171-236 4965. 191 beds.

38 Bolton Gardens, SW5 0AG (Earls Court). Tel: 0171-373 3083. 111 beds.

4 Wellgarth Road, NW11 7HR (Hampstead). Tel: 0181-458 9054. 220 beds.

84 Highgate West Hill, N6 6LU (Highgate). Tel: 0181-340 1831. 62 beds.

King George VI Memorial Hostel, Holland House, Holland Walk, W8 7QU (Kensington). Tel: 0171-937 0748. 190 beds. Set in charming Holland Park, it is the best of the London youth hostels. Advisable to book well ahead.

Details of other student and budget accommodation are freely available from the London Tourist Board at one of their Tourist Information Centres.

A Place of Your Own

Finding a Flat

There's no shortage of agents and private companies offering London apartments, many of them luxurious, others basic and frankly overpriced. Be wary – not all people are reputable. Decide what you want to pay, and stick to it. Obviously, it can be risky booking an apartment without seeing it first, and glossy brochures can be misleading.

If you're planning to stay in London for a while, it's better to look at flats from a temporary base when you arrive. The variety of properties can be bewildering, and going through a reputable agent is often the answer. Estate agents also act as letting and management agents for their clients – there is a comprehensive list in the Yellow Pages telephone directory. Also agents and individual apartment owners advertise in the *Evening Standard* newspaper. This can be a useful source, but often offers only the more expensive properties. The London Tourist Board is another good source of reputable agents.

The payment of a deposit is standard practice when renting a flat in London. However, it can be high, as much as four weeks' rent (a returnable insurance against breakages, etc.), an attempt by the owners to weed out irresponsible tenants. But many holiday let agencies ask for a deposit which is also to cover against cancellation. Try and avoid agents who charge a hefty fee for finding you accommodation (such a fee is only chargeable once you have agreed to take a property). Rental prices quoted below include all bills excluding telephone.

Flat-letting agents:

Allen House, Allen Street, W8. Tel: 0171-938 1346. 42 Kensington flats, 1-3 beds. From £870–£1,250 a week.

Apartment Services, 2 Sandwich Street, WC1H 9PL. Tel: 0171-388 3558. 60 privately-owned flats in central London, particularly Bloomsbury and Covent Garden from £150–£700 a week.

Aston's, 39 Rosary Gardens, South Kensington, SW7 4NQ. Tel: 0171-370 0737. 60 of their own designer studio and 1 bed flats accommodating 1–4 people in restored South Kensington Victorian houses. £175–£875 a week.

London Country Apartments Ltd, 161 Brighton Road, Purley, Surrey CR8 4HE. Tel: 0181-660 8167

26 flats, studios, 1–2 bed flats in Croydon and Purley, catering for executives. £210–£770 a week.

Dolphin Square, SW1V 3LX. Tel: 0171-834 3800. 152 1–3 bed flats close to the river and the Tate Gallery. £70–£197 a night including use of pool, sauna and steam room.

Holiday Flats, 1 Princess Mews, Belsize Crescent, NW3 5AP. Tel: 0171-794 1186. 30–60 privately owned 1–4 bed flats in Hampstead, St.John's Wood and Swiss Cottage. £250–£700 a week.

Holiday Flats Services Ltd, 132 Cromwell Road, London SW7 4HA. Tel: 0171-373 4477. Have a large number of flats throughout Greater London from £300 weekly for a studio to several thousand pounds for five-star luxury apartment. Brochure available.

Kensbridge Apartments, Kensgate House, 38 Emperor's Gate, SW7 4HJ. Tel: 0171-589 2923. Five Victorian houses split into studio to 2-bed apartments in Kensington and Victoria. Prices from £110–£300 a week.

Eating Out

London is one of the great culinary cities of the world. This is partly due to the breadth of cosmopolitan cuisines available and also the fact that the past decade has seen the re-evaluation of the indigenous cuisine of the British. Its once internationally scorned reputation of badly cooked, unimaginative, stodgy meals has gradually been overturned by the present generation of innovative modern British chefs.

These chefs have injected new life into traditional English recipes, indeed re-discovering many, by combining them with French and ethnic influences. They now take pride in making the best of top quality and seasonal ingredients whilst also making meals lighter. For example, you will now find dishes such as "roast best end of lamb with two sauces of lime and coriander, yogurt and mint"

(Wilson's) or "courgette flowers with lobster mousseline and a caviar butter sauce" (Sutherlands).

The traditional English practices of Sunday lunch, roast carveries, and fish and chips are still very much part of the scene and sampling them provides an insight into everyday life in England. However, choose carefully, as there is a huge difference between good and bad versions of these meals.

The main concentration of London's restaurants are to be found in the West End, with Soho providing the most interesting and widest choice, whilst Covent Garden offers good value pre-theatre suppers. The City, meanwhile, with its oyster bars and restaurants traditionally catering for the business luncher, becomes a ghost town in the evenings.

Although London's restaurants are expensive, reflecting the high cost of living, eating out in this capital has arguably never been so good. Ethnic restaurants provide some of the best value, whereas pubs and wine bars often provide good inexpensive snacks in surroundings that are preferable to a fast food hamburger joint. For a really cheap meal you can't go far wrong with a take-away of good old English fish and chips.

Restaurant Listings

Prices quoted are indicators of the cost of a three-course evening meal for two with a bottle of house wine (or appropriate beverage), not including coffee and service charge. Restaurant opening times do vary, so it is advisable to check beforehand and if required, book a table. Londoners would consider restaurants which charge over £60 for two as expensive, but the £100-plus meal is becoming increasingly common at fashionable restaurants. It is worth noting that the best value at quality restaurants is often provided by a set lunch menu.

A useful number to know is that of the **Restaurant Services**, tel: 0181-888 8080, who can supply up-to-date impartial information on London's restaurants. They also provide a free booking service.

Traditional English

Auntie's, 126 Great Portland Street, W1. Tel: 0171-387 1548. Traditional English food prepared by high-class chefs in an Edwardian style restaurant. £40

Chapter House Pizza Express, Southwark Cathedral, Montague Close, SE1. Tel: 0171-378 6446. In the unusual setting of the Chapter House of Southwark Cathedral this lunch restaurant serves good traditional food. £20

Codles, 41 Kingsland High Street, E8. Tel: 0171-254 2878. This family run Eel and Pie shop is one of the few still remaining intact. Within its beautiful tiled 19th-century interior you can dine on the traditional cockney meal of jellied eels with mash and liquor (mashed potatoes and parsley sauce). Under £6

Diana's Diner, 39 Endell Street, WC2. Tel: 0171-240 0272. No longer run by Diana, this tiny "caff" is still famous for its fry-ups and cheap hearty breakfasts. Under £15

The English House, 3 Milner Street, SW3. Tel: 0171-584 3002. Quaint chintzy English dining room within a pretty Chelsea town house. The surroundings may be a touch frilly, but the food has flair and a historic influence. The puddings are particularly good. £70

Fortnum and Mason, St James's Restaurant (4th floor), Piccadilly, W1. Tel: 0171-734 8040. Good English food, as you would expect from a restaurant located within this famous food emporium. Surprisingly not overpriced, it serves traditional cooked breakfasts and excellent roast lunches, as well as afternoon and high teas. £44

Fox & Anchor, 115 Charterhouse Street, EC1. Tel: 0171-253 4838. City pub close to Smithfield meat market that is famous for its huge English breakfasts. Very popular with meat porters and the local workforce. £15

Greens Rest & Oyster Park, Marsham Court, Marsham Street, SW1. Tel: 0171-834 9552. Close to the Houses of Parliament, this is an established haunt of MPs and government officials. Good, plain cooking. £50

Jack's Place, 12 York Road, SW11.

Tel: 0171-228 8519. For a restaurant with real London character serving good homely food, this is difficult to beat. The proprietor, Jack, can tell a good tale or two and he's not mean with the portions. Sunday lunch. £40

Kenny's, 2a Pond Place, SW3. Tel: 0171-225 2916. Opened in 1989 with the new novelty of cooking your own meat or seafood at charcoal grills set into granite tables. Fun with a group. £40

The Lindsay House, 21 Romilly Street, W1. Tel: 0171-439 0450. Sister restaurant to the English House in Chelsea, this also plays on the theme of the very English dining room, serving classy food within a traditional town house. £72

Porters, 17 Henrietta Street, WC2. Tel: 0171-836 6466. Large and noisy English pie theme restaurant with a range of savoury pies and good stodgy puddings. Also English wine and real ale. £32

The Quality Chop House, 94 Farringdon Road, EC1. Tel: 0171-837 5093. A 19th-century city clerks' dining room with its original interior of fixed wooden seating still intact. The food, however, is up-market with the likes of blue fish with fennel sauce on the menu beside plain lamb chops. £36

The Ritz, Louis XVI Restaurant, Piccadilly, W1. Tel: 0171-493 8181. Elegant Edwardian restaurant decorated in Louis XVI style. Sumptuous and refined dining. The best of English cuisine accompanied by the gentle strains of a string quartet and a magnificent view over Green Park. £100. Formal dress.

Rules, 35 Maiden Lane, WC2. Tel: 0171-836 5314/2559. Old-established dining room that is exceptionally good for English game such as grouse, wild salmon, Highland roe deer and wild boar, when in season. Also does a good roast beef, traditional puddings and real ale. £56

Simpsons-in-the-Strand, 100 Strand, WC2. Tel: 0171-836 9112. The Grand Divan Tavern is an Edwardian dining room renowned for serving the best roast beef in London. Staunchly traditional, Simpsons is as popular as ever with the English establishment. £64. Formal.

Tate Gallery Restaurant, The Tate Gallery, Millbank, SW1. Tel: 0171-

834 6754. Beautifully decorated with a mural by Rex Whistler, this fine lunch restaurant has one of the most reputed wine lists in London. £50

Wilson's, 236 Blythe Road, W14. Tel: 0171-603 7267. Has justly earned a reputation for serving one of the best Sunday lunches in town. A consistently high quality is maintained throughout the week in this dignified restaurant, where the eccentric patron may be seen in a kilt. £53

Modern European

Alastair Little, 49 Frith Street, W1. Tel: 0171-734 5183. The chef-owner is something of a celebrity for his inventive approach to food on a basic French mode. Delicious, fresh, *nouvelle* style cooking. Very trendy. Rather stark decor with a newer bar downstairs serving light meals. £68

L'Escargot, 48 Greek Street, W1. Tel: 0171-437 2679. Ever fashionable landmark in Soho popular with the theatrical and media crowd. Restaurant upstairs or cheaper brasserie on the ground floor. Modern English and French cuisine. First class wine list. £65

Hilaire, 68 Old Brompton Road, SW7. Tel: 0171-584 8993. Classy South Kensington establishment with a continuing reputation for delicious unpretentious cooking of modern international inspiration. £60

The Ivy, 1 West Street, WC2. Tel: 0171-836 4751. High-quality decor, gallery worthy art, and well thought-out food have made for the successful regeneration of the Ivy which re-opened its doors in 1990. Like its relative, Le Caprice, this is a fashionable place to be seen. £60

Kensington Place, 201 Kensington Church Street, W8. Tel: 0171-727 3184. Fashionable and informal, this New York style restaurant is always bustling. The decor is modernist and the commendable food is adventurous. £55

Leith's, 92 Kensington Park Road, W11. Tel: 0171-229 4481. Prue Leith's superb food is dominated by traditional English influences with a modern imaginative flair. Excellent vegetarian menu. Many ingredients are home-grown on her Cotswold farm. £100

French

L'Artiste Assoiffé, 122 Kensington Park Road, W11. Tel: 0171-727 4714. Carousel horses and caged parrots adorn this delightful and entertaining restaurant which is close to Portobello's antique shops. Popular with local arty types. On a good night the food is excellent. £50

Belvedere Restaurant, Holland House, Holland Park, W8. Tel: 0171-602 1238. One of the most romantic places to dine in London, located within a converted stable block in the grounds of Holland Park. Menu has an international flavour and is particularly good for fish. £65

Le Café Des Amis Du Vin, 11-14 Hanover Place, WC2. Tel: 0171-379 3444. Always crowded, largely due to its Covent Garden position and reliable French food. Typical French brasserie menu and efficient service. Bar downstairs is noisy and Salon upstairs more comfortable. No obligation to eat a full meal. £40

Le Caprice, Arlington House, Arlington Street, SW1. Tel: 0171-629 2239. Black and white café-style restaurant that is a fashionable place to graze and be seen. Pianist in the evenings. Excellent New York style Sunday brunch. £50

The Chanterelle, 119 Old Brompton Road, SW7. Tel: 0171-373 7390. Attractive, very popular little restaurant. The imaginative menu changes regularly and offers good English-style French cooking. Special supper menu (cheaper) after 10.30pm. £40

Chez Gerrard, 8 Charlotte Street, W1. Tel: 0171-636 4975. Particularly good for meat, this French bistro serves excellent steak and chips. Also good traditional cooking such as soup de poisson and Chateaubriand. Pleasant simple French decor. £50

L'Epicure, 28 Frith Street, W1. Tel: 0171-437 2829. Flaming torches mark the exterior of this restaurant which serves traditional French cooking, flambés and dishes rich with butter, cream and alcohol. Its aged decor adds to the charm. £47

Le Gavroche, 43 Upper Brook Street, W1. Tel: 0171-408 0881. Having confidently been at the top of England's restaurants for many years, its standards continue not to waver. The excellence of Albert Roux made this the first British restaurant to earn three Michelin stars. Set lunch best value. Over £100

Gavvers, 61 Lower Sloane Street, SW3. Tel: 0171-730 5983. Related to Le Gavroche, Gavvers operates on a set menu basis, providing quality and value combined with attentive service in comfortable surroundings. Set dinner at £25–30 a person.

Langan's Brasserie, Stratton Street, W1. Tel: 0171-493 6437. Langan's large reputation for attracting celebrities often overshadows the notable food. Actor Michael Caine is part-owner of this continually fashionable brasserie. £50

Le Routier, Camden Lock, Chalk Farm Road, NW1. Tel: 0171-485 0360. Situated overlooking Regent's Canal, this restaurant with its basic decor and rustic French cooking can offer a certain style of romance. Open-air dining in summer. £38

Nico Central, 35 Great Portland Street, W1. Tel: 0171-436 8846. A passionate perfectionist, Nico Ladenis serves classic French cuisine which has earned him two Michelin stars, among other awards. £60

Odins, 27 Devonshire Street, W1. Tel: 0171-935 7296. Glamorous and richly adorned with paintings by the likes of Hockney, in whose sketches the memory of the late proprietor, the flamboyant Peter Langan, lingers on. Light and delicate food with traditional English and French influences. £75

La Tante Claire, 65 Royal Hospital Road, SW3. Tel: 0171-352 6045. Two Michelin stars have been awarded to this chic, exclusive little restaurant. Imaginative modern French cooking. Recommended for those who don't flinch at spending £16 on a starter. Over £100

Simply Nico, 48 Rochester Row, SW1. Tel: 0171-630 8061. Following Nico Ladenis's opening of Chez Nico, this restaurant adopted the prefix "Simply", a new chef and a bright and airy brasserie feel. However, the food is still to be taken seriously. £64

Thierry's, 342 King's Road, SW3. Tel: 0171-352 3365. Good, unfussy traditional French food with vegetarian options. Bargain set lunch. £46

Italian

La Barca, 80 Lower Marsh SE1. Tel: 0171-928 2226. Handy for the South Bank and the Old Vic Theatre. Has earned a reputation for its ingeniously treated pasta and interesting non pasta dishes. Excellent theatre suppers. £50

Bertorelli's, 44a Floral Street, WC2. Tel: 0171-836 1868. Black and white Art Deco style restaurant that has become something of an institution in Covent Garden. Serves cheap and reliable cockney-Italian food. £50

Café Venezia, 15 New Burlington Street, W1. Tel: 0171-439 2378. Informal restaurant serving home-made pasta. £40

Cibo, 3 Russell Gardens, W14. Tel: 0171-371 6271. Comfortable and airy with intriguing art on the walls, modern northern Italian cooking and charming waiters. £50

La Famiglia, 7 Langton Street, SW10. Tel: 0171-351 0761. Successful restaurant with pleasant food and decor done the southern Italian way. Has one of the largest outdoor eating areas in London. £50

Leoni's Quo Vadis, 26 Dean Street, W1. Tel: 0171-437 4809. One of the oldest and most reputed restaurants in Soho in a building once inhabited by Karl Marx. Serves rich traditional Italian food. £50

Orso, 27 Wellington Street, WC2. Tel: 0171-240 5269. More up-market than its brother restaurant, Joe Allen (see *Late Eating*). Set in a basement with simple decor, authentic north Italian food and good service. Fashionable with actors and theatre goers alike. £56

Pizzeria Castello, 20 Walworth Road, SE1. Tel: 0171-703 2556. Always packed, Castello's has a long standing reputation for serving the cheapest and the best pizzas in town. Well worth a detour to the Elephant and Castle. £25

On the subject of pizzas, **Pizza Express** is a very civilised chain, with live jazz at the Dean Street branch. The classiest is the Pizza on the Park branch at 13 Knightsbridge, whereas **Kettners** at 29 Romilly Street, W1 is the most fashionable. The **Chicago Pizza Pie Factory** at 17 Hanover Square, W1, and branches is best for deep pan pizzas. **Pizza Hut**, all over town, is reasonable, and very cheap (around £30 for two).

San Lorenzo, 22 Beauchamp Place, SW3. Tel: 0171-584 1074. Fashionable and busy posh Knightsbridge restaurant. The menu is a mixture of the exciting and the mundane. Extraordinary decor incorporates a sliding roof for summer. £70

The River Café, Thames Wharf, Rainville Road, W6. Tel: 0181-385 3344. On the banks of the Thames near Hammersmith, designed by controversial architect, Richard Rogers, and run by his wife. Delightful northern Italian food and riverside tables. £65

Chinese

Many of London's best Chinese restaurants are to be found in Chinatown which centres around Gerrard Street. Paved over and made into something of a theme park with pagoda telephone boxes and oriental style arches, this lively area is crammed with restaurants serving mainly Cantonese cuisine. If baffled by choice, those patronised by the Chinese themselves are generally a good bet.

Chuen Cheng Ku, 17 Wardour Street, W1. Tel: 0171-437 1398. Huge, functional place that has a reputation for serving some of the best *dim sum* in town (until 6pm). Popular with locals at lunch time. £32

Fung Shing, 15 Lisle Street, WC2. Tel: 0171-437 1539. Has long been one of the best Chinatown restaurants and consequently is always packed. Some original dishes with particularly good fish. £46

The Good Food Restaurant, 8 Little Newport Street, WC2. Tel: 0171-734 2130. One of the few places still serving good food at 4.30am. Three pleasant, but very small, floors on which to eat Cantonese food. £30

Ken Lo's Memories of China, 67 Ebury Street, SW1. Tel: 0171-730 7734. Ken Lo, renowned Chinese cookery writer, owns this classy restaurant where dishes originate from the many regions of China and standards are high. Second branch within the new Chelsea Harbour complex, SW10. £80

Ley On's, 56 Wardour Street, W1. Tel: 0171-437 6465. One of the cheapest restaurants in Chinatown with a large variety of *dim sum* (served until 5pm). £30

Poon's, 4 Leicester Street, W1. Tel:

0171-437 1528. The best of several branches of Poon in Central London. Wind-dried meats are a distinctive feature on the long menu of over 200 dishes. Good value. £40

Sichuen, 56 Old Compton Street, W1. Tel: 0171-437 2069. The spicy option of Sichuen cuisine as opposed to Cantonese of nearby Chinatown. £40

Wong Kei, 41-43 Wardour Street, W1. Tel: 0171-437 8408. Regular crowds aren't deterred by the rude service for which this place is famed. Huge, with three floors, serving good value Cantonese food. Cash only. £18

Zen Central, 20 Queen Street, W1. Tel: 0171-629 8103. This fashionable sleek restaurant has gained its reputation by serving outstandingly interesting Chinese food. MSG-free. £60

Indian

London has many Indian restaurants, a pleasant legacy of its colonial past, with the most distinctive being those that specialise in the cuisine of a particular region. Concentrated areas of reasonably priced Indian restaurants can be found in Brick Lane and Southall which have large Asian communities. Drummond Street, close to Euston Station, is good for vegetarian Indian restaurants such as Ravi Shankar and Diwana Bhel Poori House, which are also notably cheap.

Bombay Brasserie, Bailey's Hotel, Courtfield Close, SW7. Tel: 0171-370 4040. The stylish decor harks back to the days of the Raj. The interesting menu is well thought-out, with dishes from many regions. The lunch-time buffet provides good value. £60

Copper Chimney, 13 Heddon Street, W1. Tel: 0171-439 2004. Chefs can be seen cooking through the large glass window at one side of this classy Indian restaurant. The menu offers several less common Indian dishes. £47

Gaylord, 79 Mortimer Street, W1. Tel: 0171-636 0808. Courteous and consistently good restaurant which is part of an international chain. £33

Great Nepalese, 48 Eversholt Street, NW1. Tel: 0171-388 6737. Specialises in the milder and less oily cuisine of Nepal incorporating a lot of chicken and lamb. Authentic and always popular. £30

Khan's, 13 Westbourne Grove, W2. Tel: 0171-727 5420. This huge Indian dining room is famous for being great value. Crowded in the evenings the atmosphere is that of constant hustle and bustle. £25

Kundan, 3 Horseferry Road, SW1. Tel: 0171-834 3434. Handy for the Houses of Parliament and popular with MPs. First-class Punjab cuisine. £40

Last Days of the Raj, 22 Drury Lane, WC2. Tel: 0171-836 1628. One of London's most respected Indian restaurants, good for Bengali dishes. £32

Papadams, 125 Great Tichfield Street, W1. Tel: 0171-323 2875. Cheerful and friendly restaurant with an excellent lunch and dinner buffet for just £6.50 a head. Also fine a la carte menu. £30

Ragam, 57 Cleveland Street, W1. Tel: 0171-636 9098. One of the few restaurants in London offering unusual specialities from the Indian coastal state of Kerala. Good, healthy and cheap. £25

The Red Fort, 77 Dean Street, W1. Tel: 0171-437 2115. Renowned Soho restaurant which offers good Mogul cooking in comfortably luxurious surroundings. Its creator, Amin Ali, is also responsible for Jamdani at 34 Charlotte Street W1, which is stylish and noted for its interesting menu. £50

Salloos, 51 Kinnerton Street, SW1. Tel: 0171-235 4444. Hidden away in a Knightsbridge mews, this high-class family run restaurant specialises in well prepared Pakistani cuisine with lamb and chicken dishes a speciality. £50

Taste of India, 25 Catherine Street, WC2. Tel: 0171-836 6591. Good value pre-theatre menus and reduced price lunches. Lighter Indian snacks are served downstairs in the Jewel in the Ground wine bar. £36

Japanese

The experience of a Japanese meal in London has always been expensive. However, in recent years several more casual and affordable restaurants have appeared. Lunchtimes and the more reasonable set menus offer a good introduction.

Ajimura, 51-53 Shelton Street, WC2.

Tel: 0171-240 0178. One of the London's oldest established Japanese restaurants. Whilst it may not be the best it is certainly one of the most reasonably priced. Lunch and theatre set menus are the best value. £40

Ikeda, 30 Brook Street, W1. Tel: 0171-629 2730. Sit at the Yakitori and Sushi bars to really get the best from the Japanese experience at this fashionable Mayfair restaurant. £70

Ikkyu, 67 Tottenham Court Road, W1. Tel: 0171-636 9280. Relaxed basement restaurant with good value, quality food and less of the usual Japanese emphasis on decor and service. Has a large Japanese following. £30

Miyama, 38 Clarges Street, W1. Tel: 0171-499 2443. Sophisticated restaurant which maintains a high degree of personal service. Two *teppan-yaki* rooms where a chef cooks sizzling dishes on a hot plate. £80

Suntory, 72 St James's Street, SW1. Tel: 0171-409 0201. London's most expensive Japanese restaurant. Excellent food is served with traditional style. Has one Michelin star. £90

Yoshino, basement, Japan Centre, 66 Brewer Street, W1. Tel: 0171-287 6622. Sit at this bar below the Japan Centre and try some of the cheapest Japanese food in town. £10

Other Ethnic Eateries

Anna's Place, 90 Mildmay Park, N1. Tel: 0171-249 9379. (Swedish). Scandinavian restaurants are very few and far between in London. Anna offers good wholesome homemade Swedish cooking within a lively wine bar setting. £40

Beotys, 79 St Martin's Lane, WC2. Tel: 0171-836 8768. (Greek). One of London's oldest Greek/Cypriot restaurants, luxurious Beotys is set in the heart of theatreland. Go for the Greek specialities rather than the international menu. £40

Blue Elephant, 4-6 Fulham Broadway, SW6. Tel: 0171-385 6595. (Thai). A tropical jungle in the middle of Fulham. Excellent food and charming service from waitresses in traditional costume. Carefully explained menu. £70–80

Chiang Mai, 48 Frith Street, W1. Tel: 0171-437 7144. (Thai). Thai restaurant modelled on the traditional stilt house. Friendly staff will help you to decipher the menu which is primarily based on the cuisine of northern Thailand and lists over 100 dishes. For the uninitiated try the set menu, otherwise experiment with the rarer dishes. £30

Daquise, 20 Thurloe Street, SW7. Tel: 0171-589 6117. (Polish). Central to London's Polish community since World War II. East European food is served in a rather basic environment with a nice relaxed café atmosphere. £25

Fakhreldine, 85 Piccadilly, W1. Tel: 0171-493 3424. (Lebanese). Overlooking Green Park, this is one of London's smartest and most established Middle Eastern restaurants. Fine Lebanese cuisine. £60

Gay Hussar, 2 Greek Street, W1. Tel: 0171-437 0973. (Hungarian). A long menu of mouth-watering dishes, such as wild cherry soup, keep this fine established Hungarian restaurant very popular. It endeavours to provide value for money. £55

Kosher Luncheon Club, Morris Kasler Hall, 13 Greatorex Street, E1. Tel: 0171-247 0039. (Jewish). The last of the East End's Kosher Luncheon Clubs is open to all. Serves superb fish as well as basic Jewish staples and desserts. Set within a large hall, it has a warm and friendly atmosphere of a meeting place. No credit cards. £20 including 10p membership.

Luba's Bistro, 6 Yeoman's Row, SW3. Tel: 0171-589 2950. (Russian). Basic restaurant serving good Euro-Russian food. Good value, but unlicensed. £26

White Tower Restaurant, 1 Percy Street, W1. Tel: 0171-636 8141. (Greek). Founded in 1938 this restaurant retains an air of a Gentleman's club. Its interesting mix of very good Greek food is served with panache. £60

Nikita's, 65 Ifield Road, SW10. Tel: 0171-352 6326 (Russian). Sophisticated restaurant located in an intimate basement with a good range of vodka, caviar and well prepared traditional Russian dishes. £60

The Penang, 41 Hereford Road, W2. Tel: 0171-229 2982. (Malaysian). Excellent Malaysian food with a home-cooked freshness at this friendly,

small and unassuming restaurant. £35

Rebato's, 169 South Lambeth Road, SW8. Tel: 0171-735 6388. (Spanish). Restaurant worth a detour. The atmosphere and decor provide a perfect setting in which to enjoy the authentic food, especially the range of *tapas*. Musicians add to the experience in the evenings. £37

Calabash, 38 King Street, WC2. Tel: 0171-836 1976. (African). Situated below the Africa Centre close to Covent Garden Piazza with dishes from many regions of the African continent. Coffee is particularly good. Also African wine and beer. £30

Fish

Geales, 2-4 Farmer Street, W8. Tel: 0171-727 7969. Cheerful and homely fish restaurant in Notting Hill. Good fish and chips cooked in beef dripping, as it's done in the north of England. £20

La Gaulette, 53 Cleveland Street, W1. Tel: 0171-580 7608. The freshest of fish, whether native or tropical, are used as the starting point for the delicious dishes prepared French Mauritian style. £60

Manzi's, 1-2 Leicester Street, WC2. Tel: 0171-734 0224. Timeless Italian-run fish restaurant close to Leicester Square. Good traditional fish dishes. £60

Rudland & Stubbs, 35-37 Greenhill Rents, Cowcross Street, EC1. Tel: 0171-253 0148. English and French-style fish dishes in a characterful setting with tiled walls and raw floorboards, around the corner from Smithfield Meat Market. £60

Sea Shell Fish Bar, 49 Lisson Grove, NW1. Tel: 0171-723 8703. Renowned fish and chip restaurant and take-away. Although, as this English delicacy goes, it is not cheap, its wide choice of fish is consistently very fresh and well cooked. £30

Sheekey's, 28-32 St Martin's Court, WC2. Tel: 0171-240 2565. Edwardian fish restaurant which reflects its theatrical surroundings. The menu includes traditional potted shrimps, fish pies and eels and mash at somewhat high prices. £65

Le Suquet, 104 Draycott Avenue, SW3. Tel: 0171-581 1785. Popular first-class chi-chi French fish restau-

rant with fresh Mediterranean style decor. £60

Vegetarian

Most restaurants have realised the need to offer vegetarian dishes and many chefs have risen to this challenge, offering interesting dishes of culinary merit. Leith's, for example, offers a separate vegetarian menu and will also cook to suit Vegans. The following are good places to eat which are primarily vegetarian.

Cranks, 8 Marshall Street, W1. Tel: 0171-437 9431. One of the longest surviving vegetarian restaurants, it offers a well established repertoire of safe vegetarian food. Wholesome and a bit tied to its self-inflicted stereotyped image of a vegetarian restaurant. Several branches in central London. £25

Food For Thought, 31 Neal Street, WC2. Tel: 0171-836 0239. Small and very crowded at lunch times, with queues for take-aways. The food is never dull. £12 (bring your own wine).

Mildred's, 58 Greek Street, W1. Tel: 0171-494 1634. Imaginative cooking attractively put together in café-style surroundings. Vegan options. £13 (bring your own wine, £1 charge).

Riverside Vegetarian, 64 High Street, Kingston-upon-Thames. Tel: 0181-546 7992. Located adjacent to the river Thames, offering an international menu of vegetarian and Vegan dishes. £30

Tearooms des Artistes, 697 Wandsworth Road, SW8. Tel: 0171-720 4028. A stylish vegetarian venue with a trendy "designer decay" look. There's nothing remotely "veggie" about the bar and the atmosphere is always great. Vegan options. £25

Late-night Eating

Billboard Café, 222 Kilburn High St, NW6. Tel: 0171-328 1374. Monday–Saturday, L/O 12.45am. Cheerful Italian restaurant with a positive American influence in its modern decor and pleasingly attentive service. The menu is imaginative, changes regularly and makes good use of fresh vegetables and herbs. Everything, including the pasta, is made on the premises.

Borshtch 'n' Tears, 46 Beauchamp Place, SW3. Tel: 0171-589 5003. L/O 1.30am daily. Zany Russian Restaurant with a sense of humour that attracts a mostly young clientele who are prepared to participate in the music and gaiety. The inexpensive menu includes Russian delicacies such as blinis and caviar, chicken kiev, golubtsy and Siberian Pilmenni. £40

Castle Tandoori Restaurant, 200 Elephant & Castle Shopping Centre, SE1. Tel: 0171-703 9130. L/O 2am. Don't let the pink Elephant and Castle shopping centre put you off a late-night curry at this inexpensive Indian restaurant and takeaway. The food is pleasantly inoffensive and the service efficient and friendly no matter what the hour.

Costa Dorada, 47-55 Hanway St, W1. Tel: 0171-677 1795. L/O 2.30am. One of London's best known late-night spots, this lively restaurant/*tapas* bar with a strong Spanish following fills up in the late evening when diners flock in for the colourful flamenco dancing and live spanish music. £56

Joe Allen, 13 Exeter Street, WC2. Tel: 0171 836 0651. L/O 1am. Continually fashionable American restaurant hidden down an alley in Covent Garden largely patronised by those involved with the media and showbiz. Booking essential. £40

Maroush II, 38 Beauchamp Place, SW3. Tel: 0171-581 5434. L/O 5am daily. Largely patronised by nocturnal Middle Eastern high rollers who congregate here after a night out at London's smarter clubs. The food, which includes Lebanese delicacies such as *sujuk* (spicy sausages) and *shish taouk* (cubes of chicken charcoal grilled), is well presented and surprisingly good value.

Mayflower, 68-70 Shaftesbury Ave, W1. Tel: 0171-734 9207. L/O 3.30am. A Chinese ever popular with nightowls and a regular haunt for those involved in the restaurant trade itself, the Mayflower, which offers an extensive range of good Cantonese dishes, manages to maintain quality as the night wears on. £35

Mr Kong, 21 Lisle St WC2. Tel: 0171-437 7341. L/O 1.45am. Renowned for seafood, Mr Kong's food is amongst the best

in Chinatown. However, the decor falls a long way short of the quality of the fare, so to get the maximum enjoyment from your meal aim to sit on the ground floor and leave the top floor to the regular Chinese patrons and the basement to someone else.

Up All Night, 325 Fulham Rd, SW10. Tel: 0171-352 1998. L/O 5.30am daily. Late-night revellers swarm here like moths to a bright light to refuel after an evening on the town. Open throughout the night, this restaurant with its plastic bistro feel, serves hamburgers, pasta and steaks at moderate prices.

Theme Restaurants

Café Pacifico, 5 Langley Street, WC2. Tel: 0171-379 7728. (Mexican). Young and loud Tex Mex joint with typical repertoire of *enchiladas*, *fajitas* and *tacos* and, of course, those essential *margueritas*. Located in a converted Covent Garden Warehouse. £30

The Beefeater, Ivory House, St Katherine's Dock, E1. Tel: 0171-408 1001. The court of Henry VIII is recreated in basement vaults close to the Tower of London. Diners eat a five-course meal with an unlimited supply of wine and ale from serving wenches whilst entertained by court jesters, minstrels, magicians, and fire eaters. Merriment continues after the meal with a disco. £60. Reserve.

Cockney Cabaret, 161 Tottenham Court Road, WC2. Tel: 0171-408 1001. Over the top evening of good old cockney entertainment in the form of Pearly Kings and Queens, buskers and flower girls within a restaurant set out like an old time London music hall. Sing along to old cockney favourites while dining on a four course dinner with unlimited wine and ale. £50. Reserve.

Canal Café Theatre, Bridge House, Delamere Terrace, W2. Tel: 0171-289 6054. Pub with a small theatre next to the Regent's Canal in Little Venice. Dine on simple food to fringe theatre and cabaret shows. Entry £3.50. Dinner £20

Flanagan's, 100 Baker Street, W1/14 Rupert Street, W1. Tel: 0171-935 0287. Edwardian style dining rooms serving good old cockney fare such as "eel and pie", "fish and chips" and

"steak and kidney pudding" with old time sing-alongs and costumed waiters.

Hard Rock Café, 150 Old Park Lane, W1. Tel: 0171-629 0382. A shrine to rock music that is not only a good restaurant, serving some of the best burgers in London, but has also become a sight on most young tourists' itineraries. Houses an exceptional collection of rock memorabilia that continues to grow. £34

Players Theatre, The Arches, Villiers Street, WC2. Tel: 0171-839 1134. Victorian-style music hall within a new purpose-built theatre. Join in with lively fun of cockney sing-alongs, comedians and musicians. Acts change regularly every two weeks. Separate supper room offers set of à la carte menu. £30. Theatre £12 (booking advisable).

Rock Island Diner, London Pavilion, Piccadilly, W1. Tel: 0171-287 5500. Fun and loud 1950s-style diner decorated with kitsch memorabilia. Several times in the evening the DJ stops spinning the discs and barmen and waitresses take a break from serving, to get up on the tables and do a dance routine. Very entertaining. £28

Smollensky's Balloon, 1 Dover Street, W1. Tel: 0171-491 1199. Friendly American-style restaurant that caters well for children with Punch and Judy shows and circus entertainment at weekends. Special menu and cocktail list for children. £35

The Water Rats, 328 Grays Inn Road, WC1. Tel: 0171-837 9861. Old-fashioned theatre within a historic pub which is adorned with old theatre posters and memorabilia. A professional theatre company puts on a new production every five weeks which might be anything from old-time musicals to Shakespeare. Dinner at 7pm (booking essential) £20. Theatre £5-£8.50.

Café Life

Fashionable places to linger a while with a drink, meet your friends, be seen, and maybe eat.

Bar Italia, 22 Frith Street, W1. Tel: 0171-228 2660. Retaining its genuine 1950s feel, this is London's most famous Italian bar. No hype, just excellent coffee, a characterful atmosphere and an interesting crowd.

Café Pelican, 45 St Martin's Lane, WC2. Tel: 0171-379 0309/0259. Chic brasserie that attracts a theatre crowd, both actors and audience alike. Serves a good repertoire of brasserie food from mid-day until 2am, with a pianist accompanying the buzz in the evenings. £50

Bar Escoba, 102 Old Brompton Road, SW7. Tel: 0171-373 2403. Very trendy *tapas* bar with Mexican beers, Latin jazz and Spanish guitar music. £36

Dome, 354 King's Road, SW3. Tel: 0171-352 7611. Pretentious place to drink, read a newspaper and watch the wild-life of the King's Road go by. Many branches around London.

Freud's, 198 Shaftesbury Avenue, WC2. Tel: 0171-240 9932. Basement bunker bar that attracts the trendy. Hosts art exhibitions, live music and on busy evenings you could be excused for thinking that a "street fashion" show is taking place. £16

Joe's Café, 126 Draycott Avenue, SW3. Tel: 0171-225 2217. Sleek and chic bar which attracts the well healed for coffee, or maybe a spot of champagne and a bite to eat, after shopping across the road at Joseph.

Lisboa Patisserie, 57 Golborne Road, W10. Tel: 0181-968 5242. Fabulous and unusual Portuguese pastries draw trendy browsers from the Portobello Road and Notting Hill into this café which is an essential part of the local Portuguese community. £6

Maison Bertaux, 28 Greek Street, W1. Tel: 0171-437 6007. This rival to Patisserie Valerie, with its own set of regulars, is certainly worth queuing for a table at. Upstairs you can tranquilly enjoy delicious pastries with tea or coffee.

Market Bar, 240a Portobello Road, W11. Tel: 0171-229 6472. Inside the shell of an old pub is this triumph of the art of the distressed interior. Decadent candelabras covered in dripping wax abound in this fashionable retreat from the bustling market. £46

Patisserie Valerie, 44 Old Compton Street, W1. Tel: 0171-437 3466. Central to Soho life, this ever popular meeting place is worshipped by its arty and intellectual regulars who crowd the place. Who could pass by the best gâteaux and croissants in town?

Soho Brasserie, 23-25 Old Compton Street, W1. Tel: 0171-439 9301/3758. The whole of its front is opened directly on to the street in the warmer months, allowing maximum "poseability". Relaxed atmosphere and international food. £44

Afternoon Tea

Traditionally the English "take Afternoon Tea" at around 3.30pm settling down to genteely indulge themselves with sandwiches, cakes and, of course, a pot of tea.

Brown's Hotel, 21-24 Albemarle Street, W1. Tel: 0171-493 6020. Tea is served formally in comfortable wood-panelled lounges with an air of civility. Expensive

Maison Sagne, 105 Marylebone High Street, W1. Tel: 0171-935 6240. This patisserie maintains an air of dignity harkening back to its origins in the 1920s. Afternoon tea is served between 3–5pm. Old-fashioned service.

Palm Court, The Waldorf Hotel, Aldwych, WC2. Tel: 0171-836 2400. The magnificent Palm Court hosts traditional tea dances. As well as partaking of tea, you take to the floor with your partner for a waltz.

Park Room, Hyde Park Hotel, 66 Knightsbridge, SW1. Tel: 0171-235 2000. Tea is served to the accompaniment of a pianist while you gently gaze at the view of Hyde Park. £60

Wisteria, 14 Middle Lane, N8. Tel: 0181-348 2669. Surely everyone's idea of the English tearoom. Quaint and cosy with home-made cakes and vegetarian food.

Living Like a Lord

A few extravagant things to do in London:

● Silver service breakfast at the Royal Garden Hotel, Kensington High Street, W8, with fabulous views over Hyde Park.

● Pick up a picnic from Harrods and go boating on the Serpentine in Hyde Park.

● Traditional roast lunch at Simpsons-in-the-Strand.

● An ice cream soda at Fortnum & Mason, Piccadilly, W1 – the most upmarket fast food in town.

● Tea dance in the elegant Palm Court of the Waldorf Hotel.

● A cocktail at the American bar, Savoy hotel, Strand WC2. Get there at 6pm for a table. (Jacket and tie).

● Dine and dance at the Roof Restaurant on the 28th floor of the Hilton, Park Lane (tel: 0171-493 8000).

Drinking Notes

Wine & Cocktail Bars

American Bar, Savoy Hotel, Strand, WC2. Tel: 0171-836 4343. London's most classic cocktail bar within the sophisticated Savoy Hotel. Jacket and tie.

Almeida Theatre Wine Bar, 1 Almeida Street, N1. Tel: 0171-359 4404. Relaxed atmosphere at this earthy theatrical wine bar. Casual.

Athenaeum Bar, Athenaeum Hotel, Piccadilly, W1. Tel: 0171-499 3436. Discrete and old-fashioned cocktail bar that offers an unrivalled selection of malt whiskies. Smart.

Bar des Amis du Vin, 11-13 Hanover Place, WC2. Tel: 0171-379 3444. Dark, atmospheric basement bar with a good solid wine list and decent French snacks reflecting the food in the restaurant above. Casual.

Brinkley's Champagne Bar, 17c Curzon Street, W1. Tel: 0171-493 4490. Glamorous Mayfair bar patronised by the rich and famous. Smart.

Cork and Bottle, 44-46 Cranbourne Street, WC2. Tel: 0171-734 7807. An excellent retreat from Leicester Square, this characterful basement wine bar offers decent food and a notable selection of wines. Casual.

Daly's, 210 Strand, WC2. Tel: 0171-583 4476. Large floor boarded wine bar across the road from the Law Courts. In addition to the decent lunches it offers breakfasts and afternoon teas. Casual.

El Vino, 47 Fleet Street, EC4. Tel: 0171-353 6786. Famous as a Fleet Street haunt for journalists and lawyers; indeed, many a meeting of intrigue is reputed to have occurred here. Now the journalists have left Fleet Street, though the lawyers remain. A good wine bar which remains a stuffy bastion of tradition, insisting on jacket and tie for men, skirt or dress for women. Refuses to serve women standing at the bar.

Green's, 36 Duke Street, SW1. Tel: 0171-930 4566. Friendly smart

Champagne bar in St James's with a gentleman's club atmosphere and traditionally courteous service, although rather expensive. Smart.

Julie's Bar, 137 Portland Road, W11. Tel: 0171-727 7985. Comfortable Holland Park bar decorated with Gothic style which has attracted a notable crowd since it opened in the 1960s. Casual.

The King's Bar, Hotel Russell, Russell Square, WC1. Tel: 0171-837 6470. Cocktails taken traditionally, shaken or stirred, in an elegant wood-panelled Edwardian lounge. Smart.

Rumours, 33 Wellington Street, WC2. Tel: 0171-836 0038. Huge lively modern bar with an endless list of cocktails where the punters get crushed along with the ice. Casual.

Truckles of Pied Bull Yard, Bury Place, WC1. Tel: 0171-404 5334. Attractive wine bar with a peaceful open courtyard close to the British Museum. Casual.

Pubs

The Albion, 10 Thornhill Road, N1. This attractive pub in a pretty area of Islington has the atmosphere, as well as the appearance, of a village pub. Cosy bars and a beer garden at the back.

Anchor, 1 Bankside, SE1. This old 18th-century riverside pub has cosy higgledy-piggledy rooms with oak beams and a minstrels gallery. Outside tables.

Angel, 21 Rotherhithe Street, SE16. Built on stilts over the Thames, this old pub dates back to the 15th century when monks from the Bermondsey Priory ran it as a tavern. The balcony and upstairs restaurant offer outstanding views of the Thames, including the Pool of London and Tower Bridge.

Black Friar, 174 Queen Victoria Street, EC4. Built in 1875 on the site of the Black Friars Monastery, this is London's only Art Nouveau pub. The spectacular marble interior carries bronze friezes depicting the activities of monks.

Bunch of Grapes, 207 Brompton Road, SW3. Fine example of a late Victorian pub which is protected by a preservation order. Complete with "snob" screens for privacy.

Dickens Inn, St Katherine's Way, E1.

Successful conversion of an old warehouse into a spit-and-sawdust pub that has an authentic feel as well as a fabulous location, facing as it does St Katherine's Dock and Tower Bridge

The Dove, 19 Upper Mall, W6. Quaint 18th-century riverside pub on a pleasant stretch of the Thames at which James Thompson is claimed to have written *Rule Britannia*. It once housed the Doves Press, whilst William Morris set up the Kelmscott Press nearby.

Freemason's Arms, 32 Downshire Hill, NW3. The last court of the old English game of Pell-Mell was located in the large garden of this pub which is situated adjacent to Hampstead Heath. Old London skittles is still played in the basement.

George Inn, 77 Borough High Street, SE1. London's sole surviving galleried coaching inn. Dating from the 17th century, it is now protected by the National Trust. At lunchtime it is awash with pin-striped suits.

The Grenadier, Old Barrack Yard, 18 Wilton Row, SW1. Hidden away in a quiet cobbled mews, this pub is a real gem. It used to be the mess of the Duke of Wellington's officers.

Lamb and Flag, 33 Rose Street, WC2. Originally known as the "Bucket of Blood", this timber building was once a venue for bare fist boxing. Its character is enhanced by its quaint skew-whiff walls and doorways.

The Mayflower, 117 Rotherhithe Street, SE16. Dark olde-worlde pub backing on to the Thames with seating outside on the jetty.

Phoenix and Firkin, 5 Windsor Walk, SE5. Firkin pubs are run by Bruce's Brewery, which believes in tradition. They brew their own beer on the premises, are decorated in the spit-and-sawdust style and host cockney-style sing-a-long nights. This particular one is situated in a large Victorian railway station which is on a bridge and has a small train running around the ceiling.

Princess Louise, 209 High Holborn, WC1. Relic from the High Victorian age with notable tiling and fittings. The gent's is worth a visit. Real ales.

Ye Olde Cheshire Cheese, 145 Fleet Street, EC4. Famous olde-worlde pub, rebuilt after the Great Fire but which still has a medieval crypt beneath it. It has been frequented through the

ages by many well known literary figures including Charles Dickens, Dr Johnson and possibly Shakespeare.

Scarsdale, 23a Edwardes Street, W8. In a secluded square close to High Street Kensington is this exceptionally pretty pub covered in foliage with tables outside the front.

Spaniards Inn, Hampstead Lane, NW3. This historic pub is situated at an old toll gate on the north side of Hampstead Heath. It dates back to the 16th century and is reputed to have been used by highwayman Dick Turpin.

Sherlock Holmes, 10 Northumberland Street, WC2. Formerly known as the Northumberland Arms, this theme pub contains memorabilia relating to Arthur Conan Doyle's famed detective and a reconstruction of Holmes's Baker Street study.

Attractions

Tours

A guided tour of London by bus or coach is the best way for new visitors to familiarise themselves with the City. All tours that are registered with the London Tourist Board use their famous Blue Badge Guides, whose ranks now number just under 1,000.

Cityrama (tel: 0171-720 6663)
A two-hour tour of London (foreign language headphones provided) in an open-topped bus. Most enjoyable on a summer's day. Departs every half hour from Grosvenor Gardens (just by Victoria railway station), Coventry Street (Piccadilly) and Russell Square, between 9am and 6pm in summer and until 4pm in winter. Cost: £9 (£4.50 under 14).

Evan Evans (tel: 0181-332 2222)
An all day comprehensive introduction to the City with emphasis on historic sites. Admittance to St. Paul's, Westminster Abbey, and the Tower of London are part of the tour. Picks up from many hotels. Cost: £39.50 (£36.50 for children under 17 years). Thames cruises also available.

Frames Rickards (tel: 0171-837 3111)

Various tours of the city in air-conditioned coaches accompanied by guides who hold the coveted "Blue Badge". The London Experience full-day tour takes in major sights such as Westminster Abbey and the Tower and costs £44 (£38 for under 16s) including admission charges, a river cruise and lunch in a riverside tavern. Other trips include the Elizabethan Banquet tour where you can enjoy an evening of feasting and entertainment in a 15th-century palace in the grounds of Hatfield House. Cost £36.50. Certain tours are provided with French, German, Spanish and Italian translations.

The Original London Transport Sightseeing Tour (tel: 0181-877 1722)

A panoramic 1½-hour tour with live commentary in a traditional red double-decker bus which is open-top in fine weather. Tours begin from three different points; Piccadilly Circus/ Haymarket, Baker Street and Victoria Street (near the station). Cost: £8 (£4 for under 16s).

London Plus (tel: 0181-877 1722)

Operated by the same people as the above, but covering a slightly wider area of central London. Allows passengers to jump on and off at 20 different locations on the route; tickets last a whole day. These Hop On/Hop Off double-deckers are clearly marked with the London Plus logo. First bus 10.30am and last bus 4pm. £8 for adults and £4 for children.

Jack the Ripper & Haunted London (tel: 0171-233 7030)

As the title suggests, an after-dark tour which explores London's more murky past and shady courtyards. Includes pub visits along the way. Evenings (from 7-11pm) on Tuesday, Wednesday, Thursday, Saturday and Sunday only. Main departure point is Fountain Square (off Buckingham Palace Road by Victoria station) but pick-ups can be arranged from individual hotels. Cost £12 (£9.50 for children under 16).

London Docklands Development Corporation (tel: 0171-512 3000)

LDDC organises tours around the 8½-sq. mile new and controversial docklands development. Departures are from the LDDC Visitor Centre, Lime Harbour, on Tuesday at 2pm, Thurs-

day at 10.30am and Sunday at 11.30am, price £6.

On the River

Thames Passenger Services Federation (TPSF) (tel: 0171-930 2062) runs a riverboat service between Hampton Court (up river) and the Thames Barrier (down river) which is an excellent way to see many major sights of London, whose history is intertwined with the river. Services vary from summer to winter with down river services tending to run all year, whilst most up river services only run between April and October. There are piers at Richmond, Kew, Putney, Westminster, Charing Cross, London Bridge, the Tower and Greenwich. TPSF runs the following special services from Westminster Pier:

Evening Cruises (1 hours) with sailings at 7.30pm and 8.15pm May–September. Tel: 0171-930 2062.

Floodlight and Supper Cruises (1½ hours) with sailings at 9pm every night except Saturday May–October. Tel: 0171-839 3572.

Luncheon Cruise (2 hours) sailing at 12.45pm Wednesday and Saturday May–October, and Sunday all year. Tel: 0171-839 3572.

Catamaran Cruisers (tel: 0171-987 1185) operate a regular service downstream to the Tower of London and Greenwich, starting from 10.30 am. Departures are from Charing Cross pier, and the adult fare is £4.40 (children £2.50). The company also offers a variety of special cruises. You could enjoy the "Floodlit Supper Cruise" between Chelsea and Tower Bridge as long as you go for the view and not the food. Cost: £15 with supper, £7.50 without.

Westminster Passenger Service Association (tel: 0171-930 4721) operates a boat service from Westminster to Hampton Court and Kew, starting at 10.15am. Fare to Hampton Court is £7 one-way; to Kew is £5. Children are just over half price. The association also has evening cruises which depart from Westminster at 8.30pm, for a fare of £4.

On the Canal

Jason's Trip, Little Venice, Bloomfield Road, W9. Tel: 0171-286 3428. Tra-

ditional painted narrow boat making 90-minute trips along the Regent's Canal between Little Venice and Camden Lock, taking in Regent's Park and the zoo. March–October. Cost: £4.75 return (£3.50 for under 14).

Jenny Wren, 250 Camden High Street, NW1. Tel: 0171-485 4433. Follows the same route, but from the other direction. Through the park, past the zoo, turning back at Little Venice. March–October. Cost £4.60 return (£2.30 children).

My Fair Lady, 250 Camden High Street, NW1. Tel: 0171-485 4433. Cruising wide-boat restaurant. Three-hour dinner cruises to Little Venice and back, year-round 7.30pm boarding. Live music. Dinner £26.95 Tuesday–Saturday. Also Sunday lunch cruise £17.95, 12.30pm boarding.

London Waterbus Company, Camden Lock Place, NW1. Tel: 0171-482 2550. From Camden Lock to Little Venice with discounted tickets to the zoo at Regent's Park. £2.20 single, £1.20 under 14. (Cockney Cruises to the Thames are available in the summer).

Walking Tours

Some walking tour operators use London Tourist Board trained Blue Badge Guides. They are a guarantee of the quality of general interest walks. Walks generally last two hours.

Cockney Walks. Tel: 0181-504 9159. Daily walks through the East End, Cockney, Jewish and working-class London, led by local historians. £4

Historical Tours. Tel: 0181-668 4019. Programme of walks includes "The London of Dickens and Shakespeare" every Sunday at 11am, starting from exit 1, Blackfriars tube station. Cost: £4.50

The Original London Walks. Tel: 0171-624 3978. Programme includes Jack the Ripper, Shakespeare, Dickens, and other historical walks. Cost: £4

Stage by Stage. Tel: 0171-328 7558. Backstage tours of London's older theatres, conducted by actors and actresses.

Tour Guides International Ltd. Tel: 0171-839 2498.

A wide variety of themed walks: Royal London, Hampstead, Dickens' Lon don, Jack the Ripper, Sherlock Holmes, Legal London and the Inns of Court, etc. Blue-badged guides available for any number of people. Other languages and group bookings available on request.

Other Visits

Parks and Gardens

Battersea Park, SW11
About 200 acres (80 hectares) of park on the south bank of the Thames overlooked by Battersea Power Station. Still bears the scars left from the funfair built for the 1951 Festival of Britain (closed 1975). Has an attractive Japanese Peace Pagoda and a small boating lake. *BR: Battersea Park.*

Green Park, SW1
The smallest of the royal parks, it stretches between Buckingham Palace and Piccadilly. On Sunday the railings bordering Piccadilly are covered with the works of London's less than best artists hopefully looking for buyers. *Tube: Green Park.*

Greenwich Park, SE10
One of London's oldest and most stunning parks. It encompasses the Old Royal Observatory and is intersected by the Greenwich Meridian. Running from the south side to the old Observatory buildings is an elegant tree-lined avenue, remains of a formal plan designed by French landscape artist, Le Notre, in the 17th century. Views from the end of this avenue are breathtaking and on a clear day you can see beyond the Maritime Museum and Wren's Naval College, over the Thames to the City beyond. This beautiful hilly park was once the hunting ground of kings and still has a herd of deer. *BR: Greenwich/Maze Hill. Can also be reached by river on the River Bus or tour boat services (see On the River).*

Hampstead Heath, NW3
Hampstead Heath is vast and interesting. Much of the park itself is hilly and wooded. Some of the best views of London are from the top of Parliament Hill, a popular spot from which to fly kites. In the summer you can swim in the open air at Highgate and Hampstead ponds or take along a picnic and listen to open-air concerts beside the lake at Kenwood House.

On the north west edge is Spaniards Inn, a 16th-century tavern where many historic figures, including Dickens, have stopped to wet their lips. Keats House is to the south. *Tube: Belsize Park or Hampstead.*

Holland Park, W8
Pretty park that feels surprisingly rural, given its proximity to Kensington High Street. The park was originally the grounds to Holland House, built as a gentleman's country residence in 1606. The house was badly damaged in the war and what remains is now part of a youth hostel. Diners eat in style at the luxurious Belvedere restaurant, in the converted stable block, and visitors browse art exhibitions in the Orangery. Peacocks still roam freely. There is an open-air theatre in the summer. *Tube: Kensington High Street.*

Hyde Park and Kensington Gardens, W2
Kensington Gardens was once the grounds of Kensington Palace but now is considered part of Hyde Park. Together they make up Central London's largest park, stretching from Millionaire's Row in Kensington to Park Lane and from Knightsbridge to Bayswater. Once a hunting ground for Henry VIII, Hyde Park became more formal during the reign of Charles I, as a fashionable place to parade. Today it is still a fashionable place to parade, but on horseback along Rotten Row. In the middle of the park is the large Serpentine lake where you can go boating or bathing. Close to the bridge which crosses the lake is the Serpentine Gallery which houses exhibitions of modern art. Look out for the Albert Memorial (to the south), the statue of Peter Pan (north) and Kensington Palace (west). At the corner near Marble Arch is Speaker's Corner where on Sunday mornings anyone can get on a soapbox and say their piece in the presence of a crowd of hecklers. *Tube: Marble Arch/Hyde Park Corner.*

Kew Royal Botanical Gardens, Kew Road, Richmond. Tel: 0181-940 1171. These beautiful gardens have been an official centre for botanical research since 1841 and today are a branch of the Ministry of Agriculture with over 60,000 different species of plants and trees from all over the world. Part of the grounds were set

out with lakes and woodland in the 18th century by landscape gardener Capability Brown and several follies, including the Chinese Pagoda, were built by Sir William Chambers. Kew has two enormous 19th-century greenhouses, the Palm House and the Temperate House, stunning examples of the achievements of Victorian engineering. Sadly, the Palm House had to undergo repairs following damage which was sustained in the violent storms of 1987 when many of Kew's old and rare species of trees were damaged or lost. The latest addition to the greenhouses is the Princess of Wales conservatory opened in 1987. The Orangery has a restaurant and bookshop. Kew Gallery houses exhibitions. Open 9.30am to dusk. Cost: £3.50 adults (£1.30 for under 16s) *Tube: Kew Gardens. Can also be reached by river on the River Bus or tour boat services (see On the River).*

Regent's Park, Marylebone Road, NW1
Situated north of the Marylebone Road, Regent's Park is well-known for its zoo and the elegant Regency houses which surround it. In June Queen Mary's Rose Garden bursts into colour and in the summer there is an open-air theatre and boating on the pond. The Regent's Canal runs along the top edge from where you can catch the Waterbus that travels between Little Venice and Camden. To the left is the London Mosque. On weekends and evenings in the summer months the park is packed with friendly matches of baseball. *Tube: Regent's Park/Great Portland Street.*

Richmond Park, Richmond, Surrey
This is the largest and most rural of the royal parks with 2,500 acres (1,000 hectares) of woods, ancient oak trees and ponds. It is still inhabited by herds of deer. Situated in the park are three lodges which were once royal residences: Pembroke, White and Thatched House Lodges. The view from Richmond Hill over the Thames Valley is famous. *Tube: Richmond.*

St James's Park, SW1
This pretty park is the oldest of the royal parks and is surrounded by palaces and government buildings. Fabulous views of Buckingham Palace and Whitehall can be seen while strolling along its paths. The Houses

of Parliament and No.10 Downing Street (residence of the Prime Minister) are in close proximity whilst St James's Palace and Nash's Carlton Terrace are to be found north of the elegant tree-lined Mall. The large lake in the centre of the park is home to various species of waterfowl. At lunchtimes in summer there are brass band concerts from the bandstand. Look out for members of the Queen's Guard passing through for the Changing of the Guard ceremony each morning. *Tube: St James's Park, Green Park or Victoria.*

Graveyards

London's graveyards are some of the most historical and interesting places to visit. Here are some, dating back to the 1800s.

Brompton Cemetery, Old Brompton Road, SW10. The octagonal chapel and circular catacombs are part of a grand plan for this 40-acre (16-hectare) cemetery which was never completed. Consecrated in 1840, this became the first state-controlled cemetery. Many soldiers are buried here because of the proximity of Chelsea Hospital. Also Sir Henry Cole, organiser of the Great Exhibition (1882), Emmeline Pankhurst, fighter for women's rights (1928) and Frederick Leyland, patron of the Pre-Raphaelites (1892).

City of London Cemetery, Alderbrook Road, Manor Park, E12. This is the largest municipal cemetery in Europe and is the resting place for than 1 million people.

Hampstead Cemetery, Fortune Green Road, NW6. Opened in 1878. Buried among its 26 acres are Kate Greenaway (1901), the Grand Duke Michael of Russia (1929) and the actress Gladys Cooper (1971).

Highgate Cemetery, Swain's Lane, Highgate, N6. The most famous of London's cemeteries. Consecrated in 1839 by the Bishop of London, it immediately became a fashionable place to be buried and, in keeping with the morbid character of the Victorians, it also became a tourist attraction. The most famous occupant is the German philosopher Karl Marx (1883). Also resting here is the female novelist George Eliot (1880) and actor Sir Ralph Richardson. Some

parts may only be visited with a guide.

Jew's Cemetery, Pound Lane, Willesden, NW10. This cemetery was consecrated in 1873. Members of the de Rothschild family are buried here.

Kensal Green Cemetery, Harrow Road, W10. This is one of the most interesting of London's Victorian cemeteries. Consecrated in 1833 and stretching over 54 acres (22 hectares), it was one of the first commercial burial grounds built to relieve the problem of overcrowding in churchyards. Three gravel tracks wind through the mass of grand tombs, many now in a sad state of decay, which mark the burial places of many eminent Victorians. Here are the tombs of the engineer, Sir Isambard Kingdom Brunel (1859), and novelists William Makepeace Thackeray (1863), Anthony Trollope (1882) and Wilkie Collins (1889).

Museums

Bethnal Green Museum of Childhood, Cambridge Heath Road, E2. Tel: 0181-980 2415. Largest collection of toys and other child-related items in the country. Lovely 18th and 19th-century toys, dolls' houses and puppets. Open year-round closed on Friday. Free. *Tube: Bethnal Green.*

British Museum, Great Russell Street, WC1. Tel: 0171-636 1555. A vast collection unrivalled anywhere in the world, set within Smirke's grand neo-classical building. Includes Egyptian mummies, the Elgin Marbles, Rosetta Stone, and the Sutton Hoo ship burial. Also art, manuscripts, prints and drawings. It would take days, if not weeks, to see it all. Open daily year-round. Free. *Tubes: Holborn, Tottenham Court Road.*

Commonwealth Institute, Kensington High Street, W8. Tel: 0171-603 4535. Museum showing the history, culture and daily life of 48 nations from the Commonwealth. Open daily. Free. *Tube: High Street Kensington.*

Design Museum, Butlers Wharf, Shad Thames, SE1. Tel: 0171-403 6933. Set within a white modernist building overlooking the Thames, this museum devotes a large amount of space to the design progress of everyday domestic items from vacuum cleaners to televisions. Has a partic-

ularly good selection of chairs. Also changing displays of graphic design and new design innovations. Open 10.30am-5pm. Admission charge. Tube: Tower Hill or London Bridge.

Florence Nightingale Museum, St Thomas's Hospital, 2 Lambeth Palace Road, SE1. Tel: 0171-620 0374. Museum of modern nursing dedicated to Florence Nightingale, who changed the course of nursing. On display are reconstructions of ward scenes from the Crimean War and her famous lamp. Closed Monday. Admission charge. *Tube: Waterloo.*

Freemason's Hall, Great Queen Street, WC2. Tel: 0171-831 9811. Permanent exhibition of the history of English Freemasonry housed within a fine Art Deco building. Here you can get an insight into this loyal society that is shrouded in secrecy. Open weekdays and Saturday morning. Free. *Tube: Holborn.*

Geffrye Museum, Kingsland Road, E2. Tel: 0171-739 9893. Located in an area associated with furniture and cabinet making, this museum is for those interested in the history of English domestic design. A series of room settings display English furniture and interior decor from Tudor times to the 1950s. Closed Monday, open bank holiday Mondays, 2-5pm. Free. *Tube: Liverpool Street (and bus).*

Geological Museum, Exhibition Road, SW7. Tel: 0171-938 8765. Now a part of the Natural History Museum (alongside), here is housed the national collection of geological finds and methods, including diamonds in their natural state. Attractions include an earthquake simulator and a video of a volcano erupting. Open: daily year-round. Free. *Tube: South Kensington.*

Horniman Museum, London Road, Forest Hill, SE23. Tel: 0181-699 2339. A beautiful Art Nouveau building is home to this odd collection of anthropological objects which includes stuffed birds, totem poles, and a large selection of musical instruments from all over the world (rumoured to be about to move). Open daily. Free. *BR: Forest Hill.*

Imperial War Museum, Lambeth Road, SE1. Tel: 0171-416 5000. This was completely re-designed in 1989 and is now an excellent museum that is as much about the frightening experience of war for everybody as it is about displays of arms and weapons. Works of art, including those by the official war artists, are on show. One of the main attractions is the Blitz Experience which takes you through a simulation of a London air-raid with realistic lighting and sound effects. Open daily. Admission charge. *Tube: Elephant and Castle, North Lambeth.*

Jewish Museum, Woburn House, Tavistock Square, WC1. Tel: 0171-388 4525. Celebrates the richness of Anglo-Jewish history and tradition with displays of ritual and religious objects including jewellery, silver, ceramics and embroidery. Closed Monday. Admission charge. *Tube: Euston Square.*

London Toy and Model Museum, 21 Craven Hill, W2. Tel: 0171-262 7905. Small and friendly museum crammed with a private collection of over 3,000 toys and models dating from the 18th century. Most are hidden safely behind glass but a few, including a giant Paddington Bear, escaped and wait in the entrance hall to welcome visitors. A model train set runs around the garden where there is also a fairground carousel and a larger train giving rides to children. Closed Monday. Admission charge. *Tube: Queensway/ Paddington.*

London Transport Museum, The Piazza, Covent Garden, WC2. Tel: 0171-379 6344. (Reopening December 1993). Here is the complete history of public transport in London dating from the early days of horse-drawn trams and the beginnings of the Underground to the present day. Many buses and carriages are on display along with exhibitions of LRT graphics. Apart from the famous map by H. C. Beck this includes a particularly excellent collection of posters designed by leading artists in the 1930s. Open daily. Admission charge. *Tube: Covent Garden.*

Museum of Garden History, St Mary-at-Lambeth, Lambeth Palace Road, SE1. Tel: 0171-261 1891. Delightful museum devoted to garden history and particularly the memory of John Tradescant and his son, famous 17th-century gardeners who introduced many flowers, shrubs and trees from Europe and America. The church of St Mary houses a collection of old gar-

den tools, changing exhibitions and a café. A small and peaceful 17th-century-style garden has been recreated in part of the graveyard. Closed Saturday. Donation. *Tube: Waterloo.*

Museum of London, London Wall, EC2. Tel: 0171-600 3699. Covers the history of London from prehistoric to modern times with exhibits including archaeological finds, the golden carriage of the Lord Mayor, a 1928 lift from Selfridges and an air-raid shelter. Closed Monday. Admission charge. *Tube: Barbican/Moorgate.*

Museum of Mankind, 6 Burlington Gardens, Piccadilly, W1. Tel: 0171-636 1555. Contains the British Museum's department of ethnography which is particularly strong on exhibits relating to tribal and village cultures from America, Oceana and Africa, dating from ancient to modern times. Open daily. Free. *Tube: Piccadilly Circus.*

Museum of the Moving Image, South Bank, SE1. Tel: 0171-401 2636. Lively and fun museum of the history of cinema and television that explains the technological developments and what goes on behind the scenes. Visitors have a chance to sit in front of the cameras themselves and become a newsreader or do a screen test for a Hollywood film. Closed Monday. Admission charge. *Tube: Waterloo.*

National Army Museum, Royal Hospital Road, SW3. Tel: 0171-730 0717. Museum covering over 500 years of the history of the British Army. On show are weapons, uniforms and war relics such as a French flag captured from the battle of Waterloo. Also an art gallery with portraits of war heroes. Open daily. Free. *Tube: Sloane Square.*

National Maritime Museum, Romney Road, Greenwich, SE10. Tel: 0181-858 4422. This is the biggest naval museum in the world with a large collection of exhibits relating to Britain's great seafaring history. On show is a display of the Battle of Trafalgar, a gallery of model warships and many maritime instruments, weapons and paintings. The 17th-century building in which the museum is housed was designed by Inigo Jones for Queen Anne and is notable as England's first Palladian-style house. Open daily. Admission charge. *BR: Greenwich/Maze Hill.*

National Postal Museum, King Edward Street, EC1. Tel: 0171-239 5420. Huge international collection of stamps which includes the Post Office's own collection with every British postal stamp issued since 1840. Open weekdays. Free. *Tube: St Paul's.*

Natural History Museum, Cromwell Road, S Kensington, SW7. Tel: 0171-938 9123. With an emphasis on man's evolution and biology, different departments are concerned with botany, zoology, mineralogy, palaeontology (study of extinct organisms) and entomology (study of insects). Some of the most popular exhibits are the dinosaur and whale skeletons on the ground floor. Now incorporates the Geological Museum. Open daily. Admission charge. *Tube: S. Kensington.*

Public Record Office Museum, Chancery Lane, WC2. Tel: 0181-876 3444. Here are the national archives, including the *Domesday Book* (1086) and the log of Nelson's ship, Victory. Open weekdays. Free. *Tube: Chancery Lane.*

Science Museum, Exhibition road, SW7. Tel: 0171-938 8000. Traces the history of science and technology to the present day and analyses their influence on industry and everyday life. Highlights include exhibits concerned with man's harnessing of power such as George Stevenson's "Rocket" and memorabilia from space exploration. The history of medicine and photography is also covered. The new Food For Thought gallery shows the impact of science and technology on food. Lots of working models to play with. Open daily. Admission charge. *Tube: S. Kensington.*

Shakespeare Globe Museum, Bear Gardens, Bankside, SE1. Tel: 0171-928 6342. Exhibition of the life and times of the famous bard and also of the excavations carried out on the Rose and Globe theatres nearby. In addition to models showing how the Rose and Globe theatres are going to be re-built, there are models of the old Blackfriar, Curtain and Swan theatres on display. Open daily. Admission charge. *Tube: London Bridge*

Sir John Soane's Museum, 13 Lincoln Inn Fields, WC2. Tel: 0171-405 2107. Soane was one of Britain's greatest Neo-Classical architects and a passionate collector. His house, which he altered over the years to accommodate his vast collection of antiquities, books, drawings and paintings, is virtually unchanged since his death. This was a stipulation in his will when he bequeathed house and contents to the nation. Soane's large and valuable collection includes Hogarth's series of 12 paintings, *The Rake's Progress* and the Sarcophagus of Seti I. Other interesting items are Sir Christopher Wren's watch and Napoleon's pistol. Highly recommended. Closed Sunday and Monday. Free. *Tube: Holborn.*

The Theatre Museum, Russell Street, WC2. Tel: 0171-836 7891. Britain's richest collection of theatrical material, dating from the time of Shakespeare to the present day. Set within a former market warehouse in the middle of West End theatreland with a fine collection of costumes, props, puppets, stage models and posters from all the performing arts. Closed Monday. Admission charge. *Tube: Covent Garden.*

Victoria and Albert Museum, Cromwell Road, S Kensington, SW7. Tel: 0171-938 8500. The arts' treasure house of Britain and the finest museum of the decorative arts in the world. This museum largely came into being to house exhibits from the Great Exhibition of 1851 with the hope that as a permanent exhibition it would help to raise the standard of British design in manufacturing. This vast collection, housed within 7 miles (11 km) of galleries, contains everything from medieval candlesticks and stained-glass windows to Chippendale furniture and Clarice Cliff ceramics. Open daily. Admission by voluntary donation. *Tube: South Kensington.*

Wellington Museum, Apsley House, 149 Piccadilly, W1. Tel: 0171-499 5676. Once the home of the Duke of Wellington, known as the Iron Duke, this house used to have the address, No. 1 London. Today it houses paintings and objects that once belonged to the Duke, who is most famous for his victory at Waterloo. Highlights include his collection of medals, Goya's portrait of Wellington astride a horse of 1812, and Canova's 11ft 4-inch (3.4-metres) high marble statue of tiny Napoleon Bonaparte (Napoleon reputedly didn't like it). Closed Monday. Admission fee. *Tube: Hyde Park Corner.*

William Morris Gallery, Lloyd Park, Forest Road, E17. Tel: 0181-527 3782. Within the Georgian House where Morris spent his childhood is a collection that pays tribute to the genius and talent of this illustrious man. It also celebrates the achievements of his colleagues who, together with Morris, were responsible for the fine work of the Arts and Crafts Movement in the 19th century. On display are textiles, furniture, silverware, ceramics, paintings and drawings by artists and craftsmen such as Burne-Jones, Rossetti, de Morgan, Mackmurdo and Morris himself. Admission free. Closed Monday. *Tube: Walthamstow Central.*

Wimbledon Lawn Tennis Museum, All England Club, Church Road, SW19. Tel: 0181-946 6131. Traces the history of tennis since its early days when women used to struggle around in long skirts and the grass was cut with horse-drawn mowers. Is full of interesting and amusing facts and memorabilia relating to Wimbledon's famous fortnight. Closed Monday. Admission charge. *Tube: Southfields.*

Art Galleries

Courtauld Institute, Somerset House, The Strand, WC2. Tel: 0171-872 0220. This fine collection which was gathered by textile baron, Samuel Courtauld, has moved from Woburn Place to the Strand. It contains many priceless masterpieces including the best collection of Post-Impressionist paintings in England with works by Cézanne, Gauguin, and Van Gogh. Open daily. Admission charge. *Tube: Temple.*

Dulwich Picture Gallery, College Road, SE21. Tel: 0181-693 5254. Designed by Sir John Soane and opened in 1814, this was the first public picture gallery in England. The 300 paintings on display are rich with Dutch and Flemish masters, including works by Rembrandt, Rubens and Van Dyck. Important works by Gainsborough and Hogarth are also on view. Closed Monday. Admission charge. *BR: North or West Dulwich.*

Leighton House, 12 Holland Park Road, W14. Tel: 0171-602 3316. Pre-Raphaelite and High Victorian paintings are exhibited within this fascinating house once occupied by the acclaimed Victorian artist Lord Leighton. Millais, Burne-Jones and Alma Tadema are among those on display. The interior of the house has a strong Eastern influence, particularly the exquisite Arab Hall which was based on a Muslim palace. This was built to incorporate Leighton's extensive collection of tiles gathered from Persia and North Africa. Also look out for tiles by William de Morgan and a mosaic frieze by Walter Crane. Many great Victorian artists lived in the vicinity of Leighton House and it is worth looking out for blue plaques bearing their names. Closed Sunday. Free. *Tube: High Street Kensington.*

National Gallery, Trafalgar Square, WC2. Tel: 0171-839 3321. Home to the nation's most important, and indeed one of the world's greatest, collections of paintings. All the leading European schools and almost every artist of note from the 13th to the 19th century is here. Open daily. Free. *Tube: Charing Cross/Leicester Square.*

National Portrait Gallery, 2 St Martin's Place, WC2. Tel: 0171-306 0055. Anybody who is anybody in British history wants to have their face on the wall of this gallery. Here are paintings, photographs and sculptures of Britain's most famous and highly respected citizens since Tudor times to the present day, including monarchs, intellectuals and, more recently, pop stars. Open daily. Free. *Tube: Leicester Square/Charing Cross.*

Photographer's Gallery, 5 & 8 Great Newport Street, WC2. Tel: 0171-831 1772. London's premier photography venue, usually holding at least two different exhibitions at any one time. The gallery's Print Room keeps an excellent selection of contemporary and historic prints for view and sale. Closed Monday. Free. *Tube: Leicester Square.*

Queen's Gallery, Adjacent to Buckingham Palace, SW1. Tel: 0171-930 4832. Temporary exhibitions of treasures from the Queens private collection are shown in this gallery which used to be the Palace chapel. Closed Monday. Admission charge. *Tube: St James's Park.*

Tate Gallery, Millbank, SW1. Tel: 0171-821 1313. One must thank the sugar magnate Henry Tate for this marvellous gallery on the bank of the Thames. Opened in 1897, based on a collection of mainly Victorian paintings, the Tate now houses the nations collection of British art dating from the 16th century, including Blake, Constable, Reynolds and Gainsborough. The Tate is also home to an important collection of international art that encompasses modern movements from French Impressionism to present day and which is particularly strong on Cubism. The new Clore Gallery was designed by James Stirling for the Turner collection. Open daily. Free. *Tube: Pimlico.*

Wallace Collection, Hertford House, Manchester Square, W1. Tel: 0171-935 0687. Outstanding collection of old masters housed in an elegant town house that once belonged to the Marquesses of Hertford. In 1900 the house and works were bequeathed to the nation. Particularly notable is the selection of paintings by 18th-century French masters, including Boucher, Fragonard, Watteau and Chardin. *The Laughing Cavalier* by Frans Hals hangs here along with several fine paintings by Rubens and Rembrandt. Also superb furniture and tableware. Open daily. Donation. *Tube: Bond Street.*

Limited Viewing

These galleries are open only when exhibiting, or by special appointment.

Barbican Art Gallery, Barbican Centre, EC2. Tel: 0171-588 5705. Large concrete complex built for the arts. The gallery, which is on the 8th floor, holds exhibitions of major importance. *Tube: Barbican/Moorgate*

Hayward Gallery, South Bank, SE1. Tel: 0171-928 3144. Another concrete jungle built as a centre for the arts, but with the attractive location of the south bank of the Thames. The Hayward hosts exhibitions of international importance which most predominantly feature 20th-century art. *Tube: Waterloo.*

ICA, Nash House, The Mall, SW1. Tel: 0171-930 3647. The Institute of Contemporary Art is the most avant-garde of London's major galleries. Two galleries show modern innovative work. Also live performance art and music. *Tube: Charing Cross/Piccadilly Circus.*

Royal Academy, Burlington House, Piccadilly, W1. Tel: 0171-439 7438. Particularly well known for the summer exhibition of thousands of works by both amateurs and professionals, all of which are on sale from June to August. Unfortunately, this exhibition has a reputation for being more notable as a social event than for the quality of work exhibited. The Academy has been holding major exhibitions since it was founded in 1768 when it played an important role in bringing social acceptability to art as a profession in Britain. *Tube: Green Park/Piccadilly Circus.*

Saatchi Collection, 98a Boundary Road, NW8. Tel: 0171-624 8299. Charles Saatchi (of Saatchi and Saatchi advertising agency fame), a leading collector of modern art, financed the building of this minimalist gallery space in St John's Wood. There are two changing exhibitions a year featuring modern art of recent decades. Restricted opening times; telephone first. *Tube: St John's Wood.*

Serpentine Gallery, Kensington Gardens, Hyde Park, W2. Tel: 0171-402 6075. Hosts interesting exhibitions of contemporary art within an airy gallery space in the centre of Hyde Park. *Tube: Lancaster Gate*

Whitechapel Art Gallery, 80 Whitechapel High Street, E1. Tel: 0171-377 0107. Fabulous Art Nouveau gallery holding exciting exhibitions of work by contemporary artists. *Tube: Aldgate East.*

'Historical Houses

Chiswick House, Burlington Lane, Chiswick, W4. Tel: 0181-995 0508 Palladian villa designed by the third Earl of Burlington for himself as a temple to the arts in 1929. Indeed, here he entertained such figures as the composer Handel and the writer Alexander Pope. Burlington was the leader of the Palladian style which established the classical ideals of the Italian Renaissance (particularly those of Palladio) in England taking over from the Baroque style. The interior of the house was designed by his colleague William Kent and includes fine examples of furniture and decoration from the period. Open daily. Admission charge. *Tube: Turnham Green/BR: Chiswick.*

Dickens House, 48 Doughty Street, WC1. Tel: 0171-405 2127. Regency house which has been faithfully restored as it would have been when Charles Dickens and his family lived here between 1837 and 1839. Here he wrote the novels *Nicholas Nickleby* and *Oliver Twist*. Contains a large array of memorabilia including his library, manuscripts, first editions, paintings and furniture. The still room and wash house with water heating copper and shallow stone sink are rare surviving examples from this period. Closed Sunday, public holidays. Admission charge. *Tube: Russell Square.*

Fenton House, Hampstead Grove, Hampstead, NW3. Tel: 0171-435 3471. William and Mary style red brick house built in 1693 which houses a fine collection of early keyboard musical instruments, European and Oriental porcelain and furniture. Lovely walled garden. Open April-October afternoons only, closed Thursday and Friday. Admission charge. *Tube: Hampstead.*

Freud Museum, 20 Maresfield Gardens, NW3. Tel: 0171-435 2002. Sigmund Freud spent the last year of his life here between 1938 and 1939 after fleeing Nazi persecution in Vienna. Many of the belongings that Freud managed to bring from Austria are on display in this house, which has remained virtually intact since his death. The highlight is naturally Freud's study, containing his famous couch, library, desk, chair and spectacles as well as his interesting and unusual collection of statues and antiquities. Closed Monday and Tuesday. Admission charge. *Tube: Finchley Road.*

Ham House, Ham Street, Richmond, Surrey. Tel: 0181-940 1950. (Reopening in 1994). Lavish late Jacobean House built in 1610 which has been restored to its former glory. Fine interior with opulent period furniture and ostentatious detailing. Also well maintained formal gardens. Closed Monday. Admission charge. *Tube: Richmond.*

Hogarth's House, Hogarth Lane,

Chiswick, W4. Tel: 0181-994 6757. This was the country home of the 18th-century satirical artist William Hogarth from 1749 to 1764. It has been well restored and now houses the largest public display of his work. Pleasant grounds. Closed Tuesday (closed for part of September and December). Free. *BR: Chiswick*.

Dr Johnson's House, 17 Gough Square, Fleet Street, EC4. Tel: 0171-353 3745. This fine example of a Georgian town house was the home of the great English essayist and lexicographer Samuel Johnson from 1748 to 1759. It now contains a first edition of Johnson's famous dictionary, which he compiled here, and portraits of Johnson and friends. Closed Sunday. Admission charge. *Tube: St Paul's/Chancery Lane*.

Keats' House, Keats' Grove, Hampstead, NW3. Tel: 0171-435 2062. The Romantic poet John Keats lived here for two years (1818-20) during which time he wrote many of his greatest poems, including *Ode to a Nightingale*. This Regency house contains manuscripts and letters and other items belonging to Keats as well as period furniture. Open daily. Voluntary donation. *Tube: Hampstead*.

Kenwood House (The Iveagh Bequest), Hampstead Lane, NW3. Tel: 0181-348 1286. Elegant country house that once belonged to the Earl of Mansfield. In 1767 he commissioned Robert Adam to remodel and extend the original 17th-century building which included the library whose interior is an excellent example of Adam's distinctive decorative style. In 1925 the house was bought by Lord Iveagh, who on his death bequeathed the estate to the nation. Most importantly, this included Iveagh's valuable art collection of masterpieces by Rembrandt, Rubens, Vermeer, Turner, Gainsborough, Reynolds and others. Also fine Georgian furniture. In the summer open-air concerts are held in the grounds which were laid out by Humphrey Repton. Open daily. Free. *Tube: Golders Green/Archway*.

Marble Hill House, Richmond Road, Twickenham, Middlesex. Tel: 0181-892 5115. Fine example of an 18th-century Palladian villa, built in 1720 for Henrietta Howard, the mistress of George II. Has been restored to its original appearance. Open daily. Free. *Tube: Richmond*.

Syon House, Syon Park, Brentford, Middlesex. Tel: 0181-560 0881. Remodelled by Robert Adam in 1766, this is undoubtedly one of the best examples of his work. Working at the same time, Capability Brown laid out the gardens. The house is still home to the Duke of Northumberland. Open April-October. Closed Monday and Tuesday. Admission charge. The Butterfly Museum is within the grounds. Admission charge. *BR: Syon Lane*.

Wesley's House, 47 City Road, EC1. Tel: 0171-253 2262. This is the house where John Wesley, the founder of Methodism in the 18th century, lived and died. Contains Wesley's personal belongings and a museum of early Methodism. Next door is the chapel he built in 1778 and the graveyard where he now lies. Closed Sunday. Free. *Tube: Old Street*.

Concerts

Rock & Pop

Rock and pop music is one of Britain's greatest exports, so what better city in the world to hear it live?

Academy Brixton, 211 Stockwell Road, SW9. Tel: 0171-326 1022. Large and lively venue with a buzzing atmosphere. Tends to attract trendy bands and crowds. Good viewing. *Tube: Brixton*.

Astoria, Charing Cross Road, WC2. Tel: 0171-434 0403. This former theatre has a large dance floor and hosts a variety of music including rock, folk, reggae and R&B. *Tube: Tottenham Court Road or Leicester Square*.

Hammersmith Apollo (formerly Odeon), Queen Caroline Street, W6. Tel: 0181-741 4868. Famous long-standing music venue that is on the tour circuit for major bands. Sitting is compulsory so it is rather like being in a cinema, but despite this, good fun is usually had by all. *Tube: Hammersmith*.

Marquee, 105 Charing Cross Road, WC2. Tel: 0171-437 6603. The legendry Marquee that was home to punk in the 1970s has been moved from its original location in Wardour Street. It is still the main venue for heavy metal rock and loud discordant music, attracting queues of young followers and old rockers. *Tube: Tottenham Court Road/Leicester Square*.

Palladium, 8 Argyle Street, W1. Tel: 0171-494 5020. One of the most grand and famous theatres in London that occasionally hosts more subdued bands and singers. *Tube: Oxford Circus*.

Rock Garden, the Piazza, Covent Garden, WC2. Tel: 0171-240 3961. Provides a stage for new unknown bands in central London. Small venue in a dark cavernous basement. *Tube: Covent Garden*.

Town & Country Club, Highgate Road, Kentish Town, NW5. Tel: 0171-284 0303. One of London's most popular music venues. This small and intimate club has a strong local atmosphere and still maintains its reputation for giving young up-and-coming bands support. It is also a favourite venue with many successful bands who like to begin their tours here. *Tube: Kentish Town*.

Wembley Arena and Stadium, Empire Way, Wembley, Middlesex. Tel: 0181-900 1234. Acoustics and viewing can be a problem at the Arena, London's largest indoor venue. However, this is dwarfed by the huge football stadium next door which has a capacity of 70,000. The stadium is for mega-concerts and, unless you arrive early to get a good viewing position, expect to watch the action on the large video screens. *Tube: Wembley Park/Wembley Central*.

Jazz

100 Club, 100 Oxford Street, W1. Tel: 0171-636 0933. Decked out in a basic manner with two bars at each end serving drinks at pub prices, this club evokes the atmosphere of a northern working men's club. A renowned venue for live jazz, rhythm and blues from established bands and young "unheard of's" alike. It is packed out every night. Closes 1am.

606 Club, 90 Lots Road, SW10. Tel: 0171-352 5953. Basement club hidden behind an elusive doorway on Lots Road which hosts live jazz every night. Here young up-and-coming musicians are encouraged to play alongside more established names. The food is good and the atmosphere relaxed; popular with musicians who come to eat, drink and join in with impromptu sessions. Closes 3am.

Bass Clef, 35 Coronet Street, N1. Tel: 0171-729 2476. This cramped basement club close to Old Street hosts popular jazz through the week, with Latin and Salsa on Friday and African dance music on Saturday. Jam sessions every Tuesday, whilst on Sunday lunchtimes entry is free to hear Big Band sounds. Closes 2am.

Dover Street Wine Bar & Restaurant, 8-9 Dover Street, W1. Tel: 0171-629 9813. Intimate basement where you can dine by candlelight to live jazz, soul or R&B.

Ronnie Scott's, 47 Frith Street, W1. Tel: 0171-439 0747. In the heart of Soho is London's most famous jazz venue attracting all the major names of the jazz world and a varied clientele. Food and service are less of an attraction than the music, atmosphere and indeed Ronnie Scott himself who opens up the entertainment with his infamous "jokes". Arrive early as it gets very crowded, especially at weekends. Closes 3am.

Classical

Barbican Arts Centre, Silk Street, EC2. Tel: 0171-638 8891. Home to the London Symphony Orchestra and the English Chamber Orchestra. This huge concrete complex built for the arts is one of London's major classical concert venues. *Tube: Barbican.*

Royal Festival Hall, South Bank, Belvedere Road, SE1. Tel: 0171-928 3002. London's premier classical music venue. Built as part of the Festival of Britain of 1951, the exterior of this hall appears somewhat dated and arouses mixed public comment on its appearance. However, it is an excellent concert hall with space for large scale performances. Next door is the **Queen Elizabeth Hall** where chamber concerts and solos are performed. Also the small **Purcell Room**. *Tube: Waterloo.*

Wigmore Hall, 36 Wigmore Street, W1. Tel: 0171-935 2141. Delightful intimate hall with seating for 550. It has a pleasant atmosphere and excellent acoustics and is most renowned for chamber recitals. Also Sunday Morning Coffee Concerts. *Tube: Bond Street.*

The Royal Albert Hall, Kensington Gore, SW7. Tel: 0171-589 3202. Erected in the memory of Prince Albert, this circular hall comes alive every summer for the Henry Wood Promenade Concerts, simply known as The Proms. The acoustics have been improved over the past few years, making this a more enjoyable venue. *Tube: Kensington High Street (10-minute walk)/South Kensington.*

Kenwood Lakeside Theatre, Hampstead Lane, NW3. Tel: 0171-973 3427. Quality open-air performances of classical music and opera in the beautiful grounds of Kenwood House. Usually includes a production by the Royal Opera. *Tube: Golders Green/Archway.*

Holland Park Open Air Theatre, Holland Park, W14. Tel: 0171-602 7856. During the warm summer months opera, dance and theatre performances are staged here in the semi-open air. *Tube: Holland Park/High Street Kensington.*

Many of London's churches also offer superb music. Three of the best are:

St John's, Smith Square, Westminster, W1, tel; 0171-222 1061. This church has been converted into a concert hall hosting chamber music and BBC lunchtime concerts. *Tube: Westminster.*

St Martin-in-the-Fields, Trafalgar Square, WC2. Tel: 0171-930 0089. Concerts are regularly held at lunchtimes and evenings within this church designed by James Gibbs. *Tube: Charing Cross.*

St Mary-le-Bow Church, Cheapside, EC2. Tel: 0171-248 5139. Thursday lunchtime recitals. This church is home to the famous Bow bells. *Tube: St Paul's.*

Ballet

Coliseum, St Martin's Lane, WC2. Tel: 0171-836 3161. Hosts performances of ballet in the summer months by the Royal Festival Ballet and visiting companies. Is particularly popular with visiting Russian Ballets. *Tube: Leicester Square.*

Sadler's Wells Theatre/Lilian Bayliss Theatre, Rosebery Avenue, EC1. Tel: 0171-278 8916. Although the famous Sadler's Wells Royal Ballet is no longer in residence here, having moved to Birmingham, this theatre is still London's leading dance venue. All styles of dance are represented by major international dance companies. *Tube: Angel.*

Royal Opera House, 48 Floral Street, WC2. Tel: 0171-240 1066. Home to the Royal Ballet and the Royal Opera. This theatre is exceptionally grand and the tickets, though expensive, sell out quickly. *Tube: Covent Garden.*

Opera

Coliseum, English National Opera, St Martin's Lane, WC2. Tel: 0171-836 3161

This elegant Edwardian theatre is easily distinguished on London's skyline by the illuminated golden globe on its roof. Home to the English National Opera (ENO) this is where English language operas are performed. Productions tend to be more theatrical than those of the Royal Opera. *Tube: Leicester Square.*

The Royal Opera House, 48 Floral Street, WC2. Tel: 0171-240 1066. More traditional than the Coliseum, this is the poshest theatre in London attracting the *crème de la crème* of the Opera world. Operas are performed in their original language and tickets are very expensive. Dressy affair. *Tube: Covent Garden*

Theatre

Getting a Ticket

The only way to get a ticket at face value is to buy it from the theatre box office. Most are open from 10am until mid-evening. You can pay by credit card over the phone for most theatres, or reserve seats three days in advance before paying. There are booking agents throughout London. Beware: some charge high fees. Two reputable ones that are open 24 hours are:

First Call at 0171-240 7200
Ticketmaster at 0171-379 4444

You can also book many of the West End shows at the **Theatre Museum**. Tel: 0171-836 2330. Touts should be ignored. They do no-one a service but themselves.

Getting a Seat

Many theatres will offer unsold seats

(standby) at knockdown rates just before a performance. Winter Wednesday matinees can be particularly good for this. The **SWET Ticket Booth** in Leicester Square also sells unsold tickets at discount rates, but charges a £1 booking fee and only accepts cash. Expect queues.

The Barbican Arts Centre, Barbican, EC2. Tel: 0171-638 8891. Home to the London Symphony Orchestra and to the Royal Shakespeare Company who sadly, due to financial difficulties, do not perform here all year round. Contains the **Barbican Theatre**, **Concert Hall** and **The Pit** which are well thought-out and comfortable with good acoustics, although they're somewhat sterile. Several different productions run concurrently. *Tube: Moorgate.* 24-hour information tel: 0171-628 2295.

National Theatre, South Bank, SE1. Tel: 0171-928 2252. Box office tel: 0171-928 2033. Three repertory theatres are housed within this concrete structure: the **Olivier**, the **Lyttelton** and the **Cottesloe**. They always provide a good and varied selection of plays. *Tube: Waterloo/Embankment.*

Cinema

There are fewer screens in London than there used to be, and the city generally doesn't radiate the same excitement about cinema as, say, New York does. Also, the scarcity of first-run cinemas means that London sometimes has to wait months for some American movies (though the blockbusters travel the Atlantic fast to take advantage of the global merchandising hype).

Most cinemas in central London (mainly close to Leicester Square) are part of the big companies and show the new releases; independent cinemas tend to be on the fringes of the central area or in the suburbs. Advance seat bookings are available. Monday night is reduced ticket price night in many West End cinemas. It's usually also cheaper to see a film during the day (and much quieter).

Repertory Cinema

These venues show regularly changing programmes of new and old English and foreign-language films.

National Film Theatre, South Bank, SE1. Tel: 0171-928 3232. Hosts the London Film Festival. Presents short seasons of films dedicated to themes such as international regions, actors and film directors. Two cinemas, bookshop and a good café. Daily membership 40p (£13.50 per year). For information, tel: 0171-633 0274.

The Electric Cinema, 191 Portobello Road, W11. Tel: 0171-792 2020. This is one of London's oldest and most beautiful cinemas. On Fridays it offers a comedy variety act followed by a late-night movie.

ICA Cinema & Cinemathèque, Nash House, The Mall, SW1. Tel: 0171-930 3647. Shows a selection of international avant-garde movies. Access to the Institute of Contemporary Art requires a £1.50 day membership.

Everyman, Hollybush Vale, NW3. Tel: 0171-431 2240. The oldest repertory cinema in the country. Originally a drill hall, then a theatre, it opened as a cinema in 1933. Shows a variety of films which change each night.

For entertainment listings consult: *What's On* (events' magazine for tourists); *Time Out* (the events' magazine Londoners read); plus *The Guardian*, *The Independent*, *The Times* and the *Evening Standard* (newspapers).

Diary of Events

January

New Year's Day Parade from Berkeley Square to Hyde Park.

London International Boat Show, Earl's Court: the world's largest.

Charles I commemoration (last Sunday): English Civil War Society dress up as Royalists from the King's army and march from Charles I's statue in Whitehall to his place of execution outside Banqueting House.

February

Crufts Dog Show, Earl's Court. Pedigree dogs compete for the world's most coveted canine prize.

Chinese New Year: colourful Chinese celebrations centring around Gerrard Street in Chinatown.

Valentine's Day (14th): the most romantic day of the year.

March

Ideal Home Exhibition, Earl's Court. Tel: 01895-677677. Exhibition of new ideas and products for the home.

Oxford and Cambridge Boat Race: annual race between university oarsmen that has taken place on the Thames between University Stone in Putney and Mortlake since 1856.

London Book Fair, Olympia.

Chelsea Antiques Fair, Old Town Hall, Kings Road, SW3: wide range of antiques on sale.

Easter Parade, Battersea Park. Tel: 0171-580 0145: carnival with floats and fancy dress costumes.

Camden Jazz Festival, Camden Town. Tel: 0171-860 5866: includes jazz, opera, dance, film and exhibitions all over Camden.

April

April Fool's Day (1 April): throughout the morning Britons go out of their way to hoodwink each other.

London Harness Horse Parade, Regent's Park. Tel: 0171-486 7905: horse parade in harness around the inner circle.

London Marathon, Greenwich Park. Tel: 0181-948 7935: one of the world's biggest, with a route from Greenwich Park to Westminster.

Queen's Birthday (21 April): the Queen's real birthday (as opposed to her official one in June) is celebrated with a gun salute in Hyde Park and at the Tower of London.

May

Chelsea Flower Show, Royal Hospital, SW3. Tel: 0171-834 4333: major horticultural show in the grounds of the Chelsea Royal Hospital.

Royal Windsor Horse Show, Windsor Park. Tel: 01298-72272: major show jumping event.

FA Cup Final, Wembley. Tel: 0171-262 4542: final of the nation's main football competition.

Oak Apple Day, Chelsea Royal Hospital: parade of the Chelsea Pensioners in memory of their founder, Charles II.

June

Beating Retreat, Horse Guards Parade, Whitehall. Tel: 0171-930 0292:

annual ceremonial display of military bands.

Derby Day, Epsom Racecourse. Tel: 01372-726311: famous flat race for 3-year-old colts and fillies.

Royal Academy Summer Exhibition, Burlington House, Piccadilly. Tel: 0171-439 7438: large exhibition of work by professional and amateur artists running until August. All works for sale.

Trooping the Colour, Horse Guards Parade. Tel: 0171-414 2357: the Queen's official birthday celebrations, with royal procession along the Mall to Horse Guards Parade for the ceremonial parade of regimental colours. Followed by the presence of the royal family on the balcony of Buckingham Palace.

Royal Ascot, Ascot Racecourse. Tel: 01344-22211: elegant and dressy race meeting attended by royalty.

Grosvenor House Antiques Fair, Grosvenor House Hotel, Park Lane. Tel: 0171-499 6363: a large and prestigious event.

Wimbledon Lawn Tennis Championships, All England Club. Tel: 0181-946 1066: world-famous fortnight of tennis played on grass courts.

July

Henley Royal Regatta, Henley-on-Thames, Oxfordshire. Tel: 01491-572153: international rowing regatta that is also an important social event. Worth a day-trip if you like drinking Pimm's.

Henry Wood Promenade Concerts, Royal Albert Hall. Tel: 0171-927 4296: series of classical concerts known as The Proms.

Royal Tournament, Earl's Court. Tel: 0171-370 8227: military displays from the Royal Army, Navy and Air Force.

Swan Upping on the Thames: all the swans on the Thames belong to the Queen, the Vintners and the Dyers and for five days every year officials can be seen rowing up and down the river registering them.

Doggett's Coat and Badge Race, London Bridge: race for single scull boats between London Bridge and Chelsea that has been a tradition since 1715.

August

Notting Hill Carnival, Ladbroke Grove (bank holiday weekend): colourful West Indian street carnival (Europe's largest) with exciting and imaginative costumes, live steel bands and reggae music.

London Riding Horse Parade, Rotten Row, Hyde Park: elegant competition for best turned-out horse and rider.

International Street Performers' Festival, Covent Garden Piazza.

September

Chelsea Antiques Fair, Old Town Hall, King's Road, SW3: contact tel: 01444-482514.

Horseman's Sunday, Church of St John and St Michael, W2: morning service dedicated to the horse with mounted vicar and congregation. Followed by procession through Hyde Park.

October

Judges' Service: marks the beginning of the legal year in Britain with a procession of judges in full attire from Westminster Abbey to the Houses of Parliament.

Horse of the Year Show, Wembley Arena. Tel: 0181-900 1234: major international competition attracting the world's top horses and riders.

Costermongers' Pearly Harvest Festival (1st Sunday), Church of St Martin-in-the-Fields, Trafalgar Square. Tel: 0171-930 0089. Pearly Kings and Queens (street traders) attend this service in their traditional attire, which is elaborately adorned with pearl buttons.

Trafalgar Day Parade: commemorates Nelson's victory at Trafalgar.

Motor Show, Earl's Court: major international car show held every two years.

November

London to Brighton Veteran Car Run (1st Sunday): hundreds of veteran cars and their proud owners start out from Hyde Park and make their way sedately to Brighton.

Lord Mayor's Show: grand procession, including the Lord Mayor's guilded coach, from the Guildhall in the City to the Royal Courts of Justice, celebrating the Mayor's election.

Remembrance Sunday (nearest the 11th): to commemorate those lost at war. Main wreath laying service at the Cenotaph, Whitehall.

State Opening of Parliament, House of Lords, Westminster. Tel: 0171-219 4272: official re-opening of Parliament (following the summer recess) by the Queen, who travels down the Mall in a state coach.

Guy Fawkes Day (5 November): traditional firework celebration of the failure to blow up the Houses of Parliament by Guy Fawkes in 1605.

Christmas Lights: switched on in Oxford and Regent streets.

December

Olympia International Horse Show, Olympia: major international show jumping championships.

Christmas Carol Services, Trafalgar Square: carols are sung here in the evenings beneath the giant tree which is presented each year by Norway. Also in many churches all over London.

"January" sales: excellent bargains can be found at these sales which seem to begin earlier and earlier each year as retailers try to take maximum advantage of pre-Christmas spending.

New Year's Eve, Trafalgar Square: thousands of people congregate here to hold hands and sing Auld Lang Syne at midnight.

Architecture

Churches & Cathedrals

Church building didn't get under way in London until AD 604, when King Ethelbert commissioned the original St Paul's Cathedral. The years after the Great Fire of 1666 and the early 19th century were the two great building periods. There are domestic churches everywhere in the London streets and some of the outstanding ones are listed below:

St Paul's Cathedral, EC4. The masterpiece of designer Sir Christopher Wren. Famous Whispering Gallery in the dome.

Westminster Abbey, SW1. Every English monarch has been crowned here since 1066.

Westminster Cathedral Ashley Place, SW1. The pre-eminent Roman Catholic church of all England. Tower offers a magnificent view.

Southwark Cathedral, Borough High Street, SE 1. The cathedral across the river, and the oldest gothic church in London.

All Hallows by the Tower, Eastcheap EC3. Originally a Saxon church (some bricks are Roman) with many later additions. Small museum, well worth a visit.

St Bartholomew the Great, Smithfield EC1. The finest Norman church in London, though much "improved" by the Victorians.

St Brides, Fleet Street, EC4. The printers' church, with Sir Christopher Wren's tallest spire. Museum in the crypt.

St Clements' Dane, Strand, WC2. Dr Johnson worshipped here, and his effigy remains.

St Helen's, Bishopsgate, EC3. An important survival from medieval London. Sumptuous interior.

St James's, Piccadilly, W1. Elegant Wren church, close to the Royal Academy. Also houses the best Brass Rubbing Centre in London.

St Margaret's, Westminster, SW1. The Parish church of the House of Commons. Many distinguished politicians have been married here, including Sir Winston Churchill. Buried here are William Caxton (1491) and Sir Walter Raleigh (1618).

St Mary Abchurch, Abchurch Yard, EC4, between Cannon Street and King William Street. The least altered of Wren's city churches.

St Mary le Bow, Cheapside, EC2. The cockney church of "bow bells" fame. One of Wren's finest, with a superb steeple.

St Paul's Church, Covent Garden Piazza, WC2. The actor's church. Many famous people are buried anonymously here.

Temple Church, off Fleet Street, EC4. Church of the 12th-century crusading order the Knights Templar.

The following churches were built by Nicholas Hawksmoor and are some of the most interesting and unusual churches in London.

Christchurch, Spitalfields, Commercial Street, E1. This is Hawksmoor's largest church, built in 1720.

St Anne, Commercial Road, Limehouse, E14. Begun in 1714 in the shape of a Greek cross with a bold Roman Baroque exterior and probably the highest church clock in London.

St George in the East, Cannon Street Road, E1. More striking for its bold angular exterior than its interior, which was bombed in 1941.

St Mary Woolnoth, Lombard Street, EC4. Built in 1724, this was one of Hawksmoor's last London churches. Comparatively small, the exterior, which is heavily rusticated, is very bold and powerful. By comparison, the interior, which was based on the Egyptian Hall of Vitruvius, is calm and serene and is indeed one of his finest.

Other Attractions

Bank of England Museum, Bartholomew Lane, EC2. Tel: 0171-601 5545. Museum explaining the history of money and the intricacies of modern money markets. Open daily. Free. *Tube: Bank.*

Banqueting House, Whitehall, SW1. Tel: 0171-930 4179. Only remaining part of the original Palace of Whitehall, designed by Inigo Jones in 1622. Built from Portland stone, this was the first Palladian-style building in England. Charles I, who was later executed outside this hall, commissioned Rubens to paint the ceiling in 1635. The Hall was originally used for state and court ceremonies, but in 1698, after suffering fire damage, it was converted into a chapel by Wren. It became the Chapel of the Horse Guards, then the Chapel Royal before becoming a museum. Closed Sunday. Admission charge. *Tube: Charing Cross/Westminster.*

Buckingham Palace, The Mall, SW1. Tel: 0171-730 3488. Since 1993 visitors have been admitted to a limited area of the building during several weeks each August and September (9.30am–5.30pm) when the Queen is not in attendance. A souvenir shop does a roaring trade. Tickets are sold at a kiosk on the corner of St James's Park opposite the palace.

Cabinet War Rooms, Clive Steps, King Charles Street, SW1. Tel: 0171-930 6961. Bomb-proof underground headquarters of the government in World War II with the Cabinet Room,

Map Room and Churchill's bedroom on show as they were during the war. Open daily. Admission charge. *Tube: Westminster.*

Changing of the Guard at Buckingham Palace, The Mall, SW1. Tel: 0171-730 3488. Takes place with full pomp and ceremony as the Queen's Guards, in their red uniforms and bearskins, march between their barracks and the Palace accompanied by a military band for a change over of guard duty. Also takes place at Whitehall and the Tower. When the Queen is in residence the Royal Standard is raised above the Palace. 11.30am daily (alternate days in winter). Free. *Tube: St James's Park.*

Chelsea Royal Hospital, Royal Hospital Road, SW3. Tel: 0171-730 0161. Built by Charles II as a home for old and injured soldiers. Designed by Wren out of red brick, it was completed in 1692. The inhabitants, who wear their smart red uniforms with pride, are called Pensioners and can often be seen walking around Chelsea. A small, but interesting museum detailing the hospital's history. Grounds are open to the public. Nearby is the National Army Museum. Closed Monday. Free. *Tube: Sloane Square.*

Cutty Sark, King William Walk, Greenwich, SE10. Tel: 0181-853 3589. The last surviving tea-clipper, the *Cutty Sark* once held all the maritime speed records before the introduction of steam ships. She now lies as a museum in dry dock. Nearby is the *Gypsy Moth IV*, the yacht Sir Francis Chichester sailed single-handed around the world in 1966-67. Closed Monday. Admission charge. *BR: Greenwich.*

Crafts Council, 44A Pentonville Road, N1. Tel: 0171-278 7700. Has regular exhibitions relating to British crafts, past and present. Closed Monday. *Tube: Piccadilly Circus.*

Greenwich Royal Observatory, Greenwich Park, SE10. Tel: 0181-858 1167. Founded by Charles II, and built by Wren in 1685, this group of buildings are home to Greenwich Mean Time and the Prime Meridian. On display are early navigational, time-keeping and measuring instruments. In 1948 the Royal Observatory moved to Sussex and this group of buildings became part of the National Maritime Museum. Open daily. Admission charge. *BR: Greenwich.*

Guildhall, King Street, EC2. Tel: 0171-606 3030. This attractive 15th-century building is the centre of London's civic government and where the Lord Mayor is elected and keeps his office. It has suffered many disasters throughout its long history, including the Great Fire of 1666 and World War II, and has been restored many times. See the ancient Great Hall with its minstrels' gallery and hanging coats of arms and banners of the City Guilds. Has an extensive medieval crypt. Open weekdays. Free. *Tube: Bank.*

Guinness World of Records, The Trocadero, Piccadilly Circus, W1. Tel: 0171-439 7331. Exhibition that attempts to bring to life superlatives that have been recorded in the world, from the tallest man to the heaviest snake. Open daily. Admission charge. *Tube: Piccadilly Circus.*

Hampton Court, East Molesey, Surrey. Tel: 0181-977 8441. Great Tudor palace on the banks of the Thames, begun by Cardinal Wolsey, but persuasively taken over by Henry VIII. William and Mary later added state apartments designed by Wren, hoping to rival Versailles in France. The interior houses a fascinating collection of period furniture and detailing, while outside the formal gardens are equally delightful. Here you can see the famous maze and the old tennis court. Open daily. Admission charge. *BR: Hampton Court.*

HMS Belfast, Morgan's Lane, Tooley Street, SE1. Tel: 0171-407 6434. World War II cruiser built in 1938. Long retired from active service, it is now a floating museum of war at sea. Open daily. Admission charge. *Tube: London Bridge.*

Houses of Parliament, Westminster, SW1. Tel: 0171-219 4273. The Palace of Westminster, with the exception of the ancient hall, was burnt down in 1834 and was rebuilt in 1852 by Charles Barry on a classical plan and given gothic detailing by Augustus Pugin. This enormous building, which contains the House of Commons and the House of Lords, has over 1,000 rooms and 2 miles of corridors. Of the three towers, St Stephen's Tower is the most famous, housing the Big Ben 13-ton bell. The public can watch sessions of both

Houses from visitors' galleries, but demand usually far outstrips capacity (debates in the Commons are televised live on TV). Open weekday afternoons and Friday all day. Free. *Tube: Westminster.*

Kensington Palace, Kensington Gardens, W8. Tel: 0171-937 9561. The primary sovereign residence between 1689 and 1760, this palace is now the London home of the Princess of Wales. It was here that Queen Victoria spent her strict childhood and learned of her accession to the throne at the age of 18. The original Jacobean house has been remodelled over the years, including alterations by Christopher Wren and William Kent. The State Apartments are open to the public and include much of interest such as Queen Victoria's toys and the Court Dress Collection. Closed Monday. Admission charge. *Tube: High Street Kensington.*

Law Courts, (Royal Courts of Justice), Strand, WC2. Tel: 0171-936 6470. Enormous structure built in the eclectic style of the Victorian Gothic Revival, designed by G. E. Street in 1868. This romantic fantasy building contains 58 law courts and a splendid great hall. Visitors can view from the public galleries. Open weekdays (no court during August summer recess). Free. *Tube: Aldwych.*

London Dungeon, 28-34 Tooley Street, SE1. Tel: 0171-403 0606. Experience the horrible side of British history in this dark cavern of medieval torture, diseases and cults. Open daily. Admission charge. *Tube: London Bridge.*

London Planetarium and Laserium, Marylebone Road, NW1. Tel: 0171-486 1121. The solar-system is revealed with a spectacular display inside this large dome. Laserium takes over in the evenings combining lasers and rock music. Open daily. Admission charge. *Tube: Baker Street.*

London Zoo, Regents Park, NW1. Tel: 0171-722 3333. This is one of the finest zoos in the world with over 8,000 animals. Look out for the famous Penguin pool and the Gorilla House built by Tecton in 1934. Open daily. Admission charge. Tube: Camden Town/Regent's Park.

Madame Tussaud's, Marylebone Road, NW1. Tel: 0171-935 6861. The world's best-known waxwork museum

and one of London's greatest tourist attractions. Many famous personalities from history and the present day have been immortalised in wax, including the Royal Family. Opinions differ about how life-like some of the exhibits are. Open daily. Admission charge (tickets combined with Planetarium available). Queues can be very long. *Tube: Baker Street.*

The Monument, Monument Street, EC3. Tel: 0171-626 2717. You can climb the 311 steps to the public gallery at the top of this 202-ft (30-metre) column for a fabulous view over London. Designed by Wren to commemorate the Great Fire of 1666 which started nearby in Pudding Lane. Closed Sunday in winter. Admission charge. *Tube: Monument.*

Old Bailey (Central Criminal Court), Newgate Street, EC4. Tel: 0171-248 3277. London's main criminal court which was built on the site of Newgate Prison. Public are permitted to watch trials. Open weekdays. Free. *Tube: St Paul's.*

Rock Circus, London Pavilion, Piccadilly Circus, W1. Tel: 0171-734 7203. Clever technology is combined with the artful wax working of Madame Tussaud's. The result is this amazing display of the history of rock and pop where stars, including Elvis and Madonna, "perform". Open daily. Admission charge. *Tube: Piccadilly Circus.*

Royal Mews, Buckingham Palace Road, SW1. Tel: 0171-930 4832. This is where the royal horses and coaches are kept. Included on view are the Golden State Coach, used for coronations since the 17th century, and the Glass Coach used for royal weddings. Open 2-4pm Wednesday & Thursday. Admission charge. *Tube: Victoria.*

Royal Naval College, King William Walk, Greenwich, SE10. Tel: 0181-858 2154. Built on the site of Greenwich Palace, this was originally designed as a maritime hospital by Wren under the instruction of William and Mary. However, in the 19th century the hospital was taken over by the Royal Naval College who are still in residence. The Painted Hall, decorated by John Thornhill, and the Chapel are open to the public. Closed every morning and all day Thursday. Free. *BR: Greenwich/Maze Hill.*

St Katherine's Dock, E1. Tel: 0171-

488 2400. One of the many docks and warehouses that once cluttered the East End of London, St Katherine's was built by Thomas Telford in 1828. Its warehouses have been attractively converted, whilst carefully retaining their character, into flats, shops, restaurants and bars and overlook the harbour which has become a marina. This is a pleasant place to stop if you are visiting the Tower and London Bridge close by. Open 24 hours daily. *Tube: Tower Hill.*

10 Downing Street, Off Whitehall, SW1. This is the Prime Minister's official London residence. Next door at number 11 lives the Chancellor of the Exchequer. Visitors have to peer through the tall railings at the road end which were erected for extra security. *Tube: Westminster/Charing Cross.*

Thames Barrier, Unity Way, Woolwich, SE18. Tel: 0181-854 1373. Built to protect London should the Thames burst its banks, this is an awe-inspiring piece of engineering and quite stunning to look at. The Visitor's Centre has displays relating to the Barrier. Open daily. Admission charge. *Riverbus or BR: Charlton*

Tower Bridge, Tower Hill, SE1. Tel: 0171-407 0922. Built as late as 1894, this is the last bridge to cross the Thames downstream and can be raised to let tall ships through. It was built in a gothic style to fit in with the Tower, with a stone facade covering the steel frame beneath. Visitors can take a lift to the overhead walkways for a fabulous view and also visit the steam room. A museum in the towers relates to the history of London's bridges. Open daily. Admission charge. *Tube: Tower Hill.*

Tower of London, Tower Hill, EC3. Tel: 0171-709 0765. This imposing medieval fortress has a long and intriguing history and is London's principal tourist attraction. First built by William the Conqueror in 1066, the oldest part is the White Tower which houses the Royal Armouries. Particularly notorious as a prison and place of execution. Those unfortunate enough to lose their heads on the block here included two of Henry VIII's wives. Also see the Crown Jewels and the ravens, which are encouraged to stay for superstitious reasons. The Beefeaters (Yeoman Warders in Tudor uni-

forms) give free guided tours. Long, long queues, especially in summer. Closed Sunday in winter. Admission charge. *Tube: Tower Hill.*

Westminster Abbey, Dean's Yard, SW1. Tel: 0171-222 5152. This cathedral dates back to the 13th century and is a fine example of English Gothic architecture. Steeped in royal history, this is where most of the kings and Queens of England have been crowned since 1066 and where many have been married and buried. The Coronation Chair is on view with the Stone of Scone. The Abbey contains memorials to many eminent British citizens, including Darwin and Newton. Among the names inscribed at Poets' Corner and Statesmen's Aisle are those of Chaucer, Dickens, Peel and Gladstone. The tomb of the Unknown Warrior is here. See the Chapels of Edward the Confessor and Henry VII and visit the museum and Chapter House. Brass-rubbing in the Cloisters. Closed during Sunday services. Nave Free. *Tube: Westminster.*

Nightlife

London may not have a reputation for being one of the world's great late-night cities, but there is still some life left in the capital after midnight. The relatively limited choice of attractions in the small hours is partly explained by the tough licensing and gaming laws and partly by the desire of the Londoner to retire early to bed. Most restaurants have wound down by 1am and clubs by 3am, leaving just a few determined cafés and shops to stagger on until the city awakes.

Nevertheless, there is something magical about being out all night in London, buying the day's newspaper before the day breaks, swapping tales over breakfast in a café, detouring home through one of the markets or watching the sun rise over the Thames.

To experience late-night London at its best, it is advisable to plan in advance, so read on to find out where you can eat, drink, listen to jazz, or just buy a newspaper whilst the rest of the city sleeps.

Dinner/Dance

Some of the best and most romantic

dine and dance places are at the big hotels:

Cleopatra Taverna, 146 Notting Hill Gate W11. Tel: 0171-727 4046. L/O 1.45am. Bright, fresh and friendly Greek restaurant which encourages diners to spend a whole evening over their *meze* (set dinner at £12.50) so as to enjoy live entertainment in the form of Greek music, belly dancing and the inevitable plate throwing (£7 for 12 plates) at their leisure.

Concordia Notte, 29 Craven Rd, W2. Tel: 0171-723 3725. L/O 1am. Set within a tastefully luxurious cavern is this sophisticated restaurant which courts the rich and famous. The superb classic Italian cuisine is accompanied by an impressive wine list, charming service and gentle dance music with which to while away the night.

Elephant on the River, 129 Grosvenor Rd, SW1. Tel: 0171-834 1621. Last orders 2am. Flamboyant riverbank neighbour of Villa dei Cesari, also serving fine Italian food in elegant surroundings and with a dance floor on which to float against a backdrop of moonlit views over the Thames.

The London Hilton Roof Restaurant, 22 Park Lane W1. Tel: 0171-493 8000. L/O 1am. Twenty-eight floors above London, the Roof Restaurant provides a sensational evening of dining and dancing with its combination of spectacular views and excellent french cuisine. The perfect setting for a memorable, but expensive, night out.

Palm Court at the **Ritz**, Piccadilly, W1. Tel: 0171-493 8181. Friday/Saturday 10pm–1am. The timeless surroundings set the tone for the nostalgic sounds of a Big Band playing old favourites from the 1920s, '30s and '40s. Whilst dinner-jacketed gentlemen escort elegant ladies on to the dance floor you can dine over a set three-course supper. Advance booking advisable.

Villa Dei Cesari, 135 Grosvenor Rd, SW1. Tel: 0171-828 7453. L/O 1.30am. An evening at this plush riverside restaurant is like being in a glamorous scene from a James Bond movie. You may rub shoulders with the rich and famous as you dance to the resident five-piece band or just enjoy the *haute cuisine* Italian food.

Drinking Bars

Angelos Club & Restaurant, 78 Westbourne Park Rd. Tel: 0171-229 0266. Licensed until 3am. Downstairs is a bustling restaurant with all the Greek trappings of plate smashing and bouzouki music, whilst upstairs is essentially a drinking club popular with local barflies. Non-members admitted at the discretion of the management.

Los Locos, 24 Russell St WC2. Tel: 0171-379 0220. L/O 11pm. The young at heart looking for a party atmosphere shouldn't be disappointed at lively Los Locos. Tex Mex food is heavy on *tortillas* whilst the real emphasis is on drinking – look out for the slammer girl with her crossfire of tequila and lemonade. The dance floor is cleared at 11.30 so that revellers can get up and strut their stuff.

Marquee Café, 20 Greek St, W1. Tel: 0171-287 3346. Licensed until 3am. Backing onto the relocated venue of the same name this café is a relaxed place to eat (enjoyable food in large portions), drink and listen to live music. Heavily influenced by music in both its decor and clientele, it is adorned with guitars and photographs of pop stars and has become a popular meeting place for those involved with the music business.

Piano Bar, Brewer Street, W1. Licensed until 3am. Only for the "gay folk", the doorman of the intriguing Piano Bar will explain of this small and intimate bar with a resident pianist whose seat gets taken over by performing patrons as the night hots up.

Ray Camino, 152 Kings Road, SW3 (071-351 3084) closes 2am. A "designer" *tapas* bar where the only Spanish authenticity may be the barman and the beer, worth noting as one of the rare bars in London where you don't have to be a member to get a late-night drink.

Nightclubs

All discos and nightclubs have a door policy. There's always someone at the door, ensuring only the right sort of people get in. At many places, it's just a matter of weeding out the jeans and sneakers. At some, though, it means your face has to fit.

To give you an idea of what to expect, these terms categorise the es-tablishments: *Smart* means civilised, well-dressed, appealing to an older audience. *Hip* means you've got to be cool and look the part; dress codes are pronounced. *Trendy* means it is just a good disco where everyone is welcome (unless, perhaps, they're wearing jeans). *Casual* means you can get away with jeans.

One-nighters are places where every evening has its own music and crowd, and you should check what it is before setting out. *Time Out* magazine gives a listing.

Annabel's, 44 Berkeley Square, W1. Tel: 0171-629 3558. This Mayfair club is the most exclusive in town. If you can get through the door, you will rub shoulders with the rich and famous, and possibly royalty. Membership is compulsory and expensive. Temporary membership, if you know a member of the club, is £100 for 3 weeks. Smart.

Busbys, 157 Charing Cross Road, WC2. Tel: 0171-734 6963. One of central London's mainstream discos hosting a wide variety of one-nighters and attracting a mixed crowd. Trendy.

Electric Ballroom, 184 Camden High Street, NW1. Tel: 0171-485 9006. This old dance hall is rather frayed at the edges, but has a huge main dance floor and is a popular place for a rave-up on a Saturday night. Has a jazz room upstairs and cheap bar prices. Smart.

Equinox, Leicester Square, WC2. Tel: 0171-437 1446. The Equinox is big in size, big in lighting and big in suburbia. Indeed, it is one of the biggest discos in Europe, attracting a young crowd in trendy dress.

The Fridge, Town Hall Parade, Brixton Hill, SW2. Tel: 0171-326 5100. The coolest and hippest venue south of the river renowned for spectacular one-nighters. Worth seeking out. Trendy.

Gossips, 69 Dean Street, W1. Tel: 0171-434 4480. Soho basement club with a variety of one-nighters catering for all musical tastes, from reggae to heavy metal. Gaz's long running "Rockin' Blues Night" on Thursday has a regular following. Trendy.

Heaven, Villiers Street, WC2. Tel: 0171-839 3852. Submerged beneath the Charing Cross development is one of the best dance clubs in town.

Gay nights are Tuesday, Wednesday, Friday and Saturday. Very casual dress code.

Hippodrome, Charing Cross Road, WC2. Tel: 0171-437 4311. One of the largest dance floors in London to shuffle around on, incorporating all the technological tricks you would expect from a 1980s-style discotheque. Popular with television and pop stars who make occasional sorties out of the Star Bar. Smart.

Jongleurs, (venues at Camden Lock and in Battersea). Tel: 0171 267 1999. Started as a stand-up comedy club operating only at weekends, Jongleurs has now widened its net to include live music, particularly its jazz club on Sunday afternoons.

Lacey's, 80-81 St Martin's Lane, WC2. Tel: 0171-240 8187. Dance-oriented venue where the music policy changes regularly. Casual.

Legends, 29 Old Burlington Street, W1. Tel: 0171-437 9933. Glossy Mayfair club which attracts a smart and trendy crowd who like to dress up and try out crazy dance moves. Hosts a variety of one-nighters. Hip.

Limelight, 136 Shaftesbury Avenue, W1. Tel: 0171-434 0572. A converted church; if you worship music, the sound system will put you in touch with Heaven. Has more style than danceability. Hip.

Le Palais, 242 Shepherd's Bush Road, W6. Tel: 0181-748 2812. West London's biggest disco, formerly the Hammersmith Palais. Glitzy Art Deco surroundings have smoothed over the rough edges that made this a famous 1970s venue. Has all the trappings of fast food restaurants, lasers and videos and is good for a boogie on a Saturday night. Disco at the end of the week, concerts otherwise. Smart.

Moonlighting, 17 Greek Street, W1. Tel: 0171-734 6308. Located where the Beat Route used to be, this comfy club largely plays soul music for a more mature clientele. Smart.

Samanthas, 3 New Burlington Street, W1. Tel: 0171-734 6249. Mainstream disco that has been around for a long time. Attracts well dressed and the more mature clubbers. Smart.

Shaftesbury's, 24 Shaftesbury Avenue, W1. Tel: 0171-734 2017. Executives and tourists enjoy raving it up at this posh mainstream disco. Not as hip as some, although occasionally hosts trendy one-nighters. Smart, with Champagne bar and brasserie.

Stringfellows, 16 Upper St Martin's Lane, WC2. Tel: 0171-240 5534. Reputed as a popular location for the paparazzi photographer and his willing victims, this club is strong on glamour, so dress accordingly.

Subterania, 12 Acklam Road, Ladbroke Grove W10. Tel: 0181-960 4590. West London's club for the 1990s with its well designed modern interior hewn out of the concrete structure of the Westway. This refreshing addition to the club scene regularly features live bands. Trendy.

Tattershall Castle, Victoria Embankment, King Street, SW1. Tel: 0171-839 6548. Disco with a difference. Dance the night away on this riverboat pub moored a stone's throw away from Trafalgar Square (Thursday, Friday and Saturday only). Casual.

Wag Club, 35 Wardour Street, W1. Tel: 0171-437 5534. This Soho club for cool cats is open until 6am at weekends. Heavy duty dance music and fresh fruit bar to keep you going. Hip.

Cabaret

Madame Jo Jo's, 8-10 Brewer St W1. Tel: 0171-734 2473. Closes 3am. Lacking in the sleaze and daring associated with Soho's past, Madame Jo Jo's still offers one of the best late-night outings in London with captivating cabaret shows from Ruby Venezuela and her male leggy lovelies in their amazing costumes.

Comedy Store, 28A Leicester Square, WC2. Tel: 01426-914433. A night at this well established venue for stand-up comedians will remind you that comedy need not always be accompanied by canned laughter. On a good night, the comedians in the audience are as famous as those on stage.

Casinos

Casinos have suffered a decline in England over the past few years. The 1968 Gaming Act succeeded in subduing gambling, preventing casinos from advertising or lists of venues being published. By law, you must be a member to enter a casino, and

membership must be applied for at least 48 hours in advance. However, Central London has a variety of casinos for all pockets, so if you wish to gamble during your stay, your hotel should be able to advise.

But then the British have always had an ambivalent approach to the world of the casino. While recent governments encouraged everyone and his auntie to participate in the stock market, casino gambling has remained hemmed in by restrictions. The 1968 Act by implication even excluded the publication of a list of venues in a book such as this as being a potential "stimulation" of gambling.

Nevertheless, 75 percent of the nations's gambling "drop" is spent in London, and mostly by visitors. They need to be dedicated gamblers, too: the Gaming Act precludes live shows or bands, and no alcoholic drink is allowed on the gaming premises. No wonder James Bond preferred to gamble abroad.

Round-the-Clock

Take Aways

Bagel Bake, 159 Brick Lane, E1. Tel: 0171-729 0616. Sunday–Thursday 6am, Friday/Saturday 24-hours. Join Londoners who ritually pile across to Brick Lane after a night out to tank up with freshly baked bagels filled with smoked salmon and cream cheese washed down with cups of hot coffee.

Burger King, 17 Leicester Square. Tel: 0171-930 0158. Monday–Saturday 4.30am, Sunday 2am. This branch of the fast food chain stays open through the night serving burgers to hungry clubbers.

Dionysius, 14 Tottenham Court Road, W1. Tel: 0171-637 5917. Sunday–Thurday 2.30am, Friday/Saturday 5.30am. Popular takeaway serving kebabs, humous, taramasalata as well as good old fish and chips to eat in or takeaway.

Ridley Road Hot Bagel Bakery, 13 Ridley Road, E8. Tel: 0171-241 1047. Open 24-hours. Grab a black cab and take a detour to Ridley Road on your way home for the fashionable late-night snack. This famous bagel hot spot in Dalston is as much of an institution as its Brick Lane rival.

Star Kebab House, 176 Earl's Court

Road SW5, 0171-244 7352. Until 3am daily. Thriving kebab house with a range of Turkish, Greek and Indian dishes in one of London's late-night neighbourhoods.

Uncle Jim's Takeaway, Kings Cross end of Grays Inn Road. Open until 7am. One of the outlets at Kings Cross for a late-night snack of fish and chips, sandwiches and kebabs.

Coffee/Breakfast

Bar Italia: 22 Frith Street, W1. Tel: 0171-437 4520. Until 4am daily. A piece of real Italy located in the centre of Soho, no matter what the hour this family-run bar is always buzzing. At weekends local trendies and genuine Italians alike queue for one of the best cappuccinos in town and a large screen at the end of the bar plays MTV when it's not showing live Italian football. On summer evenings it's fun to sit outside in true Italian style and watch a bewildering variety of people promenade through Soho.

Chelsea Bridge Snack Kiosk, open all night. Although some say that "it has been around so long that Dick Turpin used to stop there", a kiosk is reputed to have been doing hot food and teas at this location since the 1920s. Regardless of the legends, this is a long-standing landmark on the late-night landscape of London and is ever popular with early-morning truck drivers, cabbies and their passengers.

Carlo's, 65 Charterhouse St, EC1. Midnight–11am. This small café at Smithfield Market serves traditional English fry-ups to meat porters and any other comers.

Crescent Lounge, Kensington Hilton, 79 Holland Park Avenue, W11. Tel: 0171-603 3355. Licensed till 1am, open 24-hour, minimum charge £5.50. Next to the lobby of the plush Kensington Hilton with an atmosphere that evokes memories of airport lounges, this is nevertheless one of the more refined places to find a coffee after the witching hour.

Harry's, 19 Kingley St, W1. Tel: 0171-434 0309. 10pm–7am. Tucked away behind Regent Street Harry's Bar is a haven for the night-owl, serving excellent fashionable breakfasts, from bacon to smoked salmon with your scrambled eggs, all night. You could well find yourself sitting next to a very bleary-eyed star.

Rocky's, 3 New Burlington St, W1. Tel: 0171-494 3955. 9pm–3am. Cocktails until 3am with burgers, omelettes and set breakfasts, accompanied by blaring pop videos in surroundings of pink and blue neon.

Cinemas

The following have weekend all-nighters of films linked by a theme which is often kitsch or cult.

Rio Cinema, Dalston, 107 Kingsland High Street, E8. Tel: 0171-249 2722. 11.15pm programme Saturday.

Ritzy Cinema, Brixton Oval, SW2. Tel: 0171-737 2121. 11.15 programme Friday/Saturday.

Scala Cinema Club, 275-277 Pentonville Road, N1. Tel: 0171-278 0051. Programme 11.30 Saturday. Café open until 6am.

Shopping

Main Shopping Areas

London shopping falls into zones. High-street shopping is dominated by the big stores (Regent Street is much classier than Oxford Street). Knightsbridge, the King's Road, and Kensington High Street, despite their reputations, are now equally overrun by national chains. For individual shops and mini-stores, you have to venture down the side roads of Chelsea, Kensington and the West End. In the West End, Carnaby Street, once synonymous with Swinging London, is now tatty and full of souvenir shops selling plastic Beefeater dolls. Exclusive as ever are South Molton Street, Bond Street and Sloane Street.

In St Christopher's Place, W1, an alleyway just off Oxford Street, a designer village has sprung up. SW1, centring around Jermyn Street, is full of solid, traditional shopping with the emphasis on aristocratic menswear and old world grocers. SW3, Chelsea, is a real melting pot of styles, where the chic and trendy mingle on the pavements on Saturday mornings.

Covent Garden can be expensive and rather chi-chi, but has a superb range of clothes shops, including many young British designer outlets. It's also good for jewellery, arts and crafts, and one-offs like Neal's Yard, where organic foods and herbs have taken a hold.

Bloomsbury is still a rather sombre, bookish area, but has surprises if you delve a little deeper into its maze of backstreets around the British Museum and university. Soho, known for its European grocers, is a new centre for designer clothing. Don't neglect London's villages – Camden, Islington, and Portobello – all are outstanding for antiques, bric-a-brac, period clothing, jewellery and crafts.

Themed Centres

Shopping in London is being promoted more and more as a leisure industry. There is a current trend of large "themed" shopping malls springing up within interesting environments, often incorporating an added attraction such as a museum, cinema, or attractive location to entice the shopper.

Chelsea Harbour, Lots Road, SW10. Exclusive post-modernist development on the river with small sophisticated shops and service industries.

London Pavilion, Piccadilly Circus, W1. Shopping centre aimed at tourists which is dominated by the notable attractions of the Rock Circus and Rock Island Diner.

Tobacco Dock, The Highway, Wapping, E1. A nautical theme park is the attraction at this shopping village within a grade I listed dock built in 1812. Two replica sailing ships, the *Three Sisters* with an exhibition tracing the history of piracy, and the *Sea Lark*, which narrates the story of Treasure Island, are on permanent display. Open 7 days a week.

Trocadero, Piccadilly Circus, W1. The Guinness World of Records exhibition and Food Street, a themed Eastern supermarket, are more worthwhile than most of the shops at this well located tourist trap.

Whiteley's, Queensway, Bayswater, W2. At the beginning of the century this was an outstanding department store to rival Harrods and Selfridges. After closing its doors in 1981 it has been re-designed as a shopping complex containing leading chain stores, cafés and restaurants, whilst still retaining the grandeur of the original structure. It has the added attraction of central London's largest cinema complex, with 8 screens.

Department Stores

Barkers of Kensington, 63 Kensington High Street, W8. Tel: 0171-937 5432. This grand old store seems rather too dated to present any great competition to its Oxford Street counterparts. Nevertheless, still a pleasant place to shop where quality clothes, fashion accessories and household items can be found.

Conran Shop, Michelin Building, 81 Fulham Road, SW3. Tel: 0171-589 7401. Sir Terence Conran's unique and stylish shop sells designer furniture and household accessories, having the tendency to resemble a design museum. Set within the beautiful Art Nouveau tiled Michelin Building, it is worth a visit just to browse.

Debenhams, 334 Oxford Street, W1. Tel: 0171-580 3000. Re-vamped with a bright fresh image this store seems to have lost much of its personality, tending to resemble a shopping mall. Sells the variety of goods you would expect from a large department store with everything from perfumes to bed linen.

Fortnum and Mason, 181 Piccadilly, W1. Tel: 0171-734 8040. Fortnum and Mason opened their store in the 18th century with the grocery needs of the Palace in mind. They began importing exotic and unusual foodstuffs which have for centuries been the basis of the shop's success. The Queen's grocer also stocks fine clothes and household goods. At Christmas the window displays are a joy to behold and many hanker after one of their famous hampers. Pop in for a browse and to see very proper English folk buying their expensive groceries. A fashionable place to have tea.

Harrods, Knightsbridge, SW1. Tel: 0171-730 1234. One of the world's largest and most famous department stores, now owned by Egypt's El Fayed family. Since the 19th century Harrods has maintained a reputation for quality and service, priding itself on stocking the best of everything. No one should miss the fabulous displays in the Edwardian tiled food halls. Harrods sales are major events with those hungry for bargains prepared to queue a long time to be first through the door.

Liberty, Regent Street, W1. Tel: 0171-734 1234. The goods on sale in this distinctive and characterful store are still largely based along the same lines as the Oriental, Art Nouveau and Arts and Crafts furniture, wallpaper, silver, jewellery and fabrics Liberty began selling in the late 19th century. There are particularly fine furniture and fashion accessory departments and an exotic bazaar in the basement.

Marks and Spencer, 458 Oxford Street, W1. Tel: 0171-935 7954. This chain can't seem to do anything wrong. It stays clear of extremes of fashion, maintaining a good strong policy of quality merchandise that is safe, but well designed, and value for money. The whole nation seems to favour M & S underwear whilst the food department, with its gourmet ready cooked meals, goes from strength to strength. This Marble Arch branch is used to test out new lines.

Peter Jones, Sloane Square, SW1. Tel: 0171-730 3434. This King's Road branch of John Lewis promises customers that its prices cannot be beaten and assures to refund the difference if you can prove otherwise. Stocks a variety of quality goods, most notably household furnishings and appliances.

Selfridges, Oxford Street, W1. Tel: 0171-629 1234. Enormous store dating back to 1909 that is to be rivalled only by Harrods in its size and variety of quality goods.

Clothing

London's Finest

Aquascutum, 100 Regent Street, W1. Conservative classics and country separates aimed at the executive man and woman.

Austin Reed, 103-113 Regent Street, W1. Gentlemen's suits, casual menswear, women's separates. The place for horse-riding clothes and gear.

Burberry's, 18-22 Haymarket, SW1. For the famous trenchcoats, mackintoshes, and accessories in the famous plaid.

Dickens & Jones, 224-244 Regent Street, W1. Smart store for those with a more mature and conservative taste. Many top designers are represented, though there is not such a good choice for men as there is for women. Fashion consultant service. Excellent accessories.

Fenwick, 63 New Bond Street. Classy store with an extensive range of clothes and accessories for all tastes and ages, ranging from the casual and trendy to smart and chic designer wear.

Fortnum and Mason, Piccadilly, W1. Exclusive store with quality clothes; particularly good for formal suits and evening wear. Polite service from formally dressed assistants. Good range of accessories.

Harrods, Brompton Road, SW1 (Knightsbridge). Extensive selection of quality clothes for all ages and tastes. Formal menswear on the ground floor, vast designer collection for women on the first and trendy women's fashion on the fourth.

Harvey Nichols, Brompton Road, next to Harrods. London's leading fashion department store, with an excellent range of menswear in the basement. Women and children are also well catered for, with many top designers' goods under one roof.

Laura Ashley, 256 Regent Street, W1. Distinctive style of feminine clothes in pretty floral fabrics. Also home furnishings and fabrics.

Liberty's, Regent Street, W1. Well-known for scarves, ties and garments in art nouveau and floral prints. Excellent for more unusual fashion accessories and gifts.

Marks & Spencer, Oxford Street, W1. The original English high street store, with clothes for all the family. Has extended its reputation beyond quality traditional garments to fashionable items with flair. Excellent for basics, particularly jumpers and underwear. Value for money.

Selfridges, Oxford Street, W1. Wide selection of men's, women's and children's wear to rival Harrods. Everything from serious formal wear to the young and trendy "Miss Selfridge".

Simpson, 203 Piccadilly, W1. Traditional quality men's and women's clothing spread over several floors, predominantly in a classical style that is considered typically English. The store has its own range of clothes, bearing the Daks label.

Designer Gear

Antony Price, 34 Brook Street, W1. Extravagant and glamorous clothes for women who like to be seen, and are happy to pay for the privilege.

Bazaar, 4 South Molton Street, W1. Stocks the wild extremes from designer collections and is for male one-off celebrity dressing.

Ben De Lisi, 8 Silver Place, W1. Refined and feminine clothes for women who like a bit of glamour and sparkle.

Jasper Conran, 303 Brompton Road, SW1. Elegant *haute couture* that is classic with a twist.

Crolla, 35 Dover Street, W1. Famous for Baroque and eccentric English clothes for those who like a touch of decadence.

Droopy and Browns, 99 St Martin's Lane, WC2. Traditional and feminine women's clothes for special occasions; frills, flounces and classic ball gowns.

The Duffer of St George, 27 D'Arblay Street, W1. The penultimate in casual street cred for men.

Nicole Farhi, Sloane Street, SW1. Smart, yet comfortably casual, classic separates in soft fabrics.

Katherine Hamnett, 20 Sloane Street, SW1. London designer famous for her slogan T-shirts and simple, but original, clothes.

Hancher, 37 Marshall Street, W1. Flamboyant women's clothes that are variations on a classic theme.

Hyper, Hyper, 26-40 Kensington High Street, W8. Large prestigious market with stalls of brilliant young designers. A mixture of trendy street fashion and classic chic. Imaginative accessories. Worth visiting just to look around.

Jaeger, 204 Regent Street, W1. Tailored classic English clothes for men and women with formal, business and casual ranges.

Jones, 13 Floral Street, WC2. Hip outlet for avant-garde designers such as Nick Coleman and Gaultier. Also Jones's own label.

Michiko Koshino, 70 Neal Street, WC2. Be Bop and plastic gimmick clothes for fashion victims. English designer big in Japan.

Mulberry Company, 11 Gees Court, W1. Modern clothes on a classic British Imperialist theme in fabrics such as Gaberdine, wool, linen and cotton.

Accessories for the modern gentleman include Mulberry's famous leather luggage and briefcases.

Christopher New, 52 Dean Street, W1. Original and quirky menswear with style. Good for T-shirts, shirts and jumpers with distinctive designs.

Paul Smith, 41-44 Floral Street, W1. Designer famous for his bright shirts and ties. Clothes combine classic tailoring with a modern twist.

Vivienne Westwood, 60 Davies Street, W1. This is formal compared to Westwood's wacky World's End boutique on the King's Road, and is the outlet for her more tailored collections.

Workers For Freedom, 4 Lower John Street, W1. Based on folklore, clothes are natural and organic, soft and sensitive pieces of craftsmanship. Known for their refined use of applique.

Shirley Wong, 41 Old Compton Street, W1. Self-conscious women's fashion for the street-wise.

World Service, 68 Neal Street, WC2. Classic style suits and separates with a hint of the 1950s made in England for the colourful modern man who cares about his appearance.

Haute Couture

In the search for Haute Couture, the best place to start is Knightsbridge, where you will be spoilt by the choice of designer names. In pretty Beauchamp Place several small chic boutiques are to be found, including Caroline Charles, Bruce Oldfield and the Emmanuels (famous for Princess Diana's wedding dress). Around the corner in the Brompton Road is Emporio Armani with a more casual range than the other branch nearby in Sloane Street.

Indeed, Sloane Street can be rivalled only by Bond Street for its endless list of world-class designers. Here you will find Yamamoto, Lagerfeld, Krizia, Gucci, Joseph, Hermès and Yves Saint Laurent. If you cannot locate your favourite designer here you will probably discover them within Harvey Nichols or Harrods, close by. For design-conscious children, Sloane Street can offer Oilily and La Cicogna.

Bond Street, however, has an older tradition of offering the best that

money can buy. If any of London's streets were paved with gold surely it must be this one. Here, among the big international names such as Valentino, Chanel, Givenchy, Versace (in a whole new store of its own) and Pierre Cardin, are London's major jewellery houses, auction houses, and elite fine art galleries. Nearby in Grafton Street is London's very own Zandra Rhodes, creator of unique fantasies for women.

Close by in South Molton Street the tension on your wallet can be released very slightly. This street, with many upmarket fashion houses, caters to a younger fashion-conscious customer. Browns houses collections by Gaultier, Romeo Gigli, Alaia, Conran and Ozbek. Close by in Brook Street is Roland Klein, Antony Price, Comme des Garçons and Gianfranco Ferre.

For Men

London is well served for men's clothes shops. Covent Garden is full of them: quality fashion shops such as Paul Smith and Jones in Floral Street and young designers such as Michiko Koshino.

What really distinguishes London's menswear from any other is its traditional gentlemen's outfitters. Savile Row is the best known street for tailor made suits. Gieves & Hawkes at No. 1, is synonymous with hand-made and off-the-peg classic English tailoring and has a long and noble history. As does the prestigious Anderson and Sheppard at the other end of the street who have discretely tailored suits for Marlene Deitrich and Prince Charles, amongst other notables. Tommy Nutter, across the road, was the young upstart of the Row. Popular with pop and film stars, Nutter had a reputation for flamboyant and eccentric tailored suits. Huntsman & Sons, like many other tailors in the Row, has been established since the 18th century.

The St James's area, which is littered with gentlemen's clubs, is full of shops selling expensive well-made clothes, toiletries and shoes. In St James's Street is John Lobb, considered to make some of the finest hand-made shoes in the world and the fine hat maker James Lock. In

Jermyn Street is Hilditch & Key and Turnbull & Asser famed for their made-to-measure and striped shirts. Bates hat shop and Geo Trumpers traditional toiletry shop are here too. Dover Street and Burlington Gardens are also worth a visit.

If you want the look without paying the price, second-hand and period clothes shops are one option. Try Hills Dresswear at 15 Henrietta Street, WC2, which is particularly good for fine dinner suits from the 1930–50 era. For new men's classics, at affordable prices, try Blazer at 36 Long Acre. For the fashion-conscious man, Soho has off the wall designs of Junior Gaultier in Fouberts Place and The Duffer of St George in D'Arblay Street sells exclusive trendy street fashion with an American influence.

Country Look

Piccadilly and St James's are again the places to go for upmarket country clothes. In the West End, the department stores are usually well-stocked with country casuals and waterproofs; some of the sports/mountaineering suppliers around Covent Garden also have surprisingly high quality outerwear.

For the Great British Sweater, look no further than **Marks & Spencer**. Their lambswool is the cheapest in London, but the choice of styles and colours is limited. **Scottish Merchant** at 16 New Row, WC2 has fascinating Scottish made sweaters of supreme quality (and great price).

Unusual Sizes

The Base, 55 Monmouth Street, WC2. Exclusive quality clothes for larger women.

High & Mighty, 83 Knightsbridge, SW1. Classic English clothes for the larger than average gentleman. Also sport and leisurewear.

Long Tall Sally, 21-25 Chiltern Street, W1. Elegant and reasonably priced clothes for tall women. (Crispins over the road caters for customers with big feet).

The Small and Tall Shoe Shop, 71 York Street, W1. For those customers with very short or long, narrow or wide feet.

Period Clothes

London's markets and the area surrounding them are often excellent for secondhand and period clothing, particularly Portobello, Camden and Islington; also Covent Garden and Hampstead.

American Classics, 400 King's Road, SW10. American 1950s originals from baseball jackets to graduation frocks.

John Burke & Partners, 20 Pembridge Road, W11. Old-fashioned gentlemen's outfitters selling relics of a by-gone age, from top hats and tails to riding boots and bowlers.

Cobwebs, 60 Islington Park Street, N1. Small, but well maintained stock of fine men's and women's period clothing.

Cornucopia, 12 Upper Tachbrook Street, SW1. Overwhelming range of clothes and accessories with an emphasis on the eccentric, extravagant and theatrical dating from the late 19th century.

The Girl Can't Help It, 140 Essex Road, N1. Saucy and vivacious shop selling anything relating to 1940s and '50s pin-up glamour girls, from the kitsch to the collectable.

Hacketts, 65 New King's Road, SW6. Old and new gentlemen's classics including dinner suits, plus-fours, brogues and braces.

Laurence Corner, 62 Hampstead Road, NW1. Weird and wonderful collection of army surplus and theatrical costumes.

Sam Walker, 41 Neal Street, WC2. Quality classic clothes and accessories from the 1940s and '50s at modern day prices.

Spatz, 48 Monmouth Street, WC2. Vintage and period women's clothing. Also linen and soft furnishings.

Street Smart

For street fashion with style, King's Road is still the place. Young chainstore fashion which echoes the new cuts and colours of the season for teenagers is found on Oxford Street, in shops like **Hennes**, **Top Shop** and **Miss Selfridge**.

The home of street fashion is undeniably **Kensington Market**, a covered maze of shops and stalls where nearly every item comes only in black.

It's on Kensington High Street, W8. **Hyper Hyper** just across the road provides a variety of upmarket versions and adventurous collections from young designers.

Antiques

London has an enormous and widespread selection of antique shops and markets.

Over 400 of the most elite dealers are to be found in Mayfair, centring around Old Bond Street, with highly valuable collections of silver, fine art, jewellery, porcelain, carpets, furniture and antiquities.

Chelsea and Knightsbridge have a large share of fine dealers. The Fulham and the King's roads are excellent for period furniture and decorative items.

Westbourne Grove in W11 has many interesting dealers. The whole area comes to life on Friday and Saturday mornings when hordes of tourists descend on the antique arcades and stalls of the Portobello Road market.

Kensington Church Street in W8 is filled with a variety of expensive antique shops dealing in everything from fine art to porcelain.

Islington, N1, is also a popular but more expensive area with over 100 dealers. Particularly interesting is the Mall Antiques Arcade at 359 Upper Street and the adjacent Camden Passage.

Bermondsey's early-morning Friday antique market at Bermondsey Square, SE1, is a major trading event, with the best items changing hands by 10am.

Further advice and information on buying antiques in Britain as a whole can be obtained from the London and Provincial Antique Dealers' Association, 535 King's Road, SW10, tel: 0171-823 3511. They run an up-to-date computer information service on the antiques situation throughout the country and also publish their own comprehensive booklet, *Buying Antiques in Britain*, which can be purchased for £3 (plus postage).

Covered Markets

Alfies, 13-25 Church Street, NW8. London's largest covered antiques

market with over 250 dealers providing an enormous selection of antiques and collectable items. Meanwhile, outside in Church Street, are several fine shops with a particularly strong decorative arts bias.

Antiquarius, 135-141 King's Road, SW3. A whole range of antiques, decorative arts and period clothing. Can be expensive.

Chelsea Antique Market, 245-253 King's Road, SW3. Another Chelsea antique market which opened in the 1960s. This is smaller and less expensive than the others with a good range of antiquarian books and men's period clothing.

Chenil Galleries, 181-183 King's Road, SW3. Classy antiques market with fine art, furniture and objets d'art.

The Furniture Cave, 533 King's Road, SW10. Has several floors of dealers selling fine period furniture and garden ornaments.

The Galleries, 157 Tower Bridge Road, SE1. Enormous warehouse with three floors predominantly filled with furniture, and interesting pieces of architectural salvage.

Gray's Antique Market, 58 Davies Street, W1. Has a good reputation for fair dealing. Over 200 stalls dealing in a variety of antiques from art deco furniture to Victorian toys.

London Silver Vaults, Chancery House, 53 Chancery Lane, WC2. High-security vaults where stall holders trade in valuable gold and silverware.

Art

Cork Street is famous for its art galleries. Here in the **Waddington**, **Redfern**, **Nicola Jacobs** and **Odette Gilbert** galleries you can view or purchase works by major international modern masters of the class of Picasso and Hepworth. Nearby in Dering Street are three **Anthony d'Offay** galleries which feature the work of British Post-Impressionists and leading international modern artists. The work of established British artists can be found in the **Bernard Jacobson Gallery** in Clifford Street, W1, and the **Marlborough Gallery** in Albemarle Street, W1, which had Francis Bacon among its artists. For those interested in old masters there are various galleries dotted around Mayfair.

If you are looking for young British talent that won't set you back more than £2,000 then visit the **Albemarle Gallery** in Albemarle Street, or the **Austin/Desmond Gallery** at 15a Bloomsbury Square. The **Scottish Gallery** in Cork Street shows the best young talent from Scotland.

Five years ago Angela Flowers moved her gallery out of Central London to the East End. It's now called **Flowers East** at 199-205 Richmond Road, E8, but it's worth the trek to see the fine young British talent she displays within this vast white space.

An area of London that has increased its reputation over recent years for galleries showing young contemporary art is Portobello. A community of fresh and exciting galleries have sprung up in this lively area, including the **Anderson O'Day**, **Creaser**, **Todd**, and **Vanessa Devereux** galleries. Close by in Kensington Park Road is the **Special Photographers Company** which displays innovative fine art photography. The **Photographer's Gallery** in Great Newport Street, WC2 has exhibitions of major international photography and a fine collection of prints for sale in the Print Room. **Hamiltons** in Carlos Place, W1 is another major photography gallery. If you are interested in cartoons, check out the **Cartoon Gallery** at 83 Lamb's Conduit Street, WC1.

Auction Houses

London's leading auction houses for antiques and fine art are **Christie's**, 8 King Street, SW1 and **Sotheby's**, 34 New Bond Street, W1. There are also the smaller fine art auction houses of **Phillip's** at 7 Blenheim Street, W1 and **Bonham's** in Montpelier Street, SW7. **Bloomsbury Book Auctions**, 3 Hardwick Street, EC1, is the only specialist book auction house in the country, with maps and manuscripts also going under the hammer.

China & Glass

All of the big department stores have excellent china and glass departments, with a full range of styles and prices. For more upmarket English goods, try **Garrard** at 112 Regent Street and **Thomas Good**e at 19

South Audley Street, W1. **Wedgwood** is at 266-270 Regent Street; not everything here is dazzlingly expensive. Their other shop, **Waterford Wedgwood**, is at 173 Piccadilly. Bargain prices at the **Reject China Shop** at 33-35 Beauchamp Place, SW3, for discount china and kitchenware with a few imperfections.

Jewellery

Covent Garden is a good hunting ground for quality costume jewellery. Try **Accessorize** at 22 the Market; **Acsis** at 31 the Market, or **Sheer Decadence** at 44 Monmouth Street, WC2. At the other end of the scale are the breathtakingly expensive jewellers around Bond Street. **Asprey** in New Bond Street sells antique and modern jewellery and gifts; **Cartier** at 175 is as exclusive and expensive as ever, as is **Tiffany's**. **Collingwood** of Conduit Street, W1 and **Garrard's** of Regent Street are by appointment to the Queen.

Van Cleef and Arpels at 153 New Bond Street specialise in "invisibly set" stones. You can choose your own rock at the **London Diamond Centre**, Hanover Street W1, and see it mounted before you buy. For period jewellery, try **Cobra and Bellamy** at 149 Sloane Street, SW1, who specialise in 1900-50 English pieces, or **Arcade Jewellery** at 309 King's Road, for costume jewellery at affordable prices.

Perfumiers

Penhaligons, Wellington Street, WC2. Old-fashioned and beautifully packaged traditional English toiletries.
Floris, 89 Jermyn Street, W1. Expensive English flower perfumes.
Taylor of London, Sloane Street, SW3. Selling their own perfumes for men and women.

Traditional Markets

Most markets open early in the morning and close at around 2pm.
Berwick Street Market, Berwick Street, W1. Daily market that is famous for its fruit and veg at surprisingly good prices given its central location. Also sells clothes and fabrics. Monday to Saturday.

Brick Lane Market, Brick Lane, E1. Bustling East End market with a strong ethnic influence selling cheap clothes, fruit, veg and bric-a-brac. There are also many bargains of dubious origin such as bicycles and electrical goods. Sunday.
Camden Lock Market, Camden Town, NW1. This market centres around an attractive canal lock and is always packed, especially at weekends when there is lots of second-hand clothes, hand made jewellery and bric-a-brac (Saturday and Sunday). Antiques market on Thursday.
Camden Passage, Islington Green, N1. Close to Islington's cluster of quaint antique shops. This is a pretty open-air market that is popular with tourists. Wednesday and Saturday.
Columbia Road Flower Market, Columbia Road, E2. Even if you have no intention of buying, it is worth a visit on a Sunday morning just to take in the delightful colours, smells and East End bustle of this glorious flower market. Sunday.
Covent Garden Market, The Piazza, Covent Garden, WC2. Attractive market with antiques on Monday and crafts from Tuesday to Saturday. But beware: although there are some beautifully hand-crafted items, bargains are rare.
Greenwich Market, Market Square, SE10. Four good weekend markets close together where you will find second-hand books, clothes and bric-a-brac. Includes a crafts section with hand-made wares such as baskets, toys, jewellery and jumpers. Saturday and Sunday.
Leadenhall Market, Leadenhall Street, EC3. Quality meat, poultry and fish within this beautiful old Victorian covered market. Weekdays.
Leather Lane Market, EC1. Popular with Londoners, this market sells cheap household goods and clothes. Weekdays.
New Caledonian Market, Tower Bridge Road, Bermondsey, SE1. Fascinating antiques market where many traders themselves arrive as early as 4am to buy their stock. Friday.
Petticoat Lane, Middlesex Street, E1. Sunday market famous for clothes with a designer fashion market. Also household goods and food. Sunday.
Portobello Market, Portobello Road,

W11. A walk down the characterful Portobello Road starts at the top with the antique shops, takes you through the colourful vegetable market, on to the second hand clothes and bric-a-brac and ends with a fascinating array of junk and treasures spread over the pavements of Golborne Road. Saturday.

Spitalfields Market, Commercial Street, E1. In an elegant old market building, the stalls specialise in organic meat and vegetables, arts and crafts. Under the same management as Camden Lock. Mainly weekends.

Food

The food halls at **Harrods** are justly famous, but don't neglect **Fortnum's** or **Selfridges'**. SW1 and Soho are the places for old-fashioned grocers: **Justin de Blank** at 42 Elizabeth Street, and **Paxton & Whitfield** on Jermyn Street, the best cheese shop in London. Soho is the place for European delicatessens and Chinese grocers: found on Brewer Street, Berwick Street and Old Compton Street. Gerrard Street has authentic Chinese supermarkets. Neal's Yard in Covent Garden specialises in organic vegetables and wholefood.

Several supermarkets are in the centre of town. **Waitrose** at 196 King's Road is the best. **Hollywood**, 75 Charing Cross Road, is more expensive than most but is open 24 hours a day. There's **Safeway** at 23 Brunswick Square, WC1, and **Tesco** at 18-24 Warwick Way, SW1. **Sainsburys** on Cromwell Road, SW7 is where well-heeled Kensingtonians (or their nannies) go for their asparagus tips.

Toys

Hamleys, 188-196 Regent Street, W1. Six floors of toys, dolls and games and other fabulous toys.
Covent Garden Market is good for unusual (if expensive) toys.
Cabaret Mechanical Theatre, 33 the Market (£1 admission).
The Dolls House, 29 the Market.
Pollock's Toy Theatre, 44 the Market.
Snooks, 32 the Market, WC2.
Just Games at 62 Brewer Street, W1.

A Gift from England

Ideas on what to buy for the folks back home:

British Museum Shop, British Museum, WC1. A variety of tasteful gifts, some very expensive, like the superb Egyptian cats. The National Gallery and National Portrait Gallery at Trafalgar Square are good for posters, calendars and other arty gifts.
Alfred Dunhill, 30 Duke Street, SW1. Famous for traditional accessories for gentlemen.
Asprey, 165 New Bond Street, W1. If money is no object, here are the most decadent gifts in town – e.g. a leather Scrabble board.
Inderwicks, 45 Carnaby Street, W1. Hand-made pipes.
Mansfield, 30-35 Drury Lane, WC2. Antique personal accessories like pens and luggage.
Naturally British, 13 New Row, WC2. A wide selection of British goods in natural materials, including lovely sweaters and inexpensive jewellery.
London Brass Rubbing Centre, St James's Church, Piccadilly W1. In addition to brass rubbings, have your family coat-of-arms researched and painted.

VAT & Exporting

England has 17.5 percent VAT (Value Added Tax) on most goods, including clothes. Anything you buy in a department store is likely to have had VAT built into the ticket price. Most big stores (and many smaller shops selling goods like Scottish woollens or English china) operate a VAT Refund Scheme or Export Scheme. Ask the salesperson. You can get your VAT back by filling in a form which is stamped by customs. Shops may require a minimum purchase (often £50) before the customer can participate.

All the shops listed are generally open Monday-Saturday, 9am–5pm or later. Thursday night is late shopping night in Oxford and Regent streets, Wednesday night for Knightsbridge and Kensington, with many shops staying open until 7pm or 8pm.

Spectator

Cricket: Played in summer only, at the Oval, Kennington, SE11, tel: 0171-582 6000, or at the Lord's ground, St John's Wood, NW8, tel: 0171-289 1615.
The Dogs (greyhound racing): Most tracks hold two meetings a week throughout the year; days vary. Tracks: Catford, Hackney Wick, Romford, Walthamstow, Watford, Wembley, Wimbledon. The best is Walthamstow Race Track, Chingford Road, E4. Tel: 0181-531 4255.
Football (Soccer): Played throughout autumn, until late spring, culminating in the Cup Final in May at Wembley Stadium, tel: 0181-903 4864. Ring the Football Association, tel: 0171-262 4542, for information on matches.
Horse Racing: Tracks: Ascot, tel: 01344-22211, (Royal Ascot in June is one of the highlights of the English social calendar), Epsom, tel: 013727-26311, Sandown Park, tel: 01372-63072, and Windsor, tel: 01758-65234.
Rowing: The major event of the London rowing calendar is the Oxford and Cambridge university boat race, held on the Thames every March.
Tennis: Suburban Wimbledon, on the district line of the Underground, is the venue for the famous tennis championship in late June. Seats must be reserved at least six months in advance, but you can queue to watch play on the outside courts on the day of the event. All England Tennis Club, Church Road, Wimbledon, SW19. Tel: 0181-946 2244.

Time Out magazine publishes a comprehensive guide to sports, health and fitness in London.

Further Reading

Charing Cross Road is traditionally the home of bookselling. **Cecil Court** is its old-fashioned heart, selling secondhand and rare books of all kinds. **Foyle's** is the biggest store selling new books. **Waterstone's** next door has fewer volumes. W1 bookshops are more up-market: **Hatchard's** on Piccadilly features a huge variety of biographies and fiction. It's the oldest bookshop in London. Of the second-hand and rare book sellers in W1, **Quaritch** in Lower John Street is probably the best known.

Specialist bookshops abound in London. **Zwemmer's** on the Charing Cross Road is known for fine art. **Bertram Rota** at Langley Court WC2 is good for modern first editions. **Edward Stanford** on Long Acre is a travel bookshop. **Biografia** at 49 Covent Garden market has the largest selection of biographies and memoirs in the country. **French's** the theatre bookshop, is at Fitzroy Street, W1. Close to Portobello market is **The Travel Bookshop** at 13 Blenheim Crescent, W11.

There are enough books about London, of course, to adequately fill several libraries. We have selected a necessarily random selection of titles which may be of interest.

Out and Around London – North. A Geographia Guide. Helpful on what to see north of the city's limits.

R. L. and M. J. Elliot, *Where to go and What to do in the South East*. Heritage Publications. Exhaustive display of the possibilities.

Michael Elliman, Frederick Roll, *The Pink Plaque Guide to London*. GMP. An interesting view of some of the more famous London names, from a gay angle.

Hugh Mellor, *London Cemeteries,* Avebury Press. Surprisingly entertaining guide to an odd subject, full of excellent quotes about London.

David Piper, *Artist's London*. Weidenfeld and Nicholson. Fascinating images of London over the ages.

Simon Jenkins, *Companion Guide to Outer London*. Collins. Rather studied and worthy handbook to places like Kew, Richmond, Greenwich etc.

John Talbot White, *Country London*. Routledge and Kegan Paul. The author who finds great oaks in the shadow of Battersea power station.

Frank Swinnerton, *The Bookman's London*. John Baker. Lugubrious guide to where to buy books.

John Wittich, *Discovering London's Parks and Squares*. Shire publications. A bit of village London. A London-walker's notes.

Geoffrey Trease, *London: A Concise History*. Good illustrated history.

Gavin Weightman and Steve Humphries, *The Making of Modern London*. Sidgwick and Jackson. Worthy stuff, full of detail.

Gavin Stamp, *The Changing Metropolis*. Viking. Very intriguing set of early photographs of London.

Ben Weinreb and Christopher Hibbert, *The London Encyclopaedia*. Papermac/Dictionary of London. Detailed and interesting, but more a reference book than a good read.

Paul Barkshire, *Unexplored London*. Lennard Publishing. Excellent photographs of things that you might not notice.

Benny Green, *London*. Oxford University Press. Anthology of what the world has said about London in the past.

Peter Ackroyd, *Dickens' London*. Headline. Excerpts illustrating how London figured in the famous author's work.

V S Pritchett, *London Perceived*. The Hogarth Press. Atmospheric stuff.

Andrew Davies, *The Map of London*. Batsford. Fascinating study which shows how little London's streets have changed with routes.

Ian MacAuley, *Guide to Ethnic London*. Michael Haag. Where London's communities originated, and where they are now.

Mary Peplow and Debra Shipley, *London for Free*. Panther. Full of good ideas for activities, but it lacks background information.

Kathleen Denbigh, *Preserving London*. Robert Hale. Detailed on the history of the villages of London.

Other Insight Guides

Apa Publications produces three series of guidebooks to suit the needs of every traveller. The 190-title *Insight Guides* series places destinations in their total cultural context. The 110-title *Insight Pocket Guides* series provides specific recommendations from a local host. And the *Compact Guides* series structures information for handy on-the-spot reference.

Insight Guides to the United Kingdom include *Great Britain, Scotland Wales, Oxford, Glasgow, Edinburgh Ireland* and *Dublin*.

Insight Pocket Guides cover *South East England, London, Scotland* and *Ireland*. The *Compact Guides* series includes *London*.

244

ART/PHOTO CREDITS

Photography by

INDEX

A

Abbot, Diane, 48
Acton, 21
Adam, Robert, 27
Adams, John, 85
Addle Hill, 176
Adelphi, 27
Admiralty Arch, 75,104,105
African slaves, 46
Africans, 45
Agar Town, 33
"Aggie", *see* London Business Design Centre
"Alan Whicker", (cockney slang), 51
Albert Bridge, 186
Albert Memorial, 110, 129
Aldermanbury, 21
Aldersgate, 167
Aldgate, 167
Aldwych, the, 77
Alfred, (King of Wessex), 21
All Saints Road, 146
All Souls' Church, 88
Alleyn's School, 138
Alleyn, Edward, 138
Almeida, 145
Altruist, 177
Amersham, 191
Angel, 144
Angry Young Men, 58
Annabel's, 84, 124
Antiquarius, 121
Antique markets, 148, 149
Apsley House, 119, 133
Arabs, 48
archaeological findings, 21
Archer, Jeffrey, 85
architecture, 35, 99
   gothic, 99-100
Armour Collection-Tower of London, 133
Armoury, 175
Arnolfini Marriage, 132
art collections, 132
Arts Council, 80
Arts, 48
Asians, 45
Atheneaum, 80
"Augusta", 21

B

Bacchus and Ariadne, 132
Bacon, 154
Bacon, Francis, 76, 141
Baden-Powell House, 128
Baird, John Logie, 72
Baker Street, 89
Ball, John, 113
Bangladeshis, 45
Bank of England, 171, 172
Bank, 171
banking, 171
Banqueting House, 26, 94
Baptism of Christ, The, 132
Barbara Hepworth, 112
Barbican Art Gallery, 133
Barbican Centre, 174
Barbican Gallery, 133
Barbican, the, 57, 61
Barking, 32
Barrie, J.M., 110
Barry, 32
Barry, Charles, 96, 139
bars, 177
Bath, 21
Battersea bridge, 186
Battersea Power Station, 186
Battersea, 29
Battle of Hastings, 192
Battle of Trafalgar, 140
Bazalgette, Sir Joseph, 32, 184
Bear Gardens Museum, 58
Beardsley, Aubrey, 87
Beauchamp Place, 102, 127
'Bedham', *see* Bethelehem
Beckett, Thomas, 196
Bedford, 30
beer, 78
Belgrave Square, 120
Belgravia, 119
Bell Street, 177
Belloc, Hilaire, 123, 160
Bengalis, 177
Berkeley Square, 85
Berkeley Square House, 86
Berners, 30
Berry Bros and Rudd, 82
Berwick Street Market, 74, 149
Bethelehem, 25
Bethnal Green, 29, 33
Big Ben, 32, 95
Billingsgate, 148, 170
Billingsgate Market, 181
Birdcage Walk,103
Bishop's Avenue, 131, 142, 143
Bishopsgate, 22, 36, 167
"Black Death", 22
Black Friars, (pub), 154
Blackfriars, 27, 31
Blackheath, 39, 113, 141
blacks, the, 46
Blackwall, 29
Blake, William, 113
Bleak House, 30, 32, 158
Bleeding Heart Yard, 161
Blitz, the, 15, 36, 75
Bloemfontein, 41

Bloomsbury, 31, 69, 163
"Bloomsbury Group, The", 163
Blow Bladder, see King Edward Street
blue plaques, 142
boat races, 187
boat tirps, 181
Boateng, Paul, 48
Bobby, 38
Bodiam, 193
Bohemia Place, 15
Bombay Brasserie, (Indian restaurant), 128
Bond Street, 83
Boodles, 81
book market, 148
bookshops, 80
Borough, 21
Borrow, George, 125
Bouchier, Thomas, 191
Bow Bells, 51
Bow Street Runnerts, 79
Boy Scouts, 128
Branson, Richard, 131
Bread Street, 15, 25, 169
Brent Cross, (shopping centre), 40
Brent, 46
Brian Reidy Associates, 171
Brick Lane, 148, 149, 177
Brick Lane market, 17
Bridewell, 25
Bridewell Palace, 22
Brighton Centre, 195
Brighton's, 195
British Army, 122
British Boat People, 125
British Broadcasting Corporation's Bush
    House, 162
British Broadcasting Corporation, 77, 78
British Ministry of Labour, 46
British Museum, 31, 32, 120, 132, 133
British Museum and Library, 162
British Secret Service, 103
Brixton, 146-147, 149
Brixton Academy, the, 147
Brixton Prison, 147
Brixton Windmill, 147
Broadcasting House, 88
Broadstairs, 195
Broadwater Farm estate, 40
Broadway, 103
Brockway, Fenner, 162
Brompton Arcade, 127
Brompton Cemetery, 125
Brompton Oratory, 127
Brook Street, 85
Brooks', 81
Brothers Adam, 76
Brown, Capability, 111
Brune Street, 177
Brymon Express airway, 183
Buckingham House, 30
Buckingham Palace, 31, 103-105
Bucklersburgy Mosaic, 167
"bugs bunny", (cockney slang), 51
Bull's Head, (pub), 187
Bunning's Coal Exchange, 31
Burberry's, 82
Burdett-Coutts, Baroness, 33
Burlington Arcade, 83

Burlington House, 83
Bush House, 77
Busking Festival, 79
Byron, 125, 142

C

cabbies, see taxi drivers
Cabinet War Rooms, 94
Cade, Jack, 113
Caesar, Julius, 183
Cafe Royal, 87
Camberwell, 29
Cambridge, 196
Camden, 46
Camden Lock, 148
Camden Lock Market, 148
Camden market, 17
Camden Passage, 145
Camden Passage market, 149
Canaletto, Antonio, 72
Canary Wharf, 183
candlemakers, 169
Cannon Street, 169
Canterbury, 21, 196
Canute, 21
Captain Scott, 182
Carlton, 81
Carlton House, 30, 81
Carlton House Terrace, 30, 81, 105
Carlyle, 121
Carlyle, Thomas, 123
Carlyle's House, 123
Carnaby Street, 88
Carte, Richard D'Oyly, 76-77
Cash, Pat, 142
Castle, (pub), 143
castles, 192
    Bodiam Castle, 193
    Cliffe Castle, 193
    Hastings Castle, 193
    Hever Castle, 193
    Leeds Castle, 192
    Rochester's, 192
    Windsor Castle, 192
Casualty Book, 173
Catesby, Robert, 26
Cenotaph, 102
Central Criminal Court, 158
Centre Point, 35, 36
Chambers, William, 27
Chancery Lane, 158
Changing of the Guard, 104
Chapel of Edward, the Confessor, 100
Chapel of Henry VII, 100
Chapter House, 100
Charing Cross, 31
Charing Cross rail station, 76
Charing Cross Road, 80
Charles I, 113
Charles II, 69
Charterhouse Square, 157
Chartwell, 191
Chaucer, 22, 100
Cheapside, 32, 169
Cheapside Cross, 25
Cheapside market, 25
Chelsea, 29, 69, 120, 121

Chelsea Bridge, 186
Chelsea Embankment, 22, 32
Chelsea Flower Show, 122
Chelsea Harbour, 186
Chelsea Physic Garden, 123
Chelsea Pot, 122
Chelsea's King's Road, 124
Chenil Galleries and Antiquarius, 149
Chenil Galleries, 121
Chesham, 191
Chessington World of Adventure, (zoo), 193
Chester, 21
Cheyne Walk, 123
Chichester, Sir Francis, 140
Chiltern Hills, 191
Chinatown, see Gerrard Street
Chinese, 33, 45
Chinese New Year, 48
Chipping Ongar, 191
Chiswick, 187
cholera, 32
Chopin, 82, 120
Christchurch, (Spitalfields), 27
churches,
    All Souls' Church, 88
    Bow Bells, 51
    Chelsea Old Church, 123
    Christchurch, (Spitalfields), 27
    St. Anne's, (Limehouse), 27, 73
    St. Bartholomew's church, 25, 156
    St. Bride, 158
    St. Clement Dane, 158
    St. George Bloomsbury, 27
    St. George-in-the-East, 27
    St. James' church, 148, 156
    St. Margaret's Church, 99
    St. Martin-in-the-Fields, 27
    St. Mary Woolnoth, 27
    St. Mary, 186
    St. Mary-Le Bow, 175
    St. Mary-le-Strand, 27
    St. Paul's Cathedral, 22, 25, 26, 27, 35, 79, 153
    St. Stephen Walbrook, 175
    St. Stephen's Hall, 97
    St. Thomas, 25
    Westminster Abbey, 99-100
    Westminster Cathedral, 100
Churchill, Sir Winston, 95, 191
cinemas, 61
Citadel, 105
City, the, see Westminster Abbey
City, the, 167-177
    commodity markets, 170-171
    historical landmarks, 167-168
    livery company, 169
    livery halls, 167
    stock exchange, 172-173
    Tower of London, 175-176
City Barge, (pub), 187
City Corporation, 32
City Limits, 16, 57, 145
Clapham, 61
Clapham Common, 113
Clapton, Eric, 119
Clare Market, 33
Clarence House, 82, 102, 105
Claridge's Hotel, 85
Clerk's Well, 156

Clerkenwell, 25, 27, 156
Clerkenwell Green, 156
Clermont Club, 84
Cliffe Castle, 193
Clock Tower, see Gatehouse
clubs, 80-81, 124
    Empire, 72
    Hippodrome, 72
    Raymond's Revuebar, 72-73
    Ronnie Scott's jazz club, 72
Cock Lane, 157
cockney, 51
Coghlan, Monica, 85
Colchester, 21
Coldharbour Lanes, 147
Coldstream Guards, 103
Coleridge, Samuel Taylor, 142
Coliseum, the, 163
College Road, 139
Collett's London Bookshop, 80
Comedy of Errors, 160
Comedy Store, the, 61
commodity markets, 170-171
Commons, the, 32
Commonwealth Institute, 133
Conservatives, 98
Constable, 97
Conway Hill, 161
Cooper's Row, 167
Corney and Barrow, 176
Cornhill, 171
Coronation Chair, 100
Cosmo Place, 15
Cotswolds, 102
County Hall, 33, 95, 185
Court Circular, the, 102
Covent, 17, 25, 26, 29, 31, 61, 77, 78, 124, 148, 163
Covent Garden, see Covent
Coward, Noel, 58
craftsmen, 169
Cranmer, Thomas, 191
Crawford, Michael, 60
crime rate, 38
Cripplegate, 167
Criterion Brasserie, 78
Criterion, 58
Crockford's, 81
Croft, Henry, 149
Cromwell Hospital, 129
Cromwell, Oliver, 109-110, 111
Cromwell Road, 128
Crown and Greyhound, 139
Crown Jewels, 88, 175
Crown Jewels-Tower of London, 133
Croydon, 137
cruise, 17
Crystal Palace, 32, 110, 127
Cubitt, Thomas, 31, 119
cultural centres, 127
Cutty Sark, 140, 141

D

da Vinci, Leonardo, 75
Daily Express, The, 155
Daily Mirror building, the, 155
Daily Telegraph, 155

Dali, 99
Danish invasions, 21
Das Kapital, 72, 162
Davis, Angela, 41
day trips, 191-196
  countryside, 191-192
  castles, 192-193
  parks & zoos, 193-194
  resorts, (by the sea), 193
  outer suburbs, 193-194
de Gaulle, Charles, 48
Dean's Yard, 100
Decimus Burton, 119
Dekker, Thomas, 58
della Francesca, Piero, 132
Deptford, 29
Dickens, Charles, (writer), 30, 32, 119, 121, 155, 158, 161, 192
Dickens House Museum, 161, 193
Dillon's, 163
discos, 124
Disraeli, Benjamin, 86, 160
Docklands, 37, 67, 181, 182
Docklands Light Railway, 17, 182
"Dog, The", see Crown and Greyhound
Doggett's Coat and Badge Race, 187
Donne, John, 142, 153
Dorchester Hotel, 86
Dove, the, 78
Downing Street, 94
Doyle, Conan, 47, 89
Dracula, 141
"Dress Circle", (or "Royal Circle"), 60
Drury Lane, 33, 58, 79
Duke of Bedford, 26
Duke of Cumberland, 78
Duke of Edinburgh, 78
Dulwich, 31, 137, 138-139
Dulwich College Gallery, 133
Dulwich Golf Club, 138
Dulwich Picture Gallery, 133, 138-139, 161
Dulwich Wells, 139
Durham House, 32
Dutch Elm disease, 109
Dutch Garden, 112

E

Earl of Shelburne, 86
Earl's Court, 102, 125
East India Dock, 29
Eastbourne, 195
Eastenders, 149
Eaton Square, 120
Economist, The, 82
Edenbridge, 193
Egyptian Al-Fayed brothers, 127
Edward, the Confessor, 21-22, 93
Edward I, 25, 76
Edward III, 192
Edward VII, 84
El Vino, 154
Eleanor of Castile, 76
Electric Avenue, 147
Elgin Marbles, the, 32, 132, 162
Eliot, George, 123, 141
Eliot, T.S., 163
Elizabeth I, Queen, 25, 100, 139

Embassy Club, 84
Emperor of Russia, 29
Empire, 72
Engels, Frederick, 177
Epping, 191
Epping Forest, (Royal hunting reserve), 191
Eros, (Greek God), 41, 69
ethnic rioting, 47-48
Eton, 192
Eurocity Express airway, 183
Euston Road, 27, 31
Exeter, 21

F

Faber and Faber, 163
Faraday, Michael, 141
Farringdon Station, 156
Fawkes, Guy, 96
Fenchurch Street, 170
Fenton House, 133
Ferguson, Sarah, 84
Ferret and Firkin in the Ballroom up the Creek, The, (pub), 78
festivals,
  Chinese New Year, 48
  Notting Hill Carnival, 48, 145
Festival of Britain, 39
Fielding, Henry, 79
Finsburg, 26
Finsbury Park Inset club, 148
Fire of London, 133
Fitzroy Park, 142
Fitzroy Square, 61
Flask Walk, 144
Flaxman, 154
Fleet Ditch, the, 27
Fleet Street, 32, 47, 155, 158
Fletcher, Yvonne, 82
Fly-pickers, 148
Fonteyn, Dame Margot, 121
"For Hire", 54
foreign workers, 46
Forest Hill, 41, 196
"Forsyte saga", see lager
Fortnum, 17
Fortnum and Mason's, 83
Fox and Crown, 141
Foyle's, 80
Franklin, Benjamin, 76
Frederick, 81
French Impressionists, 99
French Without Tears, 58
French's Theatre Bookshop, 61
Fridge, 147
Frink, Elizabeth, 154
Frogmore Mausoleum, 192
Fry, Roger, 163
Fulham, 22
FX4, 53

G

Gainsborough, 97,132, 138,143
Gainsborough, Thomas, 72
galleries, *see* museums
Gandhi, Mahatma, 48,142
Gandhi, Marx, 48
Gardens, 142
Garlick Hill, 169
Garrards, 88
Garrick, 58, 80
Gatehouse, 82
Geffrye Museum, 133
Geldof, Bob, 121
General Eisenhower, 82
General Wolfe, 191
Geology Museum, 133
George II, 192
George III, 22, 104, 113
George IV, 81
George V, 82
George, David Lloyd, 123
George, The, 78
Gerrard Street, 48, 73
Getty, Paul, 123
Gilbert and Sullivan, 58
Gill, Eric, 112
Giltspur Street, 157
Gladstone, W.E., 81, 160
Globe, 25
Globe Theatre, 58
Gloucestor Road, 128
"Gods", The, 60
Gold State Coach, 104
Golden Age, The, 25, 27
Goldsmiths, 169
GOSH, *see* Royal Hospital for Sick Children
gothic, 99-100
government offices, 93
Gower Street, 31
Gracechurch Street, 21
Grant, Bernie, 48
Grant, Eddie, 147
Gray's Inn, 160
Greak Park, 192
Great British Public, 61
Great Eastern, the, 142
Great Exhibition, the, 32, 110, 127, 132
Great Fire, the, 15, 26-27, 31, 35, 153, 167, 169, 174
Great International Exhibition, 31
Great Marlborough Street, 87
Great Ormond St., *see* Royal Hospital for Sick Children
Greater London Council, 37, 38, 142, 185
Greek Cypriots, 46
Greeko, 45
Green House, the, 177
Green Park, 111
Greensted, 191
Greenwich, 26, 29, 138, 139-141, 181
Greenwich Obervatory, 140
Greenwich Palace, 139
Greenwich Theatre, 140
Grenadier public house, 17
Gresham, Sir Thomas, 25
Greyfriars, 25
Gribble, Herbert, 127

Grosvenor family, 86
Grosvenor House Hotel, 86
Grosvenor Square, 85
Guardian, 155
Guards' Chapel, 103
Guards' Museum, 103
Guards' Polo Club, 102
Guidlhall, 22, 170
Guiness World of Records, 73
Guinness Trust, 33
Guy Fawkes Day, 26, 96
Gwynne, Nell, 75, 82
gypsies, 139
Gypsy Hill, 139
Gypsy Moth, 140

H

Hackney Carriages, 53
Hall, Sir Benjamin, 95
Hamley's, 87
Hammersmith, 31, 78, 187
Hampstead, 137, 143
Hampstead Health, 112-113
Hampton Court, 191, 192
Hampton Court Palace, 187
Handel, 85, 142
Hangar Lane gyratory system, 40
Hard Rock Cafe, 119
Harley Street, 89
Harrod, Henry Charles, 127
Harrods, 17, 48, 125-126
Hastings, 193
Hatton Garden, 156
Hawksmoor, 27
Hay's Galleria, 183
Haymarket, 82
Hayward Gallery, 185
Hayward, the, 133
Health, 143
Heathrow Airport, 45
Hendon, 195
Hendrix, Jimi, 119
Henry VIII, 125, 139, 182, 191
Henry Wood Promenade Concerts, 130
Her Majesty's, 82
Hertford, 26
Hertford House, 89
Hever Castle, 193
High Street, 131
Highgate Cemetery, 141
Highgate, 141
Highgate Hill, 141
Hill, 175
Hilton Hotel, 86
Hippodrome, 72, 124
Historic Buildings and Monuments Commission, 142
history, 21-23
   modern, 35-41
Hockney, David, 130
Hogarth, 132
Hogarth's House, 133
Holborn, 22, 27
Holborn Viaduct, 156
Holland Park, 61, 112
Holmes, Sherlock, 47, 89
Homoeopatic Hospital, the, 163

Hope, 25
Horniman Museum, 133, 196
Horse Guards Parade, 93, 102
hospitals,
  National Hospital for Nervous Diseases, the, 163
  Homoeopatic Hospital, the, 163
  Ospedale Italiano, the, 163
  Royal Hospital for Sick Children, the, 163
House of Commons, 96, 98
House of Lords, 32, 96, 98
house boats, 125
Household Cavalry, 102
Houses of Parliament, 32, 96, 98, 124
housing, 37-40
Hudson, 163
Huguenots, 29
Hunt, Holman, 153
Hunt, Leigh, 144
Huntarian Museum, 133
Hyde Park, 25, 27, 31, 87, 109, 110
Hyde Park Corner, 69, 119, 125
Hyper Hyper, 131, 149

I

immigrants,
  Irish, 45, 46
  Pakistani, 45
  Sikh, 45
  Italian, 46
  African, 45
  Asian, 45
  Bangladeshi, 45
  Chinese, 33, 45
  Greek, 45
  Indian, 45
immigrant communities, 33
Imperial War Museum, 133
Indians, 45
Industrial Revolution, 29
Inner London, 37
Inner London Education Authority, 40
Inner Temple, 160
Inns of Court, the, 47, 158
Institute of Contemporary Arts, 81, 105
insurance, 173
International Pressing Centre, 155
Iris Garden, 112
Irish Republican Army, 112
Irish, 45, 46
Iskra, 156
Isle of Dogs, 29, 182
Islington, 46, 78, 144
Islington Spa, see New Tunbridge Wells
Ismaili Centre, 127
Italian refugees, 171
Italians, 46

J

J Floris, 102
J Lyons, (tea house), 76
Jack Straw's, 143
Jack the Ripper, 177
James, 25
James Allen Girl's School, 138
James I, 26, 113
James, Henry, 16

Jermyn Street, 82
Jesus Christ Superstar, 57
Jewel Tower, 99
Jews, 33, 45, 54, 156
Johnson, Samuel, 154
Jones, Inigo, 26, 77, 94
Jongleurs, 61
Jonson, Ben, 25, 160
Jubilee Market, 148

K

"Kangaroo Alley", see Garl's Court Exhibition Hall
Kean, Edmund, 58
Keats, 100
Keats, John 143-144
Keats' House, 133, 144
Kemp, David, 183
Kennington, 25
Kensington, 29, 32
Kensington Gardens, 110
Kensington High Road, 149
Kensington High Street, 48
Kensington Market, 131, 149
Kensington Palace, 102, 111, 130
Kensington Palace Gardens, 142
Kensington Square, 131
Kent, 195
Kent, William, 27
Kenwood House, 143
Kenwood House-Iveagh Bequest, 133
Kew, 113, 181
Kew Gardens, 187
Kew Palace, 113
Khan, Aga, 127
Kilburn, 46
King Charles I, 93, 96
King Edward Street, 157
King George II, 94, 130
King Harold, 192
King Henry III, 99, 191
King Henry VII, 99
King Henry VIII, 25, 82, 96, 99, 105
King's College, 160
King's Cross, 31
King's Head, 78, 145
King's Road, 120
Kingsway, 162
Kingsway Hall, 162
Kinsington Gardens, 129
Kipling, Rudyard, 76
Knight's Arcade, 127
Knights Templar, 160
Knightsbridge, 29, 69, 102, 125
Knightsbridge safe deposit centre, 127
Knole, 191
Kossuth, Louis, 142
Koster, Ron, 174

L

Labour Party, the, 48
Ladbroke Grove, 145
Ladies Lavatory company, 87
Ladysmith, 41
lager, 51, 78
Lambeth, 22, 25

Lambeth Bridge, 186
Lambeth Palace, 186
Lambeth Town Hall, 147
Lancashire, 45
Lancaster House, 82
Lanes, The, 195
Langham Place, 88
Lansdowne House, 86
laws of Normandy, 22
Le Sueur, 93
Leacock, Stephen, 167
Leadenhill, 170
Leather Lane, 161
Leeds Castle, 192
Leicester Square, 17, 60, 61, 74, 124, 148
Leighton House, 133
Lenin's Tomb, see Citadel
Lennon, John, 119
Les Miserables, 58
Lessons from the Varsity of Life, 128
Lewisham, 39
Liberals, 98
Liberty's, 87
Liberty, Mr., 87
Life Guards, see Royal Horse Guards
Life's Snags, 128
Liffe, 171
Light Fantastic, 74
Light of the World, The, 154
Lime Harbour, 183
Limehouse, 33
Limelight, 124
Lincoln's Inn, 25, 160
Lincoln's Inn Fields, 161
Little Boxes, 37
Little Britain, 157
Little Cloister, 100
Little Dorrit, 161
Little Gujarat, see Brent
Liverpool Street railway station, 48
livery companies, 169
livery halls, 169
Lloyd's of London, 173
Lloyds building, 17, 41
"Llyn-din", 21
Lobbs, 82
Locks and Co., 82
Lombard Street, 21, 171
Londinium, 21
London & Greenwich Railway, 31
London Bridge, 22, 27, 31, 184
London Business Design Centre, 145
London Commercial Sale Rooms, 170
London County Council, the, 37, 88, 142
London Diamond Centre, 88
London Docklands Development Corporation,
   (LDDC), 181, 182, 183
   headquarters, 183
London Experience, 74
London Marathon, the, 141
London Metal Exchange, 171
London Museum, 133
London Oratory, see Brompton Oratory
London Pavilion, 41, 73
London Planetarium, 133
London Post Office, 157
London Square, 26
London Symphony Orchestra, 174

London Transport Museum, 79, 163
London University, 31
London Wall, 167
Long Acre,
   in Covent Garden, 29
Lord B-P, 128
Lord Beaverbrook, 155
Lord Clive, 86
Lord Elgin, 132
Lord Mayor, 26, 170
Lord Mayor and Corporation, the, 25
Lord Mayor's Festival, 149
Lord Mayor's Pageant, 46
Lord Nelson, 140, 153
Lord of the Flies, 163
Lord Shaftesbury, 72, 73
Lots Road Power Station, 186
Louis XV, 75
Ludgate, 167
Ludgate Circus, 153
Lutine Bell, 173

M

M15, see British Secret Service
Madame du Barry, 75
Madame Tussaud's, 89
Madame Tussaud's Wax Museum, 133
Mafeking, 41
Main Passport Office, 103
Mall, the, 75, 81, 105
Man in the Moon, (pub), 122
Manchuria Road, 15
Mansion House, the, 170, 171
"Mappin & Webb", 41, 88
Marble Arch, 87
Marble Hill Park, 187
Marconi Wireless Telegraph Company, 77
Margate, 195
Maritime Museum, 140, 141
Maritime Turst, 141
"Market of the World", 21
markets, 148
Marlborough House, 82, 105
Martello Towers, 195
Marx, Karl, 72, 75, 141, 162
Marx Memorial Library, 156
Mary I, 139
Marylebone, 29, 88
Marylebone Park, 30
Marylebone Road, 27, 69
Mason's, 17
Mastermind, 54
Max Roach Park, 15
Maybox Group, 60
Mayfair, 27, 83, 124
Mayhew, Henry, 32
Mazzini, 156
Mctell, Ralph, 15
Medway, 192
Members of Parliament (MPs), 98
Merchant Navy, 140
Mermaid Theatre, 154
Messiah, 85, 142
Methodist Central Hall, 100
Metrocab, 53
Metropolitan, the, 33
Metropolitan Police, 89

Metropolitan police department (Met), 38
Metropolitan Policy District, 53
Michaelmas Day, 170
Michaelangel, 83
Middle Temple, 160
Middlesex Street, *see* Petticoat Lane
Midlands, 29
Milk Street, 15, 25, 169
Millbank, 97
Millbank Tower, 186
Millionaire's Rows, 142, *see* Bishop's Avenue
Milton, 100
Mirvish, Ed, 58
modern, 35-41
Monastery of St Peter, the, 21
Monet, 132
Monument, the,173, 174
Monument Yard, 174
Monuments Commission, 142
Moon, Keith, 119
Moore Henry, 99, 130, 175
More, Sir Thomas, 96
Morning Star, 155
Morocco Street, 15
Mousetrap, 57
Mozart, 72, 142
Mundania Road, 41
Murillo, 139
Museum in Docklands, 183
Museum of London, 167, 169, 183
Museum of Mankind, 48, 83,
museum district, 127
museums,
  Apsely House, 119 133
  Armour Collection-Tower of
  Bear Gardens Museum, 58
  Bequest, 133
  British Museum, 31, 32, 132,133
  Commonwealth Institute, 48, 133
  Dickens museum, 193
  dickens House Museum 161
  Horniman Museum, 133, 196
  London Transport Museum, 79, 163
  Maritime Museum, 140, 141
  Museum of London, 169
  Museum of Mankind, 48, 83, 133
  National Army Museum, 122
  Natural History Museum, 128, 133
  Naval Museum, 140
  Percival David Foundation of Chinese Art, 133
  RAF Museum, 195
  Science Museum, 128,133
  Sir John Soane Museum, 161, 133
  Victoria and Albert Museum, 32, 127, 133
My Discovery of England, 167
My Fair Lady, 79
Myddleton, Hugh, 26

N

Nag's Head, the, 78
Naipaul, V.S., 48
Naitonal Gallery, 132
Napoleon, 122
Nash, John, 30-31, 81, 111
Nat West Tower, 177
National Army Museum, 122
National Film Theatre, 39, 185
National Front, 177
National Gallery, 31, 41, 75, 133
National Hospital for Nervous Diseases, the, 163
National Portrait Gallery, 75
National Theatre, the, 39, 57, 60-61, 185, 124
National Westminster, 171
National Westminster Bank, 36
Natural History Museum, 128, 133
Naval Museum, 140
"Navigators, The", 183
Neal's Yard, 77
Nelson, 75, 110
Nelson's Column, 75
"New Commonwealth", the, 47
New River Head, 26
New Statesman, 156
Newgate, 167
Newgate Gaoland, 158
Newgate Street, 157
Newham, 181
news-agent, 47
Newton, Isaac, 142
Nicholas Nickleby, 58
night sites, 124
nightclub, *see* clubs
nightclubs, 84
Noble Street, 167
Notting Hill, 145
Notting Hill Carnival, 38, 48, 145
Nottinghamshire, 76

O

Observer, The, 154
Ode to a Nightingale, 143
Official London, 67
Old Bailey, 158
Old Bridget, 139
Old Bull and Bush, (pub), 143
Old Chelsea Town Hall, 121
Old Compton Street, 74
Old Curiosity Shop, 25
Old Grammar School, 139
Old Lady of Threadneedle Street, *see* Bank of
  England
Old Red Lion, 145
Old Vic, 58
Olivier theatre, 61
Orangery, 113
Order of the Garter, 192
Ospedale Italiano, the, 163
Oxford, 196
Oxford Street, 83, 87

P

Paddington, 29, 31
Paddle Your Own Canoe, 128
Pakistanis, 45
Palace of Whitehall, 93
Pall Mall, 80-81
Palladio, 26
Panizzi, Sir Anthony, 162
Pankhurst, Emmeline, 97
Park Crescent, 30
Park Lane, 83, 86
Parks, 109-113
Parliament, 32, 96, 98, 124

Parliament Hill Fields, 143
Parliament Square, 95
Parliament Street, 94
Parthenon Temple, 132
Patels, (village chief), 45-46, 47
Patent Office, 158
Paternoster Square, 154
Paul's Walk, 25
Peabody Trust, 33
Peace Pagoda, 186
Pearly Harvest Festival, 149
Pearly Kings and Queens, 149
Peckham, 113
Peckham Rye, 113
Peelers, 38
Pentonvilled Road, 27
Pepys, 158
Pepys, Samuel, 26, 35
Percival David Foundation of Chinese Art, 133
"Pete Marsh", 163
Peter Jones, 121
Peter Pan, 110
Petrie Ancient Egyptian Collection University
    College, 133
Petticoat Lane, 148, 177
Petticoat Lane market, 48, 51
Phantom of the Opera, 60
Pheasantry, 121
Phoenix, 58
Photographer's Gallery, 133
Piazza, 26
Picasso, 99
Piccadilly, 30, 83, 124
Piccadilly Arcade, 83
Piccadilly Book Fair, 148
Piccadilly Circus, 21, 69, 78
Piccadilly market, 148
pickpockets, 16
piers,
    Greenwich, 181
    Kew, 181
    Putney, 181
    Tower, 181
    Westminster, 181
pigeons, 75
Pit, The, 61
Pitt the Younger, 172
Plague, 26
Planetarium, 89
Plantation House, 170
Playhouse, the, 60
Poets' Corner, 100
policeman, (urban), see bobby
Polish Jews, 29
Pollock, Jackson, 99
Pool of London, 181
population, 16, 37, 45, 67
Portland, 30
Portland Place, 88
Portman, 30
Portobello Road, (antique market), 146
Portobello Road market, 149
Portuguese, 46
Posh London, 119-131
Post Office Tower, 36
Postman's Park, 112
Poultry, 169
Powell, Enoch, 48

Primrose Hill, 143
Prince Albert, 32
Prince Andrew, 84
Prince Charles, 84, 102, 120, 130
Prince of Wales, 41, 83
Prince Philip, 102
Prince Regent, 195
Princes Gate Mews, 129
Princess Anne, 102
Princess Diana, 102, 130
Princess Margaret, 84
Printing House Square, 154
Private car ownership, 54
Private Eye, 153
property prices, 182
Prospect of Whitby, (pub), 182
Prudential Assurance building, 155
Public Carriage Office, 53
Public Houses, (pubs), 78
Public Record Office, 158
Public Records Office Museum, 133
public transport, 17
public transportation, 16
publishing, 163
Pubs, 51, 78
Puddle Dock, 154
Pugin, 32
Pugin, Augustus, 96
punks, 69, 120
Putney, 181, 187

Q

Queen Anne's Gate, 103
Queen Boadicea, 15, 21, 185
Queen Elizabeth, 86,105
Queen Eizabeth Hall, 39, 124
Queen Mary, 82,105, 191
Queen Mother, the, see Queen Elizabeth
Queen Square, 163
Queen Victoria, 22, 31, 163, 192
Queen Victoria Memorial, the, 105
Queen Victoria Street, 32
Queen's Chapel, 26, 77
Queen's Gallery, the, 104,133
Queen's House, 140
Queensway, 145

R

race riots, 177
RAF Museum, 195
Raleigh, Sir Walter, 99
Ramsgate, 195
Ranelagh Gardens, 122
Rattigan, 58
Raymond's Revuebar, 72-73
Red Lion Square, 161, 162
Redoubt Fortress, 195
Reform Club, 81
Regent Street, 30, 83, 87
Regent's Canal, 17, 30, 182
Regent's Park, 17, 61, 112
Regent's Park Explosion, 112
Regent's Park Mosque, 45
Regent's Street, 148
Rembrandt, 138, 143
Remembrance Sunday, 94

Rent's Canal, 144
restaurants, 48, 124, 176, 177
  Bianchi's restaurant, 72
  Leoni's Quo Vadis, 72
  Veeraswamy's, 87
Reynolds, 132, 143
Reynolds, Sir Joshua, 154
Rhodes, Zandra, 130
Richmond Park, 113
Ritz, 83
Ritzy, the, (cinema), 147
rivers,
  Fleet, 22
  Thames, 137
  Walbrook, 22
River Thames, 137
Roach, Max, 41
Roaring Girl, 58
Rochester's, 192
Rock Garden, 79
Rococo, 122
Rogers, Richard, 173
Roman invaders, 21
Roman Wall, 167
Romans, 167
Ronan Point, 36
Ronnie Scott's jazz, 124
Ronnie Scott's jazz club, 72
Roof Garden, (restaurant), 17, 131
Rosamond's Pond, 87
Rose Garden, 112
Roseberry Avenue, 144
Rosetta Stone, the, 132, 162
Rosetti, 121
Rossetti, Christina, 141
Rossetti, Dante Gabriel, 123
Rossevelt, Franklin D, 85
Rothko, Mark, 99
Rotten Row, 110
Rovering to Success, 128
Royal Academy, the, 133, 148
Royal Academy of Arts, 83, 133
Royal Agricultural Halls, 144
Royal Albert Hall, 130
Royal Albert Memorial, 32
Royal Ascot, 102
Royal Ballet, the, 80
Royal Botanic Gardens Kew, 133
Royal Botanical Gardens, 113
Royal Colledge of Art, 130
Royal College of Music, 130
Royal College of Oranists, 130
Royal Court, 58
Royal Court and Bush, 57
Royal Court Theatre, 120
Royal Courts of Justice, 158
Royal Docks, 182, 183
Royal Exchange, 25, 171
Royal Family, the,102, 132
Royal Festival Hall, 17, 39, 185
Royal Geographical Society, 129
Royal Grenadier Guards, 103
Royal Horse Guards, 93
Royal Hospital for Sick Children, the, 163
Royal Hospital, 122
Royal Hospital Road, 123
Royal Mews, 104
Royal Navy, 140

Royal Naval College, 140, 183
Royal Observatory, 140
Royal Opera Arcade, the, 83
Royal Opera House, 79, 80, 82, 163, 195
Royal Pavilion, 195
Royal Shakespeare Company, the, 60, 174
Royal Society of Arts, 142
Royal Society, The, 82
Royal Tournament, the, 102
Royal Victoria Dock, 183
Royalty, the, 60
Rubens, 94, 138
Rubens, Sir Peter Paul, see Rubens
Rule Britannia, 78
Ruskin, John, 31
Russell Square, 163
Russian, 45
Russian Jews, 29

S

Sadler, Thomas, 144
Sadler's Wells, 144
Saeger, Pete, 37
Sainsbury's Megastore, (supermarket), 128-129
St. Anne's, (Limehouse), 27, 73
St. Bartholomew's, 157
St. Bartholomew's church, 25
St. Bartholomew's Hospital, 157
St. Bride, 158
St. Clement Dane, 158
St. George Bloomsbury, 27
St. George-in-the-East, 27
St. James', 25, 27, 124
St. James' Street, 82
St. James the Less, 82
St. James' church, 148, 156
St. James' Palace, 26, 82, 105
St. James' Park, 81, 111
St. John's Smith Square, 97
St. Katherine's Dock, 29, 182
St. Margaret's Church, 99
St. Martin's-le-Grand, 157
St. Martin-in-the-Fields, 27
St. Mary, 186
St. Mary Woolnoth, 27
St. Mary-Le Bow, 175
St. Mary-le-Strand, 27
St. Pancras Station, 33
St. Pancras, 31
St. Paul's Cathedral, 22, 25, 26, 27, 35, 79, 153
St. Paul's Cross, 25
St. Stephen Walbrook, 175
St. Stephen's Hall, 97
St. Thomas, 25
Salisbury House, 22
Samuel Pepys, 176
Sargent, 121
Savile Club, 85
Savoy, 58
Savoy Hotel, 76
Savoy Theatre, 76
Saxons, 21
schools, 138
Science Museum, 128, 133
Scottish Nationalists, the, 98
Scutari Road, 41
Senate House, 163

255

Serpentine, 87
Serpentine Art Gallery, 111
Serpentine Lake, 110
Service of Remembrance, 102
Seventh Earl of Shaftesbury, 69
Sevnoaks, 191
Seymour, Jane, 125
Shaftesbury Avenue, 163
Shah, Eddie, 155
Shakespeare, 160
Shakespeare, William, 25, 100
Shakespeare's Globe, 154
Shelley, Mary, 110
Shepherd Market, 83, 84, 85
Shepherd's Buch, 41
Shillibeer, Mr, 31
Ship, the, (pub), 176
Shoe Lane, 155
shopping, 73, 74, 82-84, 86-89, 125-127, 131, 195
Shoreditch, 25, 32
Sikhs, 45
Simpson, Mrs Wallis, 84
Simpson's, 76
Sir John Soane Museum, 161, 133
Sloane Square, 120
Sloane, Sir Hans, 120
Smith's Lawn, 102
Smithfield Meat Market, 41, 148, 156, 157, 170
Soane, Sir John 138
Social Democractic Party, the, 98
Society of West End Theatre Managers, 57
Soho, 27
Soho Brasserie, the, 124
Soho Square, 69
Somerset House, 27, 158, 184
Sommers, 30
Sotheby's, 84
South Bank Arts Centre, 185
South Bank complex, 124
Southall market, 149
Southampton, 30
Southend On Sea, 195
Southhall, 39
Southwark, 21, 22, 78
Spaniards Inn, 143
Spaniards, 46
"Spark, The", see Iskra
Speaker's Corner, (in Hyde Park), 110
Spencer, Diana, 120
Spitalfields, (fruit and vegetable market), 29, 148, 170
Spycatcher, 110
Square Africa House, 17
Stage by Stage, 58
Stalls, the, 60
Staple Inn, 25
Star of Africa, 175
State Opening, the, 98, 102
Status of Oliver Cromwell, 95
Stephens, Thomas, 45
Stepney, 25
Stinking Lane, see Newgate Street
Stock Exchange, 172-173
Stone Age, 21
Stone of Scone, 100
Strachey, Lytton, 163
Strand on the Green, 187
Strand, The, 22, 30, 32, 76, 184

Strangers' Gallery, the, 98
"Street of Shame", 153
street bazaar, 48
street performers, 79
Stringfellows, 124
striptease shows, 73
Sunflowers, 84
Surrey Docks, 182, 183
Surrey for the Derby, 102
Sutcliffe, Peter, 158
Swan, 25
Sweetings, (restaurant), 176
Sweyn, 21
Swinburne, 123
Sydney Street, 121
Sydney, Sir Philip, 160
Syon House, 187

T

Tate Gallery, 97, 132, 133, 186
Tate, Henry, 132
taxi drivers, 53-55
Taylor, Elizabeth, 142
tea dances, 17
Telecom Tower, 36, 88
Temple Bar, 69
Temple of Mithras, 167
Temples of Arts, 32
Temples of Arts and Sciences, 32
Tennyson, 100
Terriss, William, 58
textile mills, 45
Thames, 29, 31, 32, 69, 78, 95, 124, 181-187
    Docklands, 181-182
    docks, 182-183
    embankment, 184-185
    London Bridge, 183
    river activities, 187
    Tower Bridge, 183
Thames, (art publisher), 163
Thames Barrier, 183
Thames lights, 17
Thatcher, Margaret, 121, 138
Theatre Museum, 61
Theatre Royal, see Royal Opera House
Therapia Road, 41
Theroux, Paul, 48
Third Reich, 35
Thomas, Dylan, 69
Thorney Island, 21
Thorpe Park, 193
Threadneedle Street, 15
threatres, 57-61
Throgmorten Street, 15
ticket agencies, 60
ticket-buying, 60
Time Out, 16, 57, 145
Times, The, 111, 155
Titian, 132
Tobacco Dock, 182
Today, 155
Tokyo Joe's, 124
Tom Jone, 79
Tondo, 83
Tottenham Court Road, 29
Totteridge Lane new Mill Hill, 142
tourists, 16, 67

touts, 60
Tower, 29, 181
Tower Bridge, 32, 184
Tower Hamlets, 181
Tower of London, 175-176
Trafalgar Square, 17, 27, 30, 32, 74, 93, 124
Trafalgar Tavern, 141
Tramps, 124
Traveller's, 81
Trocadero Centre, 73, 124
Tropping of the Colour, 93, 102
Truefitt and Hill, 102
Tudor palace, 82
Tunbridge Wells, 144
Turf Club, 81
Turner, 97, 121, 132, 143
Turner, J.M.W., 123
Tweltfh Night, 160
Tyburn Brook, 87
Tyburn Tree, 86

U

Uncommercial Traveller, 119
Undercroft Museum, 100
Underground District line, 89
University Boat Race, 187
University College, 160
"Upper Circle" (or "Grand Circle"), 60
Upper Mall, 187
urban villages, 138

V

Van Brugh, 141
Van Brugh's Castle, 141
Van Dyck, 138
Van Eyck, Jan, 132
Van Gogh, 84, 132
Vauchall, 29
Velazquez, 132
Vermeer, 143
Victoria and Albert Museum, 32, 127, 132, 133
Victoria Embankment, 32, 184
Victoria Railway Bridge, 186
Victoria railway station, 103
Victoria Street, 100
Victoria Tower, 32, 96
Victoria Tower Gardens, 97
Vietnamese boat people, 45
villages, (urban), 67, 137-147
  Brixton, 146-147
  Dulwich, 138-139
  Greenwich, 139-141
  Hampstead, 143-145
  Highgate, 141
  Notting Hill, 145-146
Villiers Street, 76
Virgin Mary and Child, The, 75

W

Waiting for Godot, 58
Walbrook, 21
Waldorf Hotel, 17
Wallace Collection, 89, 133
Wallace, Edgar, 153
Wallace, William, 157
Wandsworth, 29, 39
Wanstead, 78
Wapping, 29, 182
Wardour Street, 74
Warkwick Road, 125
Water Gate, 76
Waterloo, 31
Waterloo Bridge, 185
Waterloo Place, 81
Waterside cafe, 174
Watts, G F, 112
wax museums, *see* Madame Tussand's
weather, 16
Webb, Sidney, 160
Well Walk, 144
Wellington Arch, 119
Wellington Barracks, 103
West End, the, 67, 69-89, 124
  clubs, 72-73, 80-81
  Marylebone, 88-89
  shopping, 82-89
  Soho, 73-74
  street performers, 79-80
  Trafalgar Square, 74-76
West Hill, 141
West India Dock, 29
West Indians, 45
West Minster, *see* Monastery of St. Peter
West Pier, 195
West Smithfield, 157
Westbourne Grove, 145
Westerham, 191
Westminster, 181
Westminster Abbey, 21, 22, 32, 33, 76, 93-105, 124
Westminster Bridge, 27, 95, 185
Westminster Cathedral, 17, 100
Westminster Hall, 22, 95-96, 98
Westminster Pier, 95, 124, 185
Westminster School, 100
Westmoreland Road, 148
Whipsnade Zoo, 193
Whistler, 87, 121
Whispering Gallery, 153
Whitechapel Art Gallery, 133
White Elephant Club, 124
White Tower, 22
White's, 81
Whitechapel, 33, 177
Whitechapel Art Gallery, 133
Whitechapel High Street, 29
Whitehall, 25, 27, 32, 93-105
Whitehall Theatre, 60
Whitestone Pond, 143
Whittington, Dick, 141
Wilberforce, William, 47
Wild Animal Kingdom, 193
Wilde, Oscar, 87
Wilfred, (bar and restaurant), 185
William, the Conqueror, 22, 175, 192

William III, 110
William Morris Gallery, 133
Wilton Place, 119
Wilton Row, 17
Wimbledon, 137
Winchester, 196
Windsor, (town), 192
Windsor Castle, 192
Windsor Horse Show, 102
Windsor Safari Park, 193
Woburn Abbey, 193
Wolsey, Cardinal, 191
Wood Street, 25, 169
Woolf, Virginia, 163
workers, 21
World War II, 15
Wosley, Cardinal, 25
Wren, Sir Christopher, 26, 35, 82, 99, 122, 130,
    140, 153, 174, 175, 183, 191

Y

Yacht Tavern, 141
Yates, Paula, 121
Ye Olde Cheshire Cheese, 78, 154
York, 21
York House, 76, 82
Yorkshire, 45
"Yorkshire Ripper, the", *see* Sutcliffe, Peter
Yukon Road, 15

Z

Zamana Gallery, 127
Zampa Road, 15
Zander Court, 15
zoos,
    Chessington World of Adventure, 193
    Regent's Park, 112
    Whipsnade Zoo, 193
    Wild Animal Kingdom, 193
    Windsor Safari Park, 193
    Woburn Abbey, 193
Zwemmer, 80